The Pigeon Tunnel

Call for the Dead

A Murder of Quality

The Spy Who Came in from the Cold

The Looking Glass War

A Small Town in Germany

The Naive and Sentimental Lover

Tinker Tailor Soldier Spy

The Honourable Schoolboy

Smiley's People

The Little Drummer Girl

A Perfect Spy

The Russia House

The Secret Pilgrim

The Night Manager

Our Game

The Tailor of Panama

Single & Single

The Constant Gardener

Absolute Friends

The Mission Song

A Most Wanted Man

Our Kind of Traitor

A Delicate Truth

The Pigeon Tunnel

Stories from My Life

JOHN LE CARRÉ

VIKING

VIKING

An imprint of Penguin Random House LLC

375 Hudson Street
New York, New York 10014
penguin.com

ISBN: 9780735220775 (hardcover)
ISBN: 9780735220799 (ebook)

Printed in the United States of America
7   9   10   8   6

Set in Electra LT Std

Contents

CONTENTS

Preface

There is scarcely a book of mine that didn't have *The Pigeon Tunnel* at some time or another as its working title. Its origin is easily explained. I was in my mid-teens when my father decided to take me on one of his gambling sprees to Monte Carlo. Close by the old casino stood the sporting club, and at its base lay a stretch of lawn and a shooting range looking out to sea. Under the lawn ran small, parallel tunnels that emerged in a row at the sea's edge. Into them were inserted live pigeons that had been hatched and trapped on the casino roof. Their job was to flutter their way along the pitch-dark tunnel until they emerged in the Mediterranean sky as targets for well-lunched sporting gentlemen who were standing or lying in wait with their shotguns. Pigeons who were missed or merely winged then did what pigeons do. They returned to the place of their birth on the casino roof, where the same traps awaited them.

Quite why this image has haunted me for so long is something the reader is perhaps better able to judge than I am.

John le Carré, January 2016

Introduction

I sit at my desk in the basement of the little Swiss chalet that I built with the profits from *The Spy Who Came in from the Cold* in a mountain village ninety minutes by train from Bern, the city to which at the age of sixteen I had fled from my English public school and where I had enrolled at Bern University. At weekends a great bunch of us students, boys and girls, mostly Bernese, would flood up to the Oberland, bunk down in mountain huts and ski our hearts out. So far as I ever knew we were the soul of probity: boys one side, girls the other, never the twain shall meet. Or if they did, I was never one of them.

The chalet sits above the village. Through my window, if I take a steep look upwards, I can glimpse the peaks of the Eiger, Mönch and Jungfrau, and most beautiful of all, the Silberhorn and the Kleines Silberhorn half a step below it: two sweetly pointed cones of ice that periodically succumb to drabness in the warm south wind called the Föhn, only to reappear days later in all their bridal glory.

Among our patron saints we have the ubiquitous composer Mendelssohn – follow the arrows for the Mendelssohn walk – the poet Goethe, though he seems to have made it only as far as the waterfalls of the Lauterbrunnental, and the poet Byron, who made it as far as the Wengernalp and hated it, protesting that the sight of our storm-ravaged forests 'reminded me of myself and my family'.

But the patron saint we most revere is undoubtedly one Ernst Gertsch, who brought fame and fortune to the village by inaugurating the Lauberhorn Ski Race in 1930, in which he himself won the

1

slalom. I was once mad enough to take part in it and, by a combination of incompetence and naked fear, came the predictable cropper. My researches tell me that, not content to become the father of ski racing, Ernst went on to give us the steel edges to our skis and steel platforms for our bindings, for which we may all be thankful to him.

The month is May, so we get a whole year's weather in one week: yesterday a couple of feet of fresh snow and not a single skier to enjoy it; today an unobstructed scorching sun, and the snow nearly gone again and the spring flowers back in business. And now this evening, thunderclouds of Payne's grey getting ready to march up the Lauterbrunnen valley like Napoleon's Grande Armée.

And probably in their wake, and because for the last days we have been spared a visit, the Föhn will return and sky, meadows and forests will be drained of colour, and the chalet will creak and fidget, and the wood smoke will roll out of the fireplace on to the carpet we paid too much for on that rainy afternoon in Interlaken in the snowless winter of whenever it was, and every clank and honk coming up from the valley will ring out like a sullen call of protest, and all birds will be confined to their nests for the duration, except for the choughs who take orders from no one. In the Föhn, don't drive a car, don't propose marriage. If you've got a headache or an urge to kill your neighbour, be consoled. It's not a hangover, it's the Föhn.

The chalet has a place in my eighty-four years of life that is quite disproportionate to its size. In the years before I built it, I came to this village as a boy, first to ski on skis of ash or hickory, using seal skins to climb uphill and leather bindings to come down again, then to walk the mountains in summer with my wise Oxford mentor, Vivian Green, later Rector of Lincoln College, who gave me by his example the inner life of George Smiley.

It's no coincidence that Smiley like Vivian loved his Swiss Alps, or like Vivian found his consolation in landscape, or like myself had a lifelong, unreconciled relationship with the German muse.

It was Vivian who put up with my maunderings about my

wayward father, Ronnie; Vivian again who, when Ronnie made one of his more spectacular bankruptcies, found the necessary cash and hauled me back to complete my studies.

In Bern I had got to know the scion of the oldest family of hotel owners in the Oberland. Without his later influence I would never have been allowed to build the chalet in the first place, for then as now no foreigner may own so much as a square foot of village land.

It was also while I was in Bern that I took my first infant steps for British Intelligence, delivering I knew not what to I knew not whom. I spend a lot of odd moments these days wondering what my life would have looked like if I hadn't bolted from my public school, or if I had bolted in a different direction. It strikes me now that everything that happened later in life was the consequence of that one impulsive adolescent decision to get out of England by the fastest available route and embrace the German muse as a substitute mother.

I wasn't a failure at school, far from it: captain of things, winner of school prizes, potential golden boy. And it was a very discreet bolt. I didn't howl and scream. I just said, 'Father, you may do with me what you will, I won't go back.' And very probably I blamed the school for my woes – and England along with it – when my real motive was to get out from under my father at all costs, which I could hardly say to him. Since then, of course, I have watched my own children do the same, though more elegantly and with a lot less fuss.

But none of that answers the central question of what direction my life might otherwise have taken. Without Bern, would I have been recruited as a teenaged errand boy of British Intelligence, doing what the trade calls *a little of this and that*? I hadn't read Maugham's *Ashenden* by then, but I had certainly read Kipling's *Kim* and any number of chauvinistic adventure stories by G. A. Henty and his ilk. Dornford Yates, John Buchan and Rider Haggard could do no wrong.

And of course, a mere four years after the war's end I was the greatest British patriot in the hemisphere. At my preparatory school we boys had become expert at identifying German spies in our ranks, and I was counted one of our better counter-espionage operatives. At my public school, our jingoistic fervour was unconfined. We did 'Corps' – military training in full uniform – twice a week. Our young teachers had returned tanned from the war and on Corps days sported their medal ribbons. My German teacher had had a wonderfully mysterious war. Our careers adviser prepared us for a lifetime's service in distant outposts of empire. The Abbey at the heart of our little town was hung with regimental flags shot to shreds in colonial wars in India, South Africa and Sudan, the shreds then restored to glory on fishnet by loving female hands.

It is therefore no sort of surprise when the Great Call came to me in the person of a thirty-something mumsy lady named Wendy from the British Embassy's visa section in Bern, that the seventeen-year-old English schoolboy punching above his weight at a foreign university should have snapped to attention and said, 'At your service, *Ma'am!*'

More difficult to explain is my wholesale embrace of German literature at a time when for many people the word *German* was synonymous with unparalleled evil. Yet, like my flight to Bern, that embrace has determined the whole later passage of my life. Without it, I would never have visited Germany in 1949 on the insistence of my Jewish refugee German teacher, never seen the flattened cities of the Ruhr, or lain sick as a dog on an old Wehrmacht mattress in a makeshift German field hospital in the Berlin Underground; or visited the concentration camps of Dachau and Bergen-Belsen while the stench still lingered in the huts, thence to return to the unruffled tranquillity of Bern, to my Thomas Mann and Hermann Hesse. I would certainly never have been assigned to intelligence duties in occupied Austria for my National Service, or studied German literature and language at Oxford, or gone on to teach them at Eton, or been posted to the British Embassy in Bonn with the cover of a junior diplomat, or written novels with German themes.

The legacy of that early immersion in things German is now pretty clear to me. It gave me my own patch of eclectic territory; it fed my incurable romanticism and my love of lyricism; it instilled in me the notion that a man's journey from cradle to grave was one unending education – hardly an original concept and probably questionable, but nevertheless. And when I came to study the dramas of Goethe, Lenz, Schiller, Kleist and Büchner, I discovered that I related equally to their classic austerity, and to their neurotic excesses. The trick, it seemed to me, was to disguise the one with the other.

*

The chalet is pushing fifty years old. Every winter season as the children grew up, they came here to ski, and this was where we had our best times together. Sometimes we did spring as well. It was here too that for four hilarious weeks in, I think, the winter of 1967 I was cloistered with Sydney Pollack, film director of *Tootsie*, *Out of Africa* and – my favourite – *They Shoot Horses, Don't They?* while we thrashed out a screenplay of my novel *A Small Town in Germany*.

The snow that winter was perfect. Sydney had never skied, never been to Switzerland. The sight of happy skiers whizzing nonchalantly past our balcony was simply too much for him. He had to be one of them, and it had to be now. He wanted me to instruct him, but thank Heaven I called up Martin Epp instead: ski teacher, legendary mountain guide and one of a rare breed to have made a solitary ascent of the north face of the Eiger.

The A-list film director from South Bend, Indiana, and the A-list mountaineer from Arosa hit it off at once. Sydney did nothing by halves. Within days, he was a competent skier. He was also seized with a passionate desire to make a movie about Martin Epp, and it soon transcended his desire to make *A Small Town in Germany*. The Eiger would play Destiny. I would write the screenplay, Martin would play himself and Sydney would be harnessed halfway up the Eiger filming him. He called his agent and told him about Martin.

He called his analyst and told him about Martin. The snow remained perfect and took its toll of Sydney's energies. Evenings, after a bath, we decided, were our best times for writing. Whether they were or not, neither movie was ever made.

Later, somewhat to my surprise, Sydney lent the chalet to Robert Redford for him to reconnoitre his movie *Downhill Racer*. Alas, I never met him, but for years afterwards, wherever I went in the village, I wore the cachet of Robert Redford's friend.

*

These are true stories told from memory – to which you are entitled to ask, what is truth, and what is memory to a creative writer in what we may delicately call the evening of his life? To the lawyer, truth is facts unadorned. Whether such facts are ever findable is another matter. To the creative writer, fact is raw material, not his taskmaster but his instrument, and his job is to make it sing. Real truth lies, if anywhere, not in facts, but in nuance.

Was there ever such a thing as *pure* memory? I doubt it. Even when we convince ourselves that we're being dispassionate, sticking to the bald facts with no self-serving decorations or omissions, pure memory remains as elusive as a bar of wet soap. Or it does for me, after a lifetime of blending experience with imagination.

Here and there, where I thought the story merited it, I have lifted bits of conversation or description from newspaper articles I wrote at the time because their freshness appealed to me, and because later memory didn't deliver the same sharpness: for example, my description of Vadim Bakatin, one-time head of the KGB. In other cases I've left the story pretty much as I wrote it at the time, just tidied it here and there, added the odd grace note to make it clearer or bring it up to date.

I don't wish to presume in my reader a great knowledge of my work – or, for that matter, any knowledge of it at all, hence the odd explanatory passage along the way. But please be assured:

nowhere have I consciously falsified an event or a story. Disguised where necessary, yes. Falsified, emphatically not. And wherever my memory is shaky, I have taken care to say so. A recently published account of my life offers thumbnail versions of one or two of the stories, so it naturally pleases me to reclaim them as my own, tell them in my own voice and invest them as best I can with my own feelings.

Some episodes have acquired a significance I wasn't aware of at the time, perhaps because of the death of a main player. Throughout a long life I kept no diary, just here and there the odd travel note or line of irretrievable dialogue: for instance, from my days with Yasser Arafat, Chairman of the PLO, before his expulsion from Lebanon; and afterwards my abortive visit to his white hotel in Tunis, the same town in which several members of his high command, billeted a few miles down the road from him, were assassinated by an Israeli hit team a few weeks after I left.

Men and women of power drew me because they were there, and because I wanted to know what made them tick. But in their presence all I seem to have done in retrospect was nod wisely, shake my head in the right places, and try a joke or two to ease the strain. Only afterwards, back in my hotel bedroom, did I fish out my mangled notepad and attempt to make sense of what I had heard and seen.

The other scribbles that survive from my travels were made for the most part not by me personally, but by the fictional characters I took along with me for protection when I ventured into the field. It was from their eye-line, not mine, and in their words, that the notes were written. When I found myself cringing in a dugout beside the Mekong River, and for the first time in my life heard bullets smacking into the mud bank above me, it was not my own quivering hand that confided my indignation to a scruffy notebook, but the hand of my courageous fictional hero, the front-line reporter Jerry Westerby, for whom being shot at was part of the daily grind. I used to think I was exceptional in this way until I met a celebrated war

7

photographer who confessed to me that it was only when he was peering through the lens of his camera that the funk left him.

Well, it never left me. But I know what he was talking about.

*

If you're ever lucky enough to score an early success as a writer, as happened to me with *The Spy Who Came in from the Cold*, for the rest of your life there's a before-the-fall and an after-the-fall. You look back at the books you wrote before the searchlight picked you out and they read like the books of your innocence; and the books after it, in your low moments, like the strivings of a man on trial. 'Trying too hard' the critics cry. I never thought I was trying too hard. I reckoned I owed it to my success to get the best out of myself, and by and large, however good or bad the best was, that was what I did.

And I love writing. I love doing what I'm doing at this moment, scribbling away like a man in hiding at a poky desk on a black-clouded early morning in May, with the mountain rain scuttling down the window and no excuse for tramping down to the railway station under an umbrella because the *International New York Times* doesn't arrive till lunchtime.

I love writing on the hoof, in notebooks on walks, in trains and cafés, then scurrying home to pick over my booty. When I am in Hampstead there is a bench I favour on the Heath, tucked under a spreading tree and set apart from its companions, and that's where I like to scribble. I have only ever written by hand. Arrogantly perhaps, I prefer to remain with the centuries-old tradition of unmechanized writing. The lapsed graphic artist in me actually enjoys drawing the words.

I love best the *privacy* of writing, which is why I don't do literary festivals and, as much as I can, stay away from interviews, even if the record doesn't look that way. There are times, usually at night, when I wish I'd never given an interview at all. First, you invent yourself, then you get to believe your invention. That is not a process that is compatible with self-knowledge.

On research trips I am partially protected by having a different name in real life. I can sign into hotels without anxiously wondering whether my name will be recognized: then when it isn't, anxiously wondering why not. When I'm obliged to come clean with the people whose experience I want to tap, results vary. One person refuses to trust me another inch, the next promotes me to Chief of the Secret Service and, over my protestations that I was only ever the lowest form of secret life, replies that I would say that, wouldn't I? After which, he proceeds to ply me with confidences I don't want, can't use and won't remember, on the mistaken assumption that I will pass them on to We Know Who. I have given a couple of examples of this serio-comic dilemma.

But the majority of the luckless souls I've bombarded in this way over the last fifty years – from middle-ranking executives in the pharmaceutical industry to bankers, mercenaries and various shades of spy – have shown me forbearance and generosity. The most generous were the war reporters and foreign correspondents who took the parasitic novelist under their wing, credited him with courage he didn't possess and allowed him to tag along.

I can't imagine setting out on my forays in South-east Asia and the Middle East without the advice and companionship of David Greenway, the much decorated South-east Asia correspondent of *Time* magazine, the *Washington Post* and the *Boston Globe*. No timid neophyte can ever have hitched his wagon to such a faithful star. On a snowy morning in 1975, he was sitting at our breakfast table here in the chalet, enjoying a brief respite from the battlefront, when his office in Washington called to tell him that the besieged city of Phnom Penh was about to fall to the Khmer Rouge. There's no road down to the valley from our village, just a little train that takes you to a bigger train that takes you to a bigger train still, and thence to Zurich airport. In a trice he had changed out of his alpine gear into a war correspondent's tacky drills and old suede shoes, kissed his wife and daughters farewell, and was pelting down the hill to the station. I pelted after him with his passport.

Famously, Greenway was one of the last US journalists to be airlifted off the roof of the besieged US Embassy in Phnom Penh. In 1981, when I was seized with dysentery at the Allenby Bridge, which connects the West Bank with Jordan, Greenway manhandled me through the mass of impatient travellers waiting to be processed, talked us through the checkpoint by sheer willpower and delivered me across the bridge.

Rereading some of the episodes I have described, I realize that either out of egotism or for the sake of a sharper story I have omitted to mention who else was in the room at the time.

I think of my conversation with the Russian physicist and political prisoner Andrei Sakharov and his wife Elena Bonner, which took place in a restaurant in what was still Leningrad, under the aegis of Human Rights Watch, three of whose members sat at the table with us, and suffered the same childish intrusions from the KGB's troop of fake photo-journalists who paraded in a ring around us, firing their old-style flash-bulb cameras in our faces. Elsewhere, I hope, others of our party have written their own accounts of that historic day.

I think back to Nicholas Elliott, the longstanding friend and colleague of the double agent Kim Philby, stalking the drawing room of our London house with a glass of brandy in his hand, and I remember too late that my wife was just as present as I was, sitting in an armchair opposite me, and just as spellbound.

And I remember, even as I write this, the evening when Elliott brought his wife Elizabeth to dinner, and we had a loved Iranian guest who spoke immaculate English with a small, rather becoming speech defect. As our Iranian guest departed, Elizabeth turned to Nicholas with a sparkle in her eyes and said excitedly:

'Did you notice his stammer, darling? *Just* like Kim!'

The long chapter about my father Ronnie goes to the back of the book rather than the beginning because, much as he would like to,

I didn't want him elbowing his way to the top of the bill. For all the hours I have spent agonizing about him, he remains as much of a mystery to me as does my mother. Unless I have indicated otherwise the stories are fresh from the mint. When I saw a need, I changed a name. The main player may be dead, but his heirs and assigns may not see the joke. I have tried to strike an orderly path through my life in the thematic, if not the chronological sense, but rather like life itself the path widened into incoherence and some stories simply became what they remain to me: stand-alone incidents, sufficient to themselves, pointing in no direction I'm aware of, told for what they have come to mean to me and because they alarm or scare or touch me, or wake me up in the middle of the night and make me laugh out loud.

With the passing of time some of the encounters I describe have acquired to my eye the status of tiny bits of history caught *in fla-grante*, which I suppose is what all older people feel. Rereading them in the whole, farce to tragedy and back again, I find them mildly irresponsible, and I'm not sure why. Perhaps it's my own life that I find irresponsible. But it's too late to do anything about that now.

*

There are many things I am disinclined to write about ever, just as there are in anyone's life. I have had two immensely loyal and devoted wives, and I owe immeasurable thanks to both, and not a few apologies. I have been neither a model husband nor a model father, and am not interested in appearing that way. Love came to me late, after many missteps. I owe my ethical education to my four sons. Of my work for British Intelligence, performed mostly in Germany, I wish to add nothing to what is already reported by others, inaccurately, elsewhere. In this I am bound by vestiges of old-fashioned loyalty to my former Services, but also by undertakings I gave to the men and women who agreed to collaborate with me. It was understood between us that the promise of confidentiality would be subject to no time limit, but extend to their children and beyond. The work we engaged in was neither perilous nor dramatic, but it involved painful soul-searching on the part of those who signed up to it. Whether today these people are alive or dead, the promise of confidentiality holds.

Spying was forced on me from birth much in the way, I suppose, that the sea was forced on C. S. Forester, or India on Paul Scott. Out of the secret world I once knew I have tried to make a theatre for the larger worlds we inhabit. First comes the imagining, then the search for the reality. Then back to the imagining, and to the desk where I'm sitting now.

1

Don't be beastly to your Secret Service

'I know what you are,' cries Denis Healey, a former British Defence Secretary in the Labour interest, at a private party to which we have both been invited, his hand outstretched as he wades towards me from the doorway. 'You're a communist spy, that's what you are, admit it.'

So I admit it, as good chaps admit everything in these cases. And everybody laughs, my slightly startled host included. And I laugh too, because I'm a good chap and can take a joke as well as the next man, and because Denis Healey may be a Big Beast in the Labour Party and a political brawler, but he's also a considerable scholar and humanist, I admire him, and he's a couple of drinks ahead of me.

'You *bastard*, Cornwell,' a middle-aged MI6 officer, once my colleague, yells down the room at me as a bunch of Washington insiders gather for a diplomatic reception hosted by the British Ambassador. 'You *utter* bastard.' He wasn't expecting to meet me, but now he has done he's glad of the opportunity to tell me what he thinks of me for insulting the honour of the Service – *our* fucking Service, for fuck's sake! – and for making clowns of men and women who love their country and can't answer back. He is standing in front of me in the hunched position of a man about to let fly, and if diplomatic hands hadn't gentled him back a step the next morning's press would have had a field day.

The cocktail chatter gradually picks up again. But not before I have established that the book that has got under his skin is not *The Spy Who Came in from the Cold*, but its successor *The Looking Glass War*, which tells a bleak story of a British-Polish agent sent on a mission into East Germany and left to rot. Unhappily, East Germany had been part of my accuser's parish in the days when we had worked together. It crosses my mind to tell him that Allen Dulles, recently retired Director of the CIA, has declared the book to be a lot closer to reality than its predecessor, but I fear that will only compound his fury.

'Heartless, aren't we? Heartless incompetents! Thanks a million!'

My furious ex-colleague is not the only one. In less fiery tones the same reproach has been made to me repeatedly over the last five decades, not as any sinister or concerted effort, but as the refrain of hurt men and women who consider they are doing a necessary job.

'Why pick on *us*? *You* know how we are *really*.' Or more nastily: 'Now that you've made your pile out of us, perhaps you'll give us a rest for a bit.'

And always, somewhere, the hangdog reminder that the Service can't answer back; that it is defenceless against bad propaganda; that its successes must go unsung; that it can be known only by its failures.

'We are definitely not as our host here describes us,' says Sir Maurice Oldfield severely to Sir Alec Guinness over lunch.

Oldfield is a former Chief of the Secret Service who was later hung out to dry by Margaret Thatcher, but at the time of our meeting he is just another old spy in retirement.

'I've always wanted to meet Sir Alec,' he told me in his homey, north-country voice when I invited him. 'Ever since I sat opposite him on the train going up from Winchester. I'd have got into conversation with him if I'd had the nerve.'

Guinness is about to play my secret agent George Smiley in the BBC's television adaptation of *Tinker Tailor Soldier Spy*, and wishes to savour the company of a real old spy. But the lunch does not proceed as smoothly as I had hoped. Over the hors d'oeuvres, Oldfield extols the ethical standards of his old Service and implies, in the nicest way, that 'young David here' has besmirched its good name. Guinness, a former naval officer, who from the moment of meeting

Oldfield has appointed himself to the upper echelons of the Secret Service, can only shake his head sagely and agree. Over the Dover sole, Oldfield takes his thesis a step further:

'It's young David and his like,' he declares across the table to Guinness while ignoring me sitting beside him, 'that make it that much harder for the Service to recruit decent officers and sources. They read his books and they're put off. It's only natural.'

To which Guinness lowers his eyelids and shakes his head in a deploring sort of way, while I pay the bill.

'You should join the Athenaeum, David,' Oldfield says kindly, implying that the Athenaeum will somehow make a better person of me. 'I'll sponsor you myself. There. You'd like that, wouldn't you?' And to Guinness, as the three of us stand on the threshold of the restaurant: 'A pleasure indeed, Alec. An honour, I must say. We shall be in touch very shortly, I'm sure.'

'We shall indeed,' Guinness replies devoutly, as the two old spies shake hands.

Unable apparently to get enough of our departing guest, Guinness gazes fondly after him as he pounds off down the pavement: a small, vigorous gentleman of purpose, striding along with his umbrella thrust ahead of him as he disappears into the crowd.

'How about another cognac for the road?' Guinness suggests, and we have hardly resumed our places before the interrogation begins:

'Those very vulgar cufflinks. Do *all* our spies wear them?'

No, Alec, I think Maurice just likes vulgar cufflinks.

'And those loud orange suede boots with crêpe soles. Are they for stealth?'

I think they're just for comfort actually, Alec. Crêpe squeaks.

'Then tell me this.' He has grabbed an empty tumbler. Tipping it to an angle, he flicks at it with his thick fingertip. 'I've seen people do *this* before' – making a show of peering meditatively into the tumbler while he continues to flick it – 'and I've seen people do *this*' – now rotating the finger round the rim in the same contemplative vein. 'But I've never seen people do *this* before' – inserting his finger into the tumbler and passing it round the inside. 'Do you think he's look-ing for dregs of poison?'

Is he being serious? The child in Guinness has never been more serious in its life. Well, I suppose if it was dregs he was looking for, he'd have drunk the poison by then, I suggest. But he prefers to ignore me.

It is a matter of entertainment history that Oldfield's suede boots, crêpe-soled or other, and his rolled umbrella thrust forward to feel out the path ahead, became essential properties for Guinness' por-trayal of George Smiley, old spy in a hurry. I haven't checked on the cufflinks recently, but I have a memory that our director thought them a little overdone and persuaded Guinness to trade them in for something less flashy.

The other legacy of our lunch was less enjoyable, if artistically more creative. Oldfield's distaste for my work – and, I suspect, for myself – struck deep root in Guinness' thespian soul, and he was not above reminding me of it when he felt the need to rack up George Smiley's sense of personal guilt; or, as he liked to imply, mine.

*

For the last hundred years and more, our British spies have con-ducted a distraught and sometimes hilarious love-hate affair with their obstreperous novelists. Like the novelists themselves they want the image, they want the glamour, but don't ask them to put up with derision or negative reviews. In the early 1900s, spy writers ranging in quality from Erskine Childers to William Le Queux and E. Phillips Oppenheim whipped up such an anti-German furore that they may fairly claim to have assisted at the birth of an established security service in the first place. Until then gentlemen supposedly did not read other gentlemen's letters; even if in reality a lot of gentlemen did. With the war of 1914–18 came the novelist Somerset Maugham, British secret agent, and by most accounts not a very good one. When Winston Churchill complained that his *Ashenden* broke the

Official Secrets Act,* Maugham, with the threat of a homosexual scandal hanging over him, burned fourteen unpublished stories and held off publication of the rest till 1928.

Compton Mackenzie, novelist, biographer and Scottish nationalist, was less easily cowed. Invalided out of the army in the First World War, he transferred to MI6 and became a competent head of British counter-intelligence in neutral Greece. However, he too often found his orders and superiors absurd and, as writers will, he had his fun of them. In 1932 he was prosecuted under the Official Secrets Act and fined £100 for his autobiographical *Greek Memories*, a book that was indeed stuffed with outrageous indiscretions. Far from learning his lesson, he wreaked his vengeance a year later with the satirical *Water on the Brain*. I have heard that in Mackenzie's file at MI5 there is a letter in enormous type addressed to the Director General and signed in the traditional green ink of the Chief of the Secret Service.

'Worst of all,' writes the Chief to his brother-in-arms on the other side of St James's Park, 'Mackenzie has revealed the actual symbols employed in Secret Service correspondence,† *some of which are still in use.*' Mackenzie's ghost must be rubbing his hands in glee.

But the most impressive of MI6's literary defectors must surely be Graham Greene, though I doubt whether he knew quite how close he came to following Mackenzie to the Old Bailey. One of my fondest memories of the late fifties is sharing a coffee with the MI5 lawyer in the Security Service's excellent canteen. He was a benign, pipe-smoking fellow, more family solicitor than bureaucrat, but that morning he was deeply troubled. An advance copy of *Our Man in Havana* had arrived on his desk, and he was halfway into it. When I said I envied him his luck, he sighed and shook his head. That fellow Greene, he said, would have to be prosecuted. Using information

* Acknowledgements to Christopher Andrew's *Secret Service*, published in 1985 by William Heinemann.
† Such correspondence traditionally started with a three-letter code for the MI6 station, followed by a number to denote the station member.

gained as a wartime officer of MI6, he had accurately portrayed the relationship between a head of station in a British Embassy and an agent in the field. He would have to go to jail.

'And it's a good book,' he complained. 'It's a *damned* good book. And that's the whole trouble.'

I combed the newspapers for news of Greene's arrest, but he remained at large. Perhaps MI5's barons had decided after all that it was better to laugh than cry. For their act of clemency, Greene rewarded them twenty years later with *The Human Factor*, which portrayed them not merely as boobies but as murderers. But MI6 must have sent a warning shot across his bows. In the foreword to *The Human Factor* he is careful to assure us that he has not infringed the Official Secrets Act. Dig out an early copy of *Our Man in Havana* and you will find a similar disclaimer.

But history suggests that our sins are eventually forgotten. Mackenzie ended his days with a knighthood, Greene with the Order of Merit.

'In your new novel, sir,' an earnest American journalist asks me, 'you have a man saying of your central character that he would not have become a traitor if he had been able to write. Can you tell me, please, what would have become of *you*, if *you* had not been able to write?'

Searching for a safe answer to this dangerous question, I wonder whether our secret services should not be grateful to their literary defectors after all. Compared with the hell we might have raised by other means, writing was as harmless as playing with our bricks. How much our poor beleaguered spies must be wishing that Edward Snowden had done the novel instead.

*

So what should I have replied to my enraged ex-colleague at the diplomatic party who looked as if he was about to knock me down? No good pointing out that in some books I have painted British

Intelligence as a more competent organization than I had ever known it to be in real life. Or that one of its most senior officers described *The Spy Who Came in from the Cold* as 'the only bloody double-agent operation that ever worked'. Or that, in describing the nostalgic war games of an isolated British department in the novel that so angered him, I might have been attempting something a bit more ambitious than a crude assault on his Service. And Heaven help me were I to maintain that if you are a novelist struggling to explore a nation's psyche, its Secret Service is not an unreasonable place to look. I would be flat on my back before I came to the main verb.

As to his Service being unable to answer back, well I would guess there is not a spy agency anywhere in the Western world that has enjoyed more mollycoddling from its domestic media than ours. *Embedded* scarcely covers it. Our systems of censorship, whether voluntary or imposed by vague and draconian legislation, our skills in artful befriending and the British public's collective submission to wholesale surveillance of dubious legality are the envy of every spook in the free and unfree world.

No good either my pointing to the many 'approved' memoirs of former members that portray the Service in the clothes in which it likes to be admired; or to the 'official histories' that draw such a forgiving veil over its more heinous misdeeds; or to the numberless cooked-up articles in our national newspapers that result from much cosier luncheons than the one I enjoyed with Maurice Oldfield.

Or how about suggesting to my furious friend that a writer who treats professional spies as fallible human beings like the rest of us is performing a modest social service – even, God help us, a democratic function, since in Britain our secret services are still, for better or worse, the spiritual home of our political, social and industrial elite?

For that, dear former colleague, is the limit of my disloyalty. And that, dear departed Lord Healey, is the limit of my communism which, come to think of it, can't be said of you in your younger days.

*

It's hard to convey, half a century on, the atmosphere of mistrust that pervaded Whitehall's corridors of secret power in the late fifties and early sixties. I was twenty-five when, in 1956, I was formally inducted into MI5 as a junior officer. Any younger, they told me, and I wouldn't have been eligible. Five, as we called it, prided itself on its maturity. Alas, no amount of maturity protected it from recruiting such luminaries as Guy Burgess and Anthony Blunt and the other sad traitors of that period whose names linger like half-forgotten football stars in the British public memory.

I had entered the Service with high expectations. My intelligence exploits to date, trivial as they were, had left me with an appetite for more. My case officers had been uniformly agreeable, efficient and considerate. They had spoken to my sense of calling and revived my lapsed public schoolboy's duty of pain. As a National Service intelligence officer in Austria, I had lived in awe of the shadowy civilians who periodically descended on our humdrum encampment in Graz and invested it with a mystique it otherwise sadly lacked. It was only when I entered their citadel that I came smartly to earth.

Spying on a decaying British Communist Party twenty-five thousand strong that had to be held together by MI5 informants did not meet my aspirations. Neither did the double standards by which the Service nurtured its own. MI5, for better or worse, was the moral arbiter of the private lives of Britain's civil servants and scientists. Under the vetting procedures of the day, homosexuals and other perceived deviants were held to be vulnerable to blackmail, and consequently debarred from secret work. But the Service seemed quite content to ignore the homosexuals in its own ranks, and its Director General openly cohabiting with his secretary during the week and his wife at weekends, even to the point of leaving written instructions for the night duty officer in case his wife called up wanting to know where he was. Yet God help the registry typist whose skirt was deemed too short or too tight, or the married desk officer who gave her the eye.

While the upper echelons of the Service were staffed by ageing survivors of the glory days of 1939–45, its middle order comprised former colonial police and district officers left over from Britain's dwindling empire. Experienced as they might be in quelling unruly natives who had the temerity to want their countries back, they were less at ease when it came to guarding the mother country they barely knew. The British working classes were as volatile and unknowable to them as were once the rioting Dervishes. Trade unions in their eyes were nothing but communist front organizations.

Meanwhile, young spy hunters such as myself, thirsting for stronger fare, were ordered not to waste their time looking for Soviet-controlled 'illegals', since it was known on unassailable authority that no such spies were operating on British soil. Known to whom, by whom, I never learned. Four years were enough. In 1960 I applied for a transfer to MI6 or, as my disgruntled employers had it, to 'those shits across the park'.

But let me in parting acknowledge one debt of gratitude to MI5 that I can never sufficiently repay. The most rigorous instruction in prose writing that I ever received came, not from any schoolteacher or university tutor, least of all from a writing school. It came from the classically educated senior officers on the top floor of MI5's headquarters in Curzon Street, Mayfair, who seized on my reports with gleeful pedantry, heaping contempt on my dangling clauses and gratuitous adverbs, scoring the margins of my deathless prose with such comments as *redundant – omit – justify – sloppy – do you really mean this?* No editor I have since encountered was so exacting, or so right.

By the spring of 1961 I had completed the MI6 initiation course, which equipped me with skills I never needed and quickly forgot. At the concluding ceremony the Service's head of training, a rugged, pink-faced veteran in tweeds, told us with tears in his eyes that we were to go home and await orders. They might take some time. The reason – which he vowed he had never dreamed he would have to utter – was that a longstanding officer of the Service, who had enjoyed its unstinted trust, had been unmasked as a Soviet double agent. His name was George Blake.

The scale of Blake's betrayal remains, even by the standards of the period, monumental: literally hundreds of British agents – Blake himself could no longer calculate how many – betrayed; covert audio operations deemed vital to the national security, such as, but not exclusively, the Berlin audio tunnel, blown before they were launched; and the entire breakdown of MI6's personnel, safe houses, order of battle and outstations across the globe. Blake, a most capable field agent in both interests, was also a God-seeker, who by the time of his unmasking had espoused Christianity, Judaism and communism in that order. Imprisoned at Wormwood Scrubs, from which he later famously escaped, he gave lessons to his fellow inmates in the Holy Koran.

Two years after receiving the unsettling news of George Blake's treachery, I was serving as a Second Secretary (Political) at the British Embassy in Bonn. Summoning me to his office late one evening, my Head of Station informed me, strictly for my own information, of what every Englishman would be reading in his evening newspaper the next day: that Kim Philby, MI6's brilliant former head of counter-intelligence, once tipped to become Chief of the Service, was also a Russian spy and, as we were only gradually allowed to know, had been one since 1937.

Later in this book you will read an account by Nicholas Elliott, Philby's friend, confidant and colleague in war and peace, of their final encounter in Beirut that led to Philby's partial confession. And it may cross your mind that Elliott's account is mysteriously short on outrage or even indignation. The reason is very simple. Spies are not policemen, neither are they quite the moral realists they like to think they are. If your mission in life is to win over traitors to your cause, you can hardly complain when one of your own, even if you loved him as a brother and cherished colleague, and shared every aspect of your secret work with him, turns out to have been obtained by someone else. It was a lesson I had taken to heart by the time I wrote *The Spy Who Came in from the Cold*. And when I came to write *Tinker Tailor Soldier Spy*, it was Kim Philby's murky lamp that lit my path.

Spying and novel writing are made for each other. Both call for a ready eye for human transgression and the many routes to betrayal. Those of us who have been inside the secret tent never really leave it. If we didn't share its habits before we entered it, we will share them ever after. For proof of this we need look no further than Graham Greene, and the anecdotal account of his self-imposed game of foxes with the FBI. Perhaps it is recorded by one of his disobliging biographers, but better not to look.

All through his later life, Greene, the novelist and former spy, was convinced that he was on the FBI blacklist of subversive pro-communists. And he had good reason, given his numerous visits to the Soviet Union, his continuing and outspoken loyalty to his friend and fellow spy Kim Philby, and his futile exertions to reconcile the Roman Catholic and communist causes. When the Berlin Wall went up, Greene had himself photographed posing on the wrong side of it, while telling the world he'd rather be there than here. Indeed, Greene's aversion to the United States and his fear of the consequences of his radical pronouncements reached such heights that he insisted that any meeting with his US publisher be conducted on the Canadian side of the border.

Came a day, then, when he was at last able to demand sight of his FBI file. It contained one entry only: that he had kept company with the politically erratic British ballerina Margot Fonteyn, when she was fighting the doomed cause of her paralysed and faithless husband, Roberto Arias.

Spying did not introduce me to secrecy. Evasion and deception were the necessary weapons of my childhood. In adolescence we are all spies of a sort, but I was a veteran. When the secret world came to claim me, it felt like a coming home. Why this was so is best left to the later chapter called 'Son of the author's father'.

2

Dr Globke's laws

Bloody Bonn was what we young British diplomats called the place in the early sixties, not out of any particular disrespect for the sleepy Rhineland spa, seat of the prince-electors of the Holy Roman Empire and birthplace of Ludwig van Beethoven, but as a sceptical doffing of the cap to our hosts' absurd dreams of moving the German capital up the road to Berlin, which we happily shared with them in the certainty it would never happen.

In 1961 the British Embassy, a sprawling industrial eyesore on the dual carriageway between Bonn and Bad Godesberg, boasted three hundred souls, the majority of them home-based rather than locally engaged. To this day I can't imagine what the rest of us got up to in the fuggy Rhineland air. Yet for me the three years in Bonn contain such seismic shifts in my life that today I think of it as the place where my past life entered its unstoppable demise, and my writing life began.

True, back in London I had had my first novel accepted by a publisher. But it wasn't till I'd been in Bonn several months that it made its modest appearance. I remember driving to Cologne airport on a damp Sunday afternoon, buying copies of the British newspapers, then parking the car and sitting down on a sheltered garden bench in Bonn and reading them alone. Reviewers were benign, if not quite as ecstatic as I had hoped. They approved of George Smiley. And suddenly that was all there was.

Probably all writers, at any stage in their lives, tend to feel that way: the weeks and months of anguish and wrong turnings; the precious finished typescript; the ritual enthusiasm of agent and publisher; the proof editing; the great expectations; the angst as the Big Day approaches; the reviews, and suddenly it's over. You wrote the book a year ago, so what are you sitting around for, instead of writing something new?

Well, in fact, I *was* writing something new.

I had begun a novel set in a public school. For background I was using Sherborne, where I had been a pupil, and Eton, where I had been a schoolmaster. There is a suggestion that I started preparing the novel while I was still teaching at Eton, but I have no memory of doing so. Rising at an unearthly hour before setting off for the Embassy, I completed the novel in short order, and sent it in. So once again, job done – except that next time round I was determined to do something grittier. I would write about the world on my doorstep.

*

By the time I had been *en poste* for a year, my remit covered all of West Germany and gave me unlimited freedom of movement and access. As one of the Embassy's travelling evangelists for Britain's entry into the Common Market, I could invite myself to town halls, political societies and mayoral parlours anywhere in West Germany. In the young West Germany's determination to appear an open, democratic society, all doors were open to the inquisitive young diplomat. I could sit all day in the Bundestag's diplomatic gallery, lunch with parliamentary journalists and advisers. I could knock on ministerial doors, attend protest rallies and lofty weekend seminars on culture and the German soul, all the while trying to fathom, fifteen years after the collapse of the Third Reich, where the old Germany ended and the new one began. In 1961 this wasn't at all easy. Or it wasn't to me.

A dictum attributed to Chancellor Konrad Adenauer, nicknamed 'The Old Man', who held the post from West Germany's foundation in 1949 until 1963, neatly summed up the problem: 'You don't throw away dirty water for as long as you haven't got any clean.' It is widely assumed that this was a veiled reference to Dr Hans Josef Maria Globke, his grey eminence on matters of national security and much else. Globke's record was impressive even by Nazi standards. Even before Hitler's rise to power, he had distinguished himself by drafting anti-Semitic laws for the Prussian government.

Two years later under his new Führer he drafted the Nuremberg Law, revoking German citizenship for all Jews and, for purposes of identification, requiring them to insert the word *Sara* or *Israel* into their names. Non-Jews who were married to Jews were ordered to get rid of their spouses. Serving under Adolf Eichmann in the Nazi Office of Jewish Affairs, he drafted a new law for the Protection of German Blood and German Honour, which sounded the signal for the Holocaust.

Simultaneously, I presume by virtue of his ardent Catholicism, Globke contrived to reinsure himself with right-wing anti-Nazi resistance groups: so much so that he was earmarked for high office should the plotters succeed in getting rid of Hitler. And perhaps this was how, when the war ended, he eluded half-hearted Allied attempts to prosecute him. Adenauer was determined to have his Globke at his side. The British did not stand in Globke's way.

Thus it happened that in 1951, a mere six years after the end of the war, and two years after the creation of West Germany as a state, Dr Hans Globke achieved a stroke of legislation on behalf of his former and present Nazi colleagues that today remains barely conceivable. Under Globke's New Law, as I shall call it, civil servants of the Hitler regime whose careers had been curtailed by circumstances beyond their control would henceforth receive full restitution of such pay, back-pay and pension rights as they would have enjoyed if the Second World War hadn't taken place, or if Germany had won it. In a word, they would be entitled to whatever promotion would have come their way had their careers proceeded without the inconvenience of an Allied victory.

The effect was immediate. The old Nazi guard clung to the plum jobs. A younger, less tarnished generation was consigned to life below stairs.

*

Now enter Dr Johannes Ullrich, scholar, archivist and lover of Bach, good red burgundy and Prussian military history. In April 1945, a few days before Berlin's military commander unconditionally surrendered to the Russians, Ullrich was doing what he had been doing for the last ten years: beavering away as curator and junior archivist of the Prussian Imperial Archive at the German Foreign Office in the Wilhelmstrasse. As the Kingdom of Prussia was dissolved in 1918, no document that passed through his hands was less than twenty-seven years old.

I have seen no pictures of Johannes, as I came to know him, in his youth, but I imagine him a quite athletic fellow, sternly dressed in the suits and stiff collars of the bygone age that was his spiritual habitat. With Hitler's rise to power he was three times urged by his superiors to join the Nazi Party, and three times he refused. Junior archivist was therefore what he remained when, in the spring of 1945, General Zhukov's Red Army advanced on the Wilhelmstrasse. Soviet troops entering Berlin had little interest in taking prisoners, but the German Foreign Office promised prisoners of high value, as well as incriminating Nazi documents.

What Johannes now did with the Russians at his door is today the stuff of legend. Wrapping the Imperial Archive in swathes of oilcloth, he loaded it on to a handcart and, disregarding a torrent of small-arms fire, mortar bombs and grenades, trundled it to a patch of soft ground, buried it and returned to his post in time to be taken prisoner.

The case against him was, by the standards of Soviet military justice, irrefutable. As a keeper of Nazi files, he was by definition an agent of fascist aggression. Of his subsequent ten years in Siberian jails, he served six in solitary and the rest in a communal cell for criminal lunatics, whose mannerisms he learned to mimic in order to survive.

In 1955, he was released under a prisoner-repatriation deal. His first act on arriving in Berlin was to lead a search party to the spot where he had buried the archive and supervise its exhumation. After which, he withdrew to recuperate.

*

Now back to Globke's New Law.

What entitlements were not due to this loyal civil servant from the Nazi era, this victim of Bolshevik brutality? Never mind his three-times refusal to join the Party. Never mind that his detestation of all things Nazi had driven him ever deeper into Prussia's imperial past. Rather ask yourself to what heights a young archivist with glowing academic credentials might not have ascended, had the Third Reich prevailed.

Johannes Ullrich, who for ten years had seen nothing of the world beyond the walls of a Siberian cell, was deemed to have spent the entire period of his incarceration as an aspirational diplomat. He was therefore entitled to the pay rises commensurate with the promotion he would have enjoyed, including back-pay, allowances, pension rights and – surely in any civil service that most desirable of perks – office space of a size appropriate to his status. Oh, and a year's paid leave, at least.

Recuperating, Johannes reads deeply in Prussian history. He re-discovers his love of red burgundy and marries a delightfully humorous Belgian interpreter who worships him. Finally the day comes when he can no longer resist the call of duty that is such an integral part of his Prussian soul. He puts on his new suit, his wife helps him tie his tie and drives him to the Foreign Office that is no longer in Berlin's Wilhelmstrasse, but in Bonn. A janitor escorts him to his room. Not *room*, he protests, but a *state apartment*, with a

3-acre desk that he swears was designed by Albert Speer. Herr Dr Johannes Ullrich, whether he likes it or not, is henceforth a senior representative of the West German Foreign Service.

*

To see Johannes in full flood, which was my good fortune on several occasions, you must picture a hunched, vigorous man in his fifties, so restlessly on the move that you could imagine him still pacing out his Siberian cell. Now he darts a quizzical glance at you over his shoulder in case he is being too much. Now he rolls his troubled eyes in horror at his own behaviour, lets out a hoot of laughter and takes another spin around the room, arms waving. But he isn't mad, like the poor prisoners he was chained up with in Siberia. He is brilliantly, unbearably sane, and once more the madness isn't in him, but around him.

First, every detail of his state apartment must be minutely described for the benefit of the spellbound dinner guests gathered at my diplomatic hiring in Königswinter beside the Rhine: the imaginary Bundesadler, the black eagle with its turned head and red claws scowling down on him from the wall – he mimes for us its disdainful sneer over its right shoulder – the ambassadorial cutlery set with its silver inkwell and penholder.

Then, pulling open an imaginary drawer of the Albert Speer 3-acre desk, he extracts for us the West German Foreign Office's own confidential internal telephone directory, bound, he tells us, in finest calf. He is holding it out to us in his empty hands, head devoutly bowed over it as he scents the leather, rolls his eyes at its quality.

Now he opens it. Very slowly. Each re-enacting is an exorcism for him, a choreographed purging of whatever came into his head the first time he saw the list of names staring at him. They are the same aristocratic names and the same owners who earned their diplomatic spurs under the ludicrous Joachim von Ribbentrop, Hitler's Foreign Minister, who from his death cell in Nuremberg continued to proclaim his love of Adolf Hitler.

They may be better diplomats now, these noble names. They may be reformed champions of the democratic way. They may, like Globke, have struck their deals with some anti-Nazi group against the day when Hitler fell. But Johannes is not of a mood to see his colleagues in this kindly light. Still watched by our small audience, he slumps into an armchair and takes a pull of the good red burgundy I have bought in his honour from the Economat where we diplomats do our privileged shopping. He is showing us that this is what he did that morning in his state apartment after he had taken a first look at the calf-bound, confidential West German Foreign Office internal telephone directory: how he flopped into a deep leather armchair with the directory open in his hands, silently reading one grand name after another, left to right in slow motion, every *von* and *zu*. We watch his eyes widen and his lips move. He stares at my wall. This is how I stared at the wall in my state apartment, he is telling us. This is how I stared at the wall of my Siberian prison.

He bounces out of my chair, or better the chair in his state apartment. He is back at Albert Speer's 3-acre desk, even if it's only a rickety mahogany sideboard next to the glass door leading to my garden. He flattens the directory on the desk with his palms. There is no telephone on my rickety sideboard but he has picked up an imaginary receiver and with the help of the forefinger of his other hand he is reading off the first extension number in the directory. We hear the *zup-zup* of an internal phone ringing out. This is Johannes, *zup-zupping* through his nose. We see his broad back arch and stiffen and hear his heels snap together in approved Prussian style. We hear the military bark, loud enough to wake my sleeping children upstairs:

'*Heil Hitler, Herr Baron! Hier Ullrich! Ich möchte mich zurückmelden!*' – Heil Hitler! This is Ullrich! I wish to report myself back for duty!

*

I wouldn't want to give the idea that I spent my three years as a dip-lomat in Germany fulminating about old Nazis in high places at a time when my Service's energies were devoted to promoting British trade and fighting communism. If I did fulminate about old Nazis – who weren't actually that old, given that in 1960 we were only half a generation away from Hitler – then I did so because I identified with the Germans my age who, in order to get on in their chosen walks of life, had to make nice to people who had participated in the ruin of their country.

What must it be like, I used to ask myself, for an aspiring young politician to know that the upper ranks of his party were adorned by such luminaries as Ernst Achenbach, who, as a senior German Embassy official in Paris during the Occupation, had personally supervised the mass deportation of French Jews to Auschwitz? Both the French and the Americans tried to put him on trial, but Achen-bach was a lawyer by trade, and had secured some kind of mysterious dispensation for himself. So instead of being hauled before the courts in Nuremberg, he set up his own lucrative law firm, defend-ing people accused of crimes identical to those he had committed. How did my aspiring young German politician respond to having an Achenbach watch over his career? I wondered. Did he just swallow and smile?

Amid all the other preoccupations of my time in Bonn and later Hamburg, Germany's unconquered past refused to let me go. Inwardly, I never succumbed to the political correctness of the day, even if outwardly I conformed. In that sense, I suppose I behaved as many Germans must have done during the 1939–45 war.

But after I had left Germany, the subject refused to let me go. With *The Spy Who Came in from the Cold* long behind me, I went back to Hamburg and sought out a German paediatrician accused of taking part in a Nazi euthanasia programme to rid the Aryan nation of useless mouths. It turned out that the case against him had been cooked up by a jealous academic rival and was baseless. I was duly chastened. In the same year, 1964, I visited the town of Ludwigsburg to talk to Erwin Schüle, Director of Baden-Württemberg's Centre for the Investigation of National Socialist Crimes. I was looking for the kind of story that later became *A Small Town in Germany*, but I hadn't yet got round to using the British Embassy in Bonn as its background. I was still too close to the experience.

Erwin Schüle turned out to be exactly as billed: decent, frank, committed to his work. And his staff of half-a-dozen or so pale young lawyers, no less. Each to his separate cubbyhole, they spent long days poring over horrific evidence gleaned from Nazi files and the skimpy testimony of witnesses. Their aim was to award atrocities to individuals who could be brought to trial, rather than military units that could not. Kneeling before children's sandpits they set out toy figures, each marked with a number. In one row, toy soldiers in uniform with guns. In the other, toy men, women and children in daily clothes. And running between them in the sand, a small trench to indicate the mass grave waiting to be filled.

Come evening, Schüle and his wife entertained me to dinner on the balcony of their house set on a forested hillside. Schüle spoke passionately of his work. It was a vocation, he said. It was an historical necessity. We agreed to meet again soon, but we didn't. In February of the following year Schüle stepped off a plane in Warsaw. He had been invited to inspect some recently discovered Nazi files. Instead, he was greeted by an enlarged facsimile of his Nazi Party membership card. Simultaneously, the Soviet government launched its own string of charges against him, including an allegation that while serving as a soldier on the Russian front he had shot dead two Russian civilians with his pistol and raped a Russian woman. Once again the charges were found to be baseless.

The lesson? The harder you looked for absolutes, the less likely you were to find them. I believe that Schüle, by the time I met him, was a decent man. But he had to live with his past and, whatever it amounted to, deal with it. How Germans of his generation did that has been one of my abiding interests. When the Baader–Meinhof era broke upon Germany, I for one was not surprised. For many young Germans, their parents' past had been buried, or denied, or simply lied out of existence. One day something was sure to boil over, and something did. And it wasn't just a few 'rowdy elements' who boiled over. It was a whole angry generation of frustrated middle-class sons and daughters who tiptoed into the fray and provided the front-line terrorists with logistical and moral support.

Could such a thing ever happen in Britain? We have long ceased to compare ourselves with Germany. Perhaps we no longer dare. Modern Germany's emergence as a self-confident, non-aggressive, democratic power – not to speak of the humanitarian example it has set – is a pill too bitter for many of us Brits to swallow. That is a sadness that I have regretted for far too long.

3

Official visit

One of my more agreeable duties while serving at the British Embassy in Bonn in the early sixties was escorting, or 'bear-leading' as the Germans have it, delegations of promising young Germans to Britain to learn from our democratic ways and – such was our proud hope – emulate them. Most were first-time parliamentarians or rising political journalists, some very bright, and all, as I only now remember, male.

The average tour lasted one week: depart Cologne airport on the Sunday evening BEA flight, receive welcoming address from British Council or Foreign Office representative, return on the following Saturday morning. Over five close-packed days, the guests would visit both Houses of Parliament; attend Question Time in the Commons; visit the High Courts of Justice and maybe the BBC; be received by government ministers and Opposition leaders of a rank determined in part by the standing of the delegates and in part by the whim of their hosts; and sample the rustic beauties of England (Windsor Castle, Runnymede for the Magna Carta, and the model English country town of Woodstock in Oxfordshire).

And come evening, they had a choice of going to the theatre or pursuing their private interests, by which was intended – see your British Council information pack – that delegates of the Catholic or Lutheran persuasion would consort with their co-religionists, socialists with their Labour comrades-in-arms, and those with more specialized private interests, such as the emerging economies of the Third World, could sit down together with their British counterparts.

For further information or requests, please don't hesitate to consult your tour guide and interpreter, meaning me.

And hesitate they didn't. Which was how it came about that at eleven o'clock of a balmy summer's Sunday evening in a West End hotel, I was standing at the concierge's desk with a ten-pound note in my hand and half-a-dozen well-refreshed young German parliamentarians leaning over my shoulder demanding female company. They had been in England for four hours, most for the first time. All they knew about London in the sixties was that it was swinging, and they were determined to swing with it. Thus far, a Scotland Yard sergeant I happened to know had recommended a nightclub in Bond Street, where 'the girls played fair and didn't diddle you'. Two black cabs had rushed us to its doors. But the doors were barred and padlocked and no lights burned. The sergeant had forgotten that in those long-gone days we had Sunday closing laws. Now, with my guests' hopes dashed, I was appealing to the concierge as a last resort, and for ten pounds he did not disappoint:

'Halfway up Curzon Street on your left-hand side, sir, and there's a blue light in the window says "French Lessons Here". If the light's out, that means the girls are busy. If it's not out, that means they're open for business. But keep it on the quiet side.'

To accompany my wards through thick and thin, or leave them to their pleasures? Their blood was up. They spoke little English, and their German was not always on the quiet side. The blue light was not out. It was of a peculiarly insinuating fluorescence, and seemed to be the only light in the street. A short garden path led to the front door. An illuminated bell button was marked 'Press'. Ignoring the concierge's advice, my delegates weren't keeping it on the quiet side. I pressed the bell. The door was opened by a large, middle-aged lady in a white kaftan and bandana headscarf.

'Yes?' she demanded indignantly, as if we had roused her from her slumbers.

I was on the point of apologizing for disturbing her, but the parliamentary member for a constituency west of Frankfurt was ahead of me.

'*We are German and we wish to learn French!*' he bellowed in his best English to roars of approval from his comrades.

Our hostess was undaunted.

'It's five pounds each for a short moment, and one at a time,' she said, with the severity of a prep-school matron.

About to leave my delegates to their specialized interests, I spotted two uniformed constables, one old, one young, approaching us down the pavement. I was wearing a black jacket and striped trousers.

'I'm from the Foreign Office. These gentlemen are my official guests.'

'Less noise,' said the older one, and they walked sedately on.

4

Fingers on the trigger

The most impressive of the politicians that I escorted to Britain during my three years at the British Embassy in Bonn was Fritz Erler, in 1963 the German Social Democratic Party's leading authority on defence and foreign policy, and widely tipped as a future chancellor of West Germany. He was also, as I knew from stints of sitting out Bundestag debates, a scathing and witty opponent of both Chancellor Adenauer and his Defence Minister, Franz Josef Strauss. And since privately I disliked the pair of them as much as Erler appeared to, I was doubly pleased to be given the job of accompanying him on a visit to London, where he would be holding talks with leading British parliamentarians of all persuasions, including the Labour leader Harold Wilson and the Prime Minister, Harold Macmillan.

The burning issue of the moment was Germany's finger on the trigger: how much say should the Bonn government have in the decision to launch US missiles from West German bases in the event of nuclear war? It was this topic that Erler had recently discussed in Washington with President Kennedy and his Defense Secretary, Robert McNamara. My job, on assignment from the Embassy, was to accompany him throughout his stay in England and generally make myself useful as his private secretary, factotum and interpreter. Although Erler, no fool, spoke more English than he let on, he liked the extra thinking time granted him by the interpreting process, and was undeterred when he was told I was not a trained interpreter. The trip was to last ten days and the schedule was tight. The Foreign Office had booked him into a suite at the Savoy

Hotel and provided me with a room a few doors down the same corridor.

Each morning around five o'clock, I bought the day's papers from a news vendor in the Strand and, with the Savoy's vacuum cleaners whizzing round my ears, sat in the hotel lounge marking up any bits of news or comment that I thought Erler should know about ahead of the day's meetings. I then dumped them on the floor outside his room, returned to mine and waited for the signal for our morning canter, which came sharp at 7.00.

Loping along beside me in his black beret and raincoat, Erler cut an austere and seemingly humourless figure, but I knew he was neither of these things. We would walk in one direction for ten minutes, each morning a different route. He would then stop, turn on his heel and, head down, hands linked behind his back, eyes fixed on the pavement, reel off the names of shops and brass plates that we had passed, while I checked them for accuracy. It was an exercise in mental discipline, he explained after a couple of such excursions, that he had acquired in Dachau concentration camp. Shortly before the outbreak of war, he was sentenced to ten years' incarceration for 'planning high treason' against the Nazi government. In 1945, while on a notorious death march of prisoners out of Dachau, he contrived to escape and lie low in Bavaria until the German surrender.

The exercise in mental discipline had evidently worked, for I don't remember him fluffing a single shop name or brass plate.

*

Our meetings over the next ten days were a Cook's Tour of Westminster's great, good and not so good. I have a pictorial memory of the faces across the table, and an aural memory of certain voices. Harold Wilson's I found particularly distracting. Lacking the detachment of the trained interpreter, I was far too interested in the vocal and physical idiosyncrasies of my subjects. I remember particularly Wilson's unlit pipe and his theatrical use of it as a stage tool. Of the substance of our supposedly high-level dialogues, I have no memory whatever. Our interlocutors appeared to have as light a grasp of defence matters as I had, which was a mercy, for although I had boned up on a list of technical terms from the macabre vocabulary of Mutually Assured Destruction (MAD), they remained as incomprehensible to me in English as they were in German. But I don't believe I ever had to trot them out, and today I doubt I would recognize them.

Only one encounter remains indelibly fixed in my memory, visually, aurally and in substance, and that was the grand climax of our ten-day tour: putative future Chancellor Fritz Erler meets incumbent British Prime Minister Harold Macmillan at 10 Downing Street.

*

We are in mid-September 1963. In March of that year, Secretary of State for War John Profumo had made his personal statement to the Commons denying any improper association with a Miss Christine Keeler, an English nightclub girl living under the protection of Stephen Ward, a fashionable London osteopath. That a married War Secretary should keep a mistress might be reprehensible, but not unheard of. That he might be sharing her, as Keeler claimed, with the Naval Attaché from the Soviet Embassy in London was excessive. The scapegoat was the luckless osteopath Stephen Ward who, after a trumped-up trial, killed himself without waiting for the verdict. By June, Profumo had resigned from government and Parliament. By October, Macmillan too had resigned, pleading ill health. Erler's encounter with him took place in September, just weeks before he threw in the towel.

We arrived at 10 Downing Street late, never a good start. The government car that had been sent for us failed to show up, and I had been reduced to stepping into the middle of the road in my black coat and striped trousers, forcing a passing driver to stop and asking him to take us to 10 Downing Street as fast as possible.

Understandably, the driver, a young man in a suit with a woman passenger at his side, thought I was mad. But his passenger rebuked him. 'Go on, do it. Or they'll be late,' she said, and the young man bit his lip and did as he was told. We clambered into the back, Erler gave the young man his card, said any time they came to Bonn. But we were still ten minutes late.

Ushered into Macmillan's office, we made our apologies and sat down. Macmillan sat motionless behind his desk, his liver-spotted hands before him. His Private Secretary, Philip de Zulueta, Welsh Guardsman, soon to be knight of the realm, sat at his side. Erler regretted in German that the car was late. I seconded him in English. Beneath the prime ministerial hands lay a sheet of glass, and under it, in typed letters large enough to read upside down, lay a prime ministerial briefing paper with Erler's curriculum vitae. The word *Dachau* was written large. While Macmillan spoke, his hands travelled over the glass as if reading braille. His patrician slur, perfectly captured by Peter Cook in the satirical *Beyond the Fringe*, was like an old gramophone record running at a very low speed. A trail of unstoppable tears leaked from the corner of his right eye, down a groove and into his shirt collar.

After a few courteous words of welcome, delivered with halting Edwardian charm – have they made you comfortable? are they looking after you? are they providing you with the right people to talk to? – Macmillan asked Erler with evident curiosity what he had come to talk about, a question that, at the least, took Erler by surprise.

'*Verteidigung*,' he replied.

Defence.

Thus informed, Macmillan consulted his brief, and I can only assume that his eye, like mine, again caught the word *Dachau*, for he brightened.

'Well then, Herr Erler,' he declared with sudden energy. '*You* suffered in the *Second* World War, and *I* suffered in the *First* World War.'

Pause for needless translation by self.

Another exchange of courtesies. Is Erler a family man? Yes, Erler concedes, he is a family man. I duly translate. At Macmillan's request he enumerates his children and adds that his wife is also politically engaged. I translate that too.

'And you have been talking to America's *defence experts*, they tell me,' Macmillan went on in a tone of jocular surprise after another examination of the large print under the sheet of glass.

'*Ja.*'

Yes.

'And do you also have *defence experts* in your party?' Macmillan enquires as one beleaguered statesman commiserating with another.

'*Ja,*' Erler replies more sharply than I would have wished.

Yes.

Hiatus. I glance at de Zulueta, trying to enlist his support. It is not to be enlisted. After a week of Erler at close quarters, I am all too familiar with his impatience when a dialogue fails to come up to expectation. I know that he is not afraid to show his disappointment. I know how thoroughly he has prepared himself for this meeting above all others.

'They come to me, you see,' Macmillan complains wistfully. 'These *defence experts*. As I expect they come to you too. And they say to me, the bombs are going to fall *here*, and the bombs are going to fall *there*' – the prime ministerial hands distributing the bombs across the glass – 'but *you* suffered in the Second World War, and *I* suffered in the First World War!' – that sense of discovery again – 'And you and I know that the bombs will fall wherever they're going to fall!'

Somehow I translated this. Even in German it took a third of the time Macmillan had needed, and sounded twice as ridiculous. When I had done, Erler ruminated for a while. When he ruminated, the muscles in his gaunt face had a way of rising and falling independently. Suddenly he stood up, reached for his beret and thanked Macmillan for his time. He was waiting for me to stand too, so I did. Macmillan, as surprised as we all were, half-raised himself for the handshake and slumped down again. As we headed for the door, Erler turned to me and gave vent to his exasperation:

'Dieser Mann ist nicht mehr regierungsfähig.'

This man is no longer capable of government. It is a formulation that strikes the German ear as odd. Perhaps he was quoting from something he had recently read or heard. Either way, de Zulueta heard it too and, worse still, knew German. A furious *'I heard that'*, hissed into my passing ear, confirmed it.

This time the government car was waiting for us. But Erler preferred the walk, head down, hands linked behind his back, eyes fixed on the pavement. Back in Bonn, I sent him a copy of *The Spy Who Came in from the Cold*, which had just come out, and confessed my authorship. When Christmas came round, he spoke kindly of it in the German press. That same December he was elected the official leader of the German parliamentary opposition. Three years later he had died of cancer.

5

To whomsoever it may concern

Everyone over fifty remembers where they were that day, but stretch and heave as I may, I don't remember who I was with. So if you were the distinguished German guest sitting at my left side in St Pancras Town Hall on the night of 22 November 1963, perhaps you will be kind enough to make yourself known. You were undoubtedly distinguished, for why else would the British government have invited you? It is also my memory that our visit to St Pancras Town Hall had been billed as a bit of relaxation for you at the end of a tiring day, a chance for you to sit back and observe our British grass-roots democracy at work.

And grass roots they surely were. The hall was packed to the eaves by a lot of angry people. The yelling was so loud I could barely make out the insults that were being hurled at the platform, let alone translate them for you. Grim-faced stewards with arms folded stood along the walls, and if anyone had broken ranks we could have been in for a free-for-all. I believe we had been offered Special Branch protection, and that you had declined it. I remember wishing I had overruled you. Squashed into the centre stalls, we were a long way from the nearest bolt-hole.

The object of the crowd's outrage stood on the platform, giving as good as he got. Quintin Hogg, formerly Viscount Hailsham, had disclaimed his peerage to fight the St Marylebone seat in the Tory interest. A fight was what he liked and what he was getting. A month earlier, Harold Macmillan had resigned. A general election loomed. Though the name won't ring many bells these days, least of all abroad, Quintin Hogg, aka Lord Hailsham, was in 1963 the pugnacious British archetype of a bygone age. Etonian, classicist, wartime soldier, lawyer, mountaineer, homophobe and vociferous Christian conservative, he was above all a political showman, famous for his bombast and pugnacity. In the thirties, in common with many of his party, he had toyed with appeasement before throwing in his lot with Churchill. After the war, he became that archetypal nearly-man of politics everywhere, constantly tipped for high office, only to be left sitting in the waiting room – but tonight, and to the end of his long life, the upper-class British brawler the electorate loved to hate.

I no longer remember Hogg's points of argument that night, if I even got to hear them above the tumult. But I remember, as anyone would in those days, his red-faced truculence, his too-short trousers and black lace-up boots set apart like a wrestler's, his puffy, agricultural face and curled fists; and, yes, that booming upper-class roar prevailing against the crowd's howls that I was trying to translate for the benefit of whoever I was accompanying.

Enter left of stage a Shakespearean messenger. I remember a small, grey man, half on tiptoe. He sidles up to Hogg and murmurs into his right ear. Hogg's arms, until now flailing in remonstrance or derision, flop to his sides. His eyes close, and open. He tilts his strangely elongated head to hear again the words that are being murmured to him. The Churchillian glower is replaced by disbelief, then utter surrender. In a humbled voice he excuses himself, and with the erectness of a man going to the scaffold, exits, followed by the messenger. To a few hopefuls he has quit the field, and they scream their abuse after him. Slowly the room is overtaken by an uneasy quiet. Hogg returns, his face ashen, his movements stiff and self-conscious. Not a sound greets him. Still he waits, head bowed as he gathers strength. He lifts his head and we see tears streaming down his cheeks.

Finally, he says it. For now, and for all time. A statement so finite, so unarguable, that unlike any other he has made tonight, it will never be contested.

'I have just been informed that President Kennedy has been assassinated. The meeting is over.'

*

It is ten years later. A Foreign Service friend invites me to a grand dinner at All Souls College, Oxford, in honour of an extinct benefactor. We are all men, which I believe in those days was the rule. Nobody is young. The food is exquisite; the erudite conversation, what I can understand of it, refined. Between each phase of the feast we process from one candlelit dining room to another, each more beautiful than the last, each with a long table set in ageless College silver. As we change rooms, so the seating arrangement changes with us, which is how at the second – or was it third? – remove I find myself placed next to the same Quintin Hogg, or as his name card now proclaims him, the recently created Baron Hailsham of St Marylebone. Having renounced his earlier title in order to enter the Commons, the former Mr Hogg has provided himself with a new title in order to return to the Lords.

I'm not good at small talk at the best of times, least of all when I am landed with a combative Tory peer with political views that, insofar as I have any, fly directly in the face of my own. The venerable scholar to my left is expounding eloquently on a subject of which I know nothing. The venerable scholar across the table is arguing a point of Greek mythology. I am not sound on Greek mythology. But the Baron Hailsham on my right, having taken one look at my place card, has lapsed into a silence so disapproving, so morose and absolute that in all courtesy I feel compelled to end it. Today I cannot explain what quirk of social manners forbade me to refer to the moment when news of Kennedy's assassination was brought to him at St Pancras Town Hall. Perhaps I supposed he would have no wish to be reminded of such a public display of emotion.

For want of a better subject, I talk about myself. I explain that I am a writer by profession, I unveil my pen-name, which does not enthral him. Or perhaps he knows it already, which accounts for his despond-ency. I say I am fortunate to have a house in Hampstead, but live mostly in West Cornwall. I extol the beauties of the Cornish coun-tryside. I ask him whether he too has somewhere in the country where he can stretch out at weekends. Now at least he must respond. He has indeed such a place, and tells me so in three exasperated words:

'Hailsham, you fool.'

6

Wheels of British justice

In the mid-summer of 1963, an eminent West German lawmaker who was in my care in London as an official guest of Her Majesty's government voiced a wish to see the wheels of British justice turning, and voiced it in the presence of no less a luminary than the Lord Chancellor of England himself, whose name was Dilhorne, but before that, Manningham-Buller – or, as his colleagues on the bench preferred to call him, Bullying Manner.

A Lord Chancellor is the member of the cabinet responsible for the management of the nation's law courts. If political influence is to be brought to bear on a particular trial, which Heaven forbid, then the Lord Chancellor is the most likely person to do the job. The topic of our meeting, in which Dilhorne had displayed not an ounce of interest, had been the recruitment and training of young judges for the German bench. For my eminent German guest, this was a crucial matter affecting the future of the German legal profession in the wake of Nazism. For Lord Dilhorne it was a needless claim on his valuable time, and he let it show.

But as we rose to take our leave, he did at least manage to ask our guest, if perfunctorily, whether there was anything he could do to make his stay in Britain more agreeable: to which he replied – feistily, I'm pleased to say – yes, there was indeed something. He would like to look in on the criminal trial of Stephen Ward, charged with living off the immoral earnings of Christine Keeler, whose part in the Profumo scandal I have described in an earlier chapter. Dilhorne, who had played a leading role in concocting the disgraceful case against Ward, coloured, and then through gritted teeth said, 'Of course.'

And thus it was that a couple of days later my German guest and I found ourselves seated cheek by jowl in No. 1 Court at the Old Bailey, directly behind the accused Stephen Ward. His counsel was delivering some kind of final statement in defence of him, and the judge, whose hostility to Ward was matched only by that of the pros-ecuting counsel, was making it as hard for him as he could. I believe, but can no longer be certain, that Mandy Rice-Davies was sitting somewhere in the public gallery, but she has received so much pub-licity that my imagination may have put her there. Mandy, for those too young to have relished her refreshing contributions to the trial, was a model, dancer, showgirl and flatmate of Christine Keeler.

But I do remember with certainty the exhaustion in Ward's face as, aware that we were some sort of VIPs, he turned to greet us: the fraught, aquiline profile, skin stretched tight, the rigid smile and exophthalmic eyes reddened and ringed with tiredness; and the husky smoker's voice, playing it for nonchalance.

'How'm I doing, you reckon?' he asked suddenly of both of us at once.

You do not expect, as a rule, actors on stage to turn round and chat casually with you in the middle of a drama. Answering for both of us, I assured him that he was doing just fine, but I didn't believe myself. A couple of days later, without waiting for the verdict, Ward killed himself. Lord Dilhorne and his fellow conspirators had got their man.

7

Ivan Serov's defection

In the early sixties, with the Cold War at its height, junior British diplomats serving abroad were not encouraged to fraternize with their Soviet opposite numbers. Any such contact, be it accidental, social or official, had immediately to be referred to their superiors, preferably before the event. It therefore caused something of a flurry in official dovecotes when I was obliged to confess to my department in London that for the better part of a couple of weeks I had been in daily contact with a senior member of the Soviet Embassy in Bonn, and that no third person had been present at our meetings.

How this had come about was as much a surprise to me as it was to my masters. The West German domestic political scene, which it was my duty to report on, was undergoing one of its periodical convulsions. The editor of *Der Spiegel* was in jail for infringing Germany's secrecy laws, and Franz Josef Strauss, the Bavarian minister who had put him there, stood accused of sharp practice in the procurement of Starfighter jet aeroplanes for the German air force. Each new day brought titillating snippets of Bavarian lowlife, featuring a cast of pimps, loose ladies and shady middle men.

So it was only natural that I should do what I always did at times of political turmoil: hurry down to the West German parliament to take up my seat in the diplomats' gallery, and grab any opportunity to slip downstairs and take soundings among my parliamentary contacts. It was on my return to the gallery from one such sortie that I was surprised to find my seat occupied by a plump, genial gentleman in his fifties with tufted eyebrows and rimless spectacles, and sporting a voluminous grey suit which, surprisingly considering the time of year, included a waistcoat that was a couple of sizes too short for his ample stomach.

When I say 'my seat', this is merely because the gallery, which was small and perched like a box at the opera on the back wall of the Bundestag chamber, was always in my experience unaccountably empty save for a CIA officer called, unconvincingly, Herr Schulz, who, having taken one look at me and sensing probably a contaminating influence, sat as far from me as possible. But today there was just the one plump gentleman. I smile at him. He beams fondly at me. I sit myself a couple of chairs along from him. The debate on the floor is in full flood. We listen, separately and intently, aware of one another's concentration. Come lunch break we stand up, fuss over who goes through the door first, make our separate ways downstairs to the Bundestag canteen, and from different tables smile politely to one another over our soups of the day. A couple of parliamentary aides join me, but my neighbour from the diplomatic gallery remains alone. Our soups consumed, we return to our seats in the gallery. The parliamentary session ends. We go our ways.

Next morning when I arrive, there he is in my chair again, beaming at me. And come lunchtime there he is all alone, taking his soup, while I gossip with a couple of lobby journalists. Should I invite him to join us? He's a fellow diplomat, after all. Should I go and sit with him? My urge to empathize is, as so often, groundless: the man is perfectly happy reading his *Frankfurter Allgemeine*. In the afternoon he doesn't appear, but it's a summer's Friday and the Bundestag is putting up the shutters.

But come next Monday, I have barely sat down in my old seat when he enters, one finger to his lips out of deference to the uproar below while he offers me his spongy hand in greeting: but with such an air of familiarity that I am seized with a guilty conviction that he knows me and I don't know him; that we've met each other on Bonn's endless diplomatic cocktail merry-go-round; that he's remembered the encounter all along, and I haven't.

Worse still, to judge from his age and bearing, there is every prob-
ability that he is one of Bonn's numberless minor ambassadors. And
one thing minor ambassadors don't like is other diplomats, especially young ones, not recognizing them. It takes another four days
for the truth to declare itself. We are both note takers: he in a ruled
notebook of poor quality, held together by a red elastic band that he
eases back into position after each entry; I in a pocket-sized pad of
plain paper, my jottings lightly strewn with furtive caricatures of the
Bundestag's leading players. So it is perhaps inevitable that one dull
afternoon during a recess I should find my neighbour leaning mis-
chievously across the empty chair between us and enquiring whether
he may take a peek; at which no sooner granted than his eyes squeeze
themselves into slits behind his spectacles and his upper body
squirms with mirth as, with the flourish of a magician, he spirits a
dog-eared visiting card from his waistcoat pocket and observes me
while I read it, first in Russian, then, for the benighted, in English:

*Mr Ivan Serov, Second Secretary, Embassy of the USSR, Bonn,
West Germany.*

And hand-printed along the bottom in spidery capitals of black
ink, also in English: *CULTURAL.*

*

Even today, I hear our ensuing conversation from a distance:

'You want drink some time?'

A drink would be great.

'You like music?'

Very much. I am in fact tone deaf.

'You married?'

Indeed I am. Are you?

'My wife Olga, she like music too. You got house?'

In Königswinter. Why lie? My address is there in the diplomatic
list for him to read any time he wants.

'Big house?'

Four bedrooms, I reply without counting.

'You got phone number?'

I give him my phone number. He writes it down. He gives me his.
I give him my card: Second Secretary (Political).

'You play music? Piano?'

I'd like to, but I'm afraid I don't.

'You just make lousy pictures of Adenauer, okay?' – with a huge
pat on the shoulder and roars of laughter. 'Listen. I got too small
apartment. We make music, everybody complain. You call me once,
okay? Invite us your house, we play you good music. I am Ivan, okay?'

David.

*

Rule One of the Cold War: nothing, absolutely nothing, is what it
seems. Everyone has a second motive, if not a third. A Soviet official
openly invites himself and his wife to the house of a Western diplomat *he doesn't even know*? Who's making a pass at who in this
situation? Put another way, what had I said or done to encourage
such an improbable proposal in the first place? Let's go over this
again, David. You say you never met him before. Now you say you
may have done?

A decision was reached, not mine to ask who by. I should invite
Serov to my house exactly as he suggested. By telephone, not in writing. I should call the number he gave me, which was the official
number of the Soviet Embassy in Bad Godesberg. I should state my
name and ask to speak to Cultural Attaché Serov. Each of these
seemingly normal acts was spelt out to me with huge precision. On
being connected with Serov – if I am – I should enquire casually
what day and hour suit him and his wife best for that musical event
we discussed. I should aim for as early a date as possible, since potential defectors were prey to impulse. I should be sure to convey my
compliments to his wife, whose inclusion in the approach – whose
mere acknowledgement – was exceptional in such cases.

On the telephone, Serov was brusque. He spoke as if he vaguely remembered me, said he would consult his diary and call me back. Goodbye. My masters predicted that it was the last I would hear of him. A day later he called me back, I guessed from another phone since he sounded more like his jolly self.

Okay, eight o'clock Friday, David?

Both of you, Ivan?

Sure. Serova, she come also.

Great, Ivan. See you eight o'clock. And my best to your wife.

*

Throughout the day, sound technicians dispatched from London had been fiddling with the wiring in our living room, and my wife was worried about scratches in the paintwork. At the appointed hour an enormous chauffeur-driven ZiL limousine with blackened windows rolled into our drive and came slowly to a halt. A rear door opened and Ivan emerged, rump first, like Alfred Hitchcock in one of his own movies, pulling a man-sized cello after him. Then nobody. Was he alone after all? No, he was not. The other rear door is opening, the one I can't see from the porch. I am about to have my first glimpse of Serova. But it's not Serova. It's a tall, agile man in a sharp, single-breasted black suit.

'Say hullo to Dimitri,' Serov announces on the doorstep. 'He come instead of my wife.'

Dimitri says he loves music too.

Before dinner, Serov, evidently no stranger to the bottle, drank whatever was offered him and wolfed a plateload of canapés before playing us an overture from Mozart on his cello, which we applauded, Dimitri loudest. Over a dinner of venison, which Serov greatly relished, Dimitri enlightened us about recent Soviet accomplishments in the arts, space travel and the furtherance of world peace. After dinner, Ivan played us a difficult composition by Stravinsky. We applauded that too, again led by Dimitri. At ten o'clock the ZiL

53

rolled back into the drive, and Ivan left bearing his cello, with Dimitri at his side.

A few weeks later, Ivan was recalled to Moscow. I was never allowed to know what was in his file, whether he was KGB or GRU, or whether his real name was indeed Serov, so I am free to remember him in my own way: as *Cultural Serov*, as I called him to myself, jovial lover of the arts, who now and then flirted wistfully with the idea of coming over to the West. Perhaps he had put out a few signals to that effect, without any great intention of seeing them through. And almost certainly he was working either for the KGB or the GRU, since it's hard to imagine he would otherwise have enjoyed such freedom of movement. So for 'cultural', read 'spy'. In short: just another Russian torn between love of country and the unrealizable dream of a freer life.

Did he see me as a fellow spy? Another Schulz? If the KGB had done their homework, they could hardly have failed to spot me for what I was. I had never taken a Diplomatic Service exam, never attended one of those country-house jamborees where potential diplomats are allegedly tested for their social graces. I had never been on a Foreign Office course, or seen the inside of the Foreign Office's headquarters in Whitehall. I had arrived in Bonn from nowhere, speaking indecently fluent German.

And if all that wasn't enough to mark me out as a spook, there were the hawk-eyed Foreign Service wives, who maintained as beady a watch on their husbands' rivals for promotion, medals and eventual knighthoods as any KGB researcher. One look at my credentials and they knew they needn't worry about me any more. I wasn't family. I was a Friend, which is how respectable British foreign servants describe the spies they are reluctantly obliged to count among their number.

8

A legacy

The year is 2003. A bullet-proof, chauffeur-driven Mercedes picks me up at crack of dawn from my Munich hotel and drives me the half-dozen miles to the agreeable Bavarian town of Pullach, industries brewing, since lapsed, and spying, which is eternal. My appointment is for a working breakfast with Dr August Hanning, at that time reigning *Präsident* of the German Intelligence Service, the BND, and a sprinkling of his senior colleagues. From the guarded gateway we pass low buildings half hidden by trees and decked in camouflage netting to a pleasant white-painted country house more typical of Germany's north than south. Dr Hanning stands waiting on the doorstep. We have a little time, he says. Would I care to take a look around the shop? Thank you, Dr Hanning, I would like to very much.

During my foreign service in Bonn and Hamburg more than thirty years earlier, I had had no contact with the BND. I had not, as the jargon has it, been 'declared'; least of all had I entered its fabled headquarters. But when the Berlin Wall came down – an event unforetold by any intelligence service – and the British Embassy in Bonn, to its amazement, was obliged to pack its bags and remove itself to Berlin, our Ambassador of the day bravely took it into his head to invite me to Bonn to celebrate the occasion. In the intervening years I had written a novel called *A Small Town in Germany* which spared neither the British Embassy nor the provisional Bonn government. In predicating – wrongly – a West German lurch to the far right, I had contrived a conspiracy between British diplomats and

West German officials which had led to the death of an Embassy employee bent on exposing an inconvenient truth.

I was not therefore expecting to be anyone's dream of the ideal person to be ringing down the curtain on the old Embassy, or welcoming in the new, but the British Ambassador, a most civilized man, preferred to think otherwise. Not content with having me deliver a (I hope) jolly address at the closing ceremony, he invited to his residence beside the Rhine every real-life counterpart of the fictional German officials that my novel had maligned, requiring of each of them, as the price of a fine dinner, a speech delivered in character.

And Dr August Hanning, posing as the least attractive member of my fictional ensemble, had risen sportingly and wittily to the occasion. It was a gesture that I took gratefully to heart.

*

We are in Pullach, it is more than a decade later, Germany is thoroughly reunited, and Hanning is waiting for me on the doorstep of his handsome white house. Though I have never been here, I know, like anyone else, the bare bones of the BND's history: how General Reinhard Gehlen, chief of Hitler's military intelligence staff on the Eastern Front, had at some unclear point towards the end of the war spirited his precious Soviet archive to Bavaria, buried it, then cut a deal with the American OSS, forerunner of the CIA, whereby he handed over his archive, his staff and himself in return for instatement as head of an anti-Soviet spying agency under American command, to be called the Gehlen Organisation or, to the initiated, the Org.

There are stages in between, naturally, even a courtship of sorts. In 1945 Gehlen is flown to Washington, still technically a US captive. Allen Dulles, America's top spy and founding Director of the CIA, looks him over and decides he likes the cut of his jib. Gehlen is treated, flattered, taken to a baseball match, but preserves that

56

taciturn and remote image that in the spy world passes all too easily for inscrutable depth. Nobody seems to know or care that, while spying for the Führer in Russia, he fell for a Soviet deception plan that rendered much of his archive valueless. It's a new war, and Gehlen is our man. In 1946, now presumably no longer captive, he is installed as chief of West Germany's embryonic overseas intelligence service under the protection of the CIA. Old comrades from Nazi days form the core of his staff. Controlled amnesia relegates the past to history.

In arbitrarily deciding that former or present Nazis were loyal by definition to the anti-communist flag, Dulles and his Western allies had of course deluded themselves on the grand scale. As every schoolchild knows, anyone with a murky past is a sitting duck for blackmail. Add now the smouldering resentment of military defeat, the loss of pride, unspoken outrage at the Allied mass bombing of your beloved home town – Dresden, for instance – and you have as potent a recipe for recruitment as the KGB and Stasi could possibly wish for.

The case of Heinz Felfe speaks for many. In 1961, when he was finally arrested – I happened to be in Bonn at the time – Felfe, a son of Dresden, had spied for the Nazi SD, Britain's MI6, East Germany's Stasi and the Soviet KGB in that order – oh, and of course for the BND, where he was a prized player in games of cat-and-mouse against the Soviet intelligence services. And well he might be, since his Soviet and East German paymasters fed him any spare agents they had on their books for their star man inside the Org to unmask and claim the glory. So precious indeed was Felfe to his Soviet masters that they set up a dedicated KGB unit in East Germany solely to manage their agent, process his intelligence and further his brilliant career inside the Org.

By 1956, when the Org acquired the grand title of Federal Intelligence Service, or Bundesnachrichtendienst, Felfe and a fellow conspirator named Clemens, also a son of Dresden and a leading player in the BND, had supplied the Russians with the BND's entire order of battle, including the identities of ninety-seven field officers serving under deep cover abroad, which must have been something like a grand slam. But Gehlen, always a poseur and something of a fantasist, contrived to sit tight until 1968, at the end of which time 90 per cent of his agents in East Germany were working for the Stasi, while back home in Pullach sixteen members of his extended family were on the BND payroll.

Nobody can do corporate rot more discreetly than the spies. Nobody does better mission creep. Nobody knows better how to create an image of mysterious omniscience and hide behind it. Nobody does a better job of pretending to be a cut above a public that has no choice but to pay top price for second-rate intelligence whose lure lies in the gothic secrecy of its procurement, rather than its intrinsic worth. In all of which, the BND, to say the least, is not alone.

*

We are in Pullach, we have a little time, and my host is giving me the tour of this handsome, rather English-style country house. I am impressed, as I suspect he wishes me to be, by the imposing conference room with its shiny long table, twentieth-century landscapes and pleasing outlook on to an inner courtyard, where sculptures of strength-through-joy boys and girls on plinths strike heroic postures at each other.

'Doctor Hanning, this is really remarkable,' I say politely.

To which, with the faintest of smiles, Hanning answers, 'Yes. Martin Bormann had pretty good taste.'

I am following him down a steep stone staircase, flight after flight of it, until we stand in Martin Bormann's personalized version of Hitler's *Führerbunker*, complete with beds, telephones, latrines and ventilation pumps, and whatever else was needful to the survival of Hitler's most favoured henchman. And all of it, Hanning assures me with his same wry smile as I stare stupidly round me, officially listed as a protected monument under Bavarian state law.

So this is where they brought Gehlen in 1947, I'm thinking. To this house. And gave him his rations, and clean bedding, and his Nazi-era files, and card indices, and his old Nazi-era staff, while uncoordinated teams of Nazi hunters chased around after Martin Bormann, and the world tried to absorb the indescribable horrors of Belsen, Dachau, Buchenwald, Auschwitz and the rest. This is where Reinhard Gehlen and his Nazi secret policemen were installed: in Bormann's country residence that he won't be requiring any time soon. One minute Hitler's not-very-good spymaster is in flight from the Russian fury, the next he is the pampered favourite of his new best friends, the victorious Americans.

Well, perhaps at my age I shouldn't have looked so surprised. And my host's smile tells me as much. Wasn't I once in the profession myself? Wasn't my own former Service energetically trading intelligence with the Gestapo right up to 1939? Wasn't it on friendly terms with Muammar Gaddafi's chief of secret police right up to the last days of Gaddafi's rule – terms friendly enough to pack up his political enemies, even pregnant ones, and see them rendered to Tripoli to be locked up, and interrogated with all the best enhancements?

It's time for us to climb back up the long stone staircase for our working breakfast. As we arrive at the top – I think we are in the main hallway to the house, but can't be sure – two faces from the past greet me from what I take to be Pullach's wall of fame: Admiral Wilhelm Canaris, chief of Hitler's Abwehr from 1935 to 1944, and our friend General Reinhard Gehlen, the BND's first *Präsident*. Canaris, a dyed-in-the-wool Nazi but no fan of Hitler, played a double game with Germany's right-wing resistance groups, but also with British Intelligence, with whom he remained in sporadic contact throughout the war. His duplicity caught up with him in 1945, when he was summarily tried and horribly executed by the SS: a brave and muddled hero of some sort, and certainly no anti-Semite, but a traitor to his country's leadership for all that. As to Gehlen, also a wartime traitor, it is hard to know in the cold light of history what is left to admire in him beyond deviousness, plausibility and a con artist's powers of self-persuasion.

So is that *all of it*, I wonder, surveying these two uncomfortable faces? Are these two flawed men the only role models from its past that the BND has to offer to its shiny-eyed new entrants? Think of the treats that await our British new entrants to the secret world! Every spy service mythologizes itself, but the Brits are a class apart. Forget our dismal showing in the Cold War, when the KGB outwitted and out-penetrated us at almost every turn. Hark back instead to the Second World War, which to believe our television and tabloid press is where our national pride is most safely invested. Look at our brilliant Bletchley Park codebreakers! Look at our ingenious Double-Cross System, and the great deceptions of the D-Day landings, at our intrepid SOE radio operators and saboteurs dropped behind enemy lines! With such heroes as these marching before them, how can our new recruits fail to be inspired by their Service's past?

Above all: we won, so we get to write the history.

But the poor old BND has no such heart-warming tradition, however mythologized, to offer its recruits. It can't crow, for instance, about the Abwehr's Operation North Pole, otherwise known as the England Game, a deception that over three years fooled SOE into dispatching fifty brave Dutch agents to certain death and worse in occupied Holland. German achievements in the field of decryption were also impressive – but to what end? It can't celebrate the undoubted counter-intelligence skills of Klaus Barbie, former Gestapo chief in Lyon, recruited to the BND's ranks as an informant in 1966. Barbie, it emerged only after a prolonged Allied cover-up, had personally tortured scores of members of the French Resistance. Sentenced to life, he died in the prison where he had perpetrated his worst atrocities. But not before he had apparently been recruited by the CIA to hunt down Che Guevara.

*

As I write this, Dr Hanning, now in private practice as a lawyer, stands in the crossfire of a German parliamentary committee charged with investigating the activities of foreign intelligence services in Germany, and the possible collusion or cooperation of German spy agencies. Like all inquiries held behind closed doors, this one is very public. Accusations, innuendo and unsourced media briefings abound. The most sensational charge is, on the face of it, scarcely credible: that the BND and its signals intelligence wing, deliberately or by bureaucratic negligence, has since 2002 helped the US National Security Agency to spy on Germany's own citizens and institutions.

On the evidence so far, this cannot be the case. In 2002 an agreement was struck between the BND and the NSA which stated categorically that German targets were a no-go area. Filters were put in place to make the agreement stick. So did the filters fail? And if they did, was their failure due to human or technical error – or merely the consequence of laxity over time? And did the NSA, having spotted the failure, perhaps decide there was no need to trouble their German allies with it?

The most likely outcome of the Committee's deliberations, in the view of Bundestag watchers better informed than myself, is that the Chancellor's Office will be found to have failed in its statutory duty to oversee the BND; the BND to have failed to oversee itself; and that, while there was cooperation with American intelligence, there was no collusion. And probably by the time you read this, yet more complexities will have emerged, and fresh ambiguities, and nobody will be held to blame except history.

And perhaps in the end history is indeed the only culprit. When American signals intelligence first cast its web over the young West Germany in the early post-war years, Adenauer's fledgling government did whatever it was told, and it was told very little. Over time that relationship may have changed, but only cosmetically. The NSA continued to spy at will without BND supervision, and it's hard to imagine that this habit didn't include, from day one, spying on anything that moved in the host country. Spies spy because they can.

To imagine that the BND at any time exercised effective control over the NSA strikes me as unreal: least of all, when it came to the NSA's selection of German and European targets. Today the NSA's message is loud and clear: if you want us to tell you about the terror threat in your own country, shut up and knuckle down.

In the wake of the Snowden revelations, Britain of course has held comparable inquiries of its own, and reached the same sort of botched conclusion. They too touched upon such ticklish matters as the extent to which our signals intelligence arm was doing for America what America was legally forbidden to do for itself. But the British public, for all the furore, is weaned on secrecy and encouraged by spoon-fed media to be docile about violations of its privacy. Where laws have been broken, they have been hastily rehashed to accommodate the breach. Where protest rumbles on, the right-wing press scotches it. If loyalty to the United States is undermined, it is reasoned, who shall we be then?

Germany, on the other hand, having known fascism and communism in a single lifetime, does not take lightly to state spies who pry into the affairs of its honest citizens; least of all when they do so at the bidding and to the benefit of a foreign superpower and supposed ally. What in Britain is called the Special Relationship, in Germany is called treason. Nevertheless, my guess is that, in these turbulent times, no clear verdict will have emerged by the time this book goes to press. The German parliament will have had its say, the greater cause of counter-terror will have been invoked, and Germany's worried citizens will have been advised not to bite the hand that protects them, even if it has wandered now and then.

But if against all odds the worst case were proved, what would there be left to say in mitigation? Only perhaps that, like anybody else who is confused about his upbringing, the BND didn't know quite who to be. Two-way trading with an over-mighty intelligence agency is never going to be an easy ride at the best of times, least of all when you're trading with the country that put you on earth, changed your first nappies, gave you your pocket money, checked your homework and pointed you where to go. And it's harder still when that parent country has delegated swathes of its own foreign policy to its spies, a thing the United States has done rather too frequently in recent years.

9

The innocence of Murat Kurnaz

I am sitting in an upstairs hotel bedroom in Bremen, north Germany, overlooking a school athletics track. The year is 2006. Murat Kurnaz, a Turkish-German, born, brought up and educated in Bremen, has just been released after five years of incarceration in Guantánamo. Before Guantánamo, he was arrested in Pakistan, sold to the Americans for three thousand dollars, held for two months in a US torture centre in Kandahar, electrocuted, beaten senseless, waterboarded and hung from a hook until, for all his great physical strength, he nearly died. However, by the time he had been held in Guantánamo for a year, both his American and German interrogators – two from the BND and one from Germany's domestic security service – had concluded that he was harmless, naive and no risk to German, American or Israeli interests.

Yet here is a paradox that I cannot begin to reconcile, explain, let alone judge. At the time that I made Kurnaz's acquaintance, I had no idea that Dr Hanning, my fellow guest at the Ambassador's table in Bonn, and my host at Pullach, had played any part in Kurnaz's destiny, let alone a significant one. Now I was hearing that, only weeks previously at a meeting of Germany's top civil servants and heads of intelligence, Hanning, as *Präsident* of the BND, had voted, in apparent defiance of the advice given by members of his own Service, against Kurnaz's return. If Kurnaz should go anywhere, then back to Turkey where he belonged. And more tortuously: that Kurnaz could not be trusted *not* to have been a terrorist in the past, or *not* to become one in the future: thus, apparently, Hanning.

In 2004, while Kurnaz was still imprisoned in Guantánamo, the police and security services of the state of Bremen announced that since Kurnaz had failed to renew his permit of residence, which in the meantime had expired – a pardonable omission, you might suppose, given the shortage of pen, ink, postage stamps and writing paper in the cages of Guantánamo – he was henceforth banished from his mother's home.

Although a court of law briskly overturned Bremen's edict, Hanning has not to this day publicly altered his position.

But if I think myself back sixty-odd years to the Cold War days when, from a much humbler position, I too was invited to pass judgement on people who for better or worse fell into certain categories – former communist sympathizers, suspected fellow-travellers, secret Party card holders and the rest – I find myself caught in the same impossible bind. Superficially, the young Kurnaz on paper ticked a lot of boxes. In Bremen he had attended a mosque known to propagate radicalism. Before setting out for Pakistan he had sprouted a beard and urged greater Koranic observance on his parents. When he did set out, he did so secretly, without telling his parents – not a good start. His mother was so alarmed that she took herself to the police, protesting that her son had been radicalized in the Abu Bakr mosque, was reading jihadist literature and intended to fight jihad in Chechnya or Pakistan. Other Bremen Turks, for whatever motives, came forward with similar tales. As well they might. Suspicion, despair and mutual recrimination were tearing their community apart. Had not the entire plot against the Twin Towers been hatched by fellow Muslims just up the road in Hamburg? For his part, Kurnaz has consistently maintained that his only purpose in travelling to Pakistan was to advance his Muslim education. That none of the ticked boxes produced a terrorist is a matter of history. Kurnaz committed no crime, and suffered unspeakably for his innocence. But take me back to those days, confront me with the same ticked boxes and a similar climate of fear, and I cannot imagine myself rushing to Kurnaz's defence.

*

Seated comfortably in the hotel room in Bremen, sipping coffee, I ask Kurnaz how he managed to communicate with his fellow inmates in adjoining punishment cells, despite the fact that all such communication was forbidden on pain of summary beatings and deprivals, to which Kurnaz was particularly prone on account of both his dogged disposition and huge bulk, which must have fitted poorly into a cage where he could neither sit nor stand for twenty-three hours of each day.

You had to be careful, he says, after the pause for thought that I am getting used to. Not just of the guards, but of other prisoners. You never asked anyone why they were there. You never asked them whether they were Al Qaeda. But when you're squatting night and day a couple of feet away from another prisoner, it was only natural that sooner or later you try to make contact.

There was first the minuscule hand basin, but that was for the more general sort of contact. At an agreed hour – he was not willing to say how the hour was agreed, since many of his fellow enemy combatants were still incarcerated* – they would refrain from using their hand basins and whisper down the plug hole. You couldn't hear actual words, but the collective rumble that came back gave a sense of belonging.

Then there was the polystyrene soup cup that was put in your food-trap with a chunk of old bread beside it. You drank the soup, then you broke a thumbnail-sized piece off the lip of the cup and hoped the guard wouldn't make anything of it. Then with your fingernail, which you had let grow for the purpose, you made an

---

* As we go to print, eighty inmates remain, of whom roughly half have been cleared for release.

indentation in Arabic from the Koran. You kept back a bit of your bread, chewed it into a pellet and let it harden. You pulled a thread out of your jump suit, bound one end of the thread round the pellet of bread, and the other round the piece of polystyrene. Using the pellet as a weight, you tossed it through the bars to your neighbour, who then drew the cotton thread and the piece of polystyrene into his cage.

And, in due course, you'd get a letter back.

For an innocent man who even by the elusive legal standards of Guantánamo is held to have been wrongfully imprisoned for five years and is now at last to be sent home, it was only right and proper that Kurnaz should be awarded his own dedicated aeroplane to transport him from Guantánamo to Ramstein Air Base in Germany on his release. For the journey, he was provided with clean under-clothes, a pair of jeans and a white T-shirt. For his further comfort, ten US soldiers were detailed to watch over him on the flight, and when he was handed over to the German reception party, the American officer in command offered his German opposite number a less weighty, more convenient pair of handcuffs for Kurnaz's onward journey, to which the German officer, to his eternal glory, replied:

'He has committed no crime. Here in Germany he is a free man.'

*

This was not, however, August Hanning's view.

In 2002, Hanning had denounced Kurnaz as a menace to German security. Since then, his reasons for overriding the German and American interrogators had not to my knowledge been explained. Nevertheless, five years later, in 2007, speaking now in his capacity as intelligence supremo in the Ministry of the Interior, Hanning not only repeated his opposition to Kurnaz's residence in Germany – an active issue, given that Kurnaz was by now back on German soil – but castigated the BND interrogators, who had formerly been under his direct command and had declared Kurnaz harmless, for exceeding their competence.

And when I myself emerged, if belatedly, as a supporter of Kurnaz's cause, Hanning, whom I continue to hold in high regard, gave me a friendly warning that my sympathy was misplaced, but offered no reason. And since no such reason has ever come to public light, or to the knowledge of Kurnaz's respected lawyer, I felt unable to follow his advice. So was there perhaps a higher cause? I almost want to believe so. Was the demonization of Kurnaz a political necessity of some sort? Was Hanning, whom I know as an honourable man, falling on his sword?

Not long ago, Kurnaz came to England to promote the book he had written about his experiences.* It had been well received in Germany and translated into a number of languages. I had given it an enthusiastic endorsement. Before beginning his tour, he spent time with us in Hampstead, where at the suggestion of Philippe Sands QC, the human rights lawyer, he was invited without notice to speak to the pupils of University College School. He accepted, and spoke as he always speaks: simply and carefully, in the fluent English he taught himself in Guantánamo, not least at the hands of his inquisitors. To a packed audience of mixed students of different beliefs or none, he said that his Muslim faith alone had enabled him to survive. He refused to blame his guards or his torturers. As usual, he made no mention of Hanning or any other German official or politician who had militated against his return. He explained how, on his release, he had given his jailers his home address in Germany for the day when the burden of what they had done became too heavy for them. Only when he is describing his obligation to the fellow prisoners he has left behind does he betray emotion. He will never be silent, he says, for as long as there is one man left in Guantánamo. When he had finished, there

* *Five Years of my Life*, published by Palgrave Macmillan.

was such a rush to shake his hand that an orderly queue had to be formed.

In my novel *A Most Wanted Man* there is a German-born Turkish man of Murat's age, religion and background. He is called Melik, and he pays a similar price for sins he did not commit. In his bulk, speech and manner he bears a strong resemblance to Murat Kurnaz.

10

Going out into the field

My writing desk in Cornwall is built into the attic of a granite barn built on a cliff edge. Looking ahead of me on a sunny July morning, I see only the Atlantic painted a ridiculously perfect Mediterranean blue. A regatta of spindly sailing boats leans against a leisurely eastern breeze. Friends who come to visit us think we are either mad or blessed depending on the weather, and today we are blessed. On this end-point of land, it can round on you any time it feels the urge. Days and nights of storm-force wind, then truce and sudden silence. Any time of year, a fat cloud of fog can park itself on our headland, and no amount of rain can persuade it to remove itself.

A couple of hundred yards inland, in a tumbledown cottage attached to an old farmstead with the beautiful name of Boscawen Rose, lives a family of barn owls. I have seen them together only once: two adults and a row of four chicks lined up on a broken windowsill for the family photograph I had no time to take. Since then I have maintained a relationship with one adult only – or so I have arbitrarily decided, though for all I know it could be any one of the extended family, because the chicks are long ago full-grown. This father owl, as I am determined to imagine him, is my secret sharer who, long before he skims past my west window, transmits by means unknown to me an early warning of his arrival. I am scribbling away, head down and lost, as I hope, to the real world; but I am never too late to spot his golden-white shadow skimming low over the ground beneath my window. He has no predators I know of. Neither the cliff ravens nor the peregrine falcons are inclined to tangle with him.

This barn owl is also surveillance-conscious to a degree that we human spies would consider psychic. Steep grazing land tips down to the sea. He can be hovering over it, eighteen inches above the long grass as he shapes to swoop on an unsuspecting vole. But if I so much as think of raising my head, he aborts the operation and ducks over the cliff. Come evening if I am lucky he will have forgotten me, and there he is again, with only the tips of his milk-and-honey wings trembling. And this time I have promised myself not to lift my head.

*

On a sunny spring day in 1974, I arrived in Hong Kong to discover that somebody had built a tunnel under the sea between the island of Hong Kong and mainland Kowloon without my knowledge. I had just turned in the corrected proofs of my novel *Tinker Tailor Soldier Spy*. Any moment, finished copies would be rolling off the presses. Among the book's supposed pleasures was a pursuit by Star Ferry across the straits between Kowloon and Hong Kong Island. To my everlasting shame I had dared to write the passage here in Cornwall with the help of an outdated guidebook. Now I was paying the price.

The hotel possessed a fax machine. I had a bound proof copy of my novel in my luggage. I dug it out. I telephoned my agent in the middle of his night and implored him to persuade the publishers to hold the presses. Was it too late for America? He would find out, but feared it was. After a couple more drives through the tunnel with a notepad on my knee, I faxed a revised text to London and swore I would never again set a scene in a place I hadn't visited. And my agent was right: it was too late for the American first edition.

But the lesson I had learned wasn't just about research. It told me that in midlife I was getting fat and lazy and living off a fund of past experience that was running out. It was time to take on unfamiliar worlds. A dictum of Graham Greene's was ringing somewhere in my ear: something to the effect that if you were reporting on human pain, you had a duty to share it.

Whether the tunnel was really to blame, or whether I made the perception later is immaterial. What I know for sure is, from the tunnel onwards, I hoisted my backpack and, fancying myself some sort of wanderer in the German Romantic tradition, set out in search of experience: first to Cambodia and Vietnam, afterwards to Israel and the Palestinians, then to Russia, Central America, Kenya and the Eastern Congo. It's a journey that has continued one way or another for the last forty-odd years, and I shall always think of Hong Kong as its starting point.

Within days I had the good luck to strike up an acquaintance with the same David (H. D. S.) Greenway who later pelted down the icy footpath from my chalet without his passport to become one of the last Americans to leave Phnom Penh. He was thinking about taking a swing through the war zones for the *Washington Post*. Would I care to tag along? Forty-eight hours later I was lying scared stiff beside him in a shallow foxhole, peering at Khmer Rouge sharpshooters embedded on the opposite bank of the Mekong River.

Nobody had ever shot at me before. I had entered a world where everyone seemed to have more courage than I had, whether they were war correspondents or ordinary people going about their daily business in the knowledge that their city was entirely surrounded by Khmer Rouge fighters at a few miles distance, that they were liable to be bombarded at any time of day or night, and that the American-backed forces under Lon Nol were ineffective. True, I was new to it all, and they were old hands. And maybe if you live with danger long enough, you do indeed get used to it – even, Heaven help us, dependent on it. Later, in Beirut, I almost came to believe that. Or maybe I am just one of those people who are unable to accept the inevitability of human conflict.

Everyone has their own take on human courage and it's always subjective. Everyone wonders what their own breaking point will be, when and how it will come, and how their performance will compare with other people's. Of myself, I know only that the nearest I came to showing courage was when I was suppressing its opposite, which may be the definition of a natural-born coward. And mostly such moments came when those around me were showing greater courage than came naturally to me; and, by their example, lent me theirs. And of all of those people, the bravest I met on my travels – some would say the craziest, although I would not be among them – was a diminutive French provincial businesswoman from Metz named Yvette Pierpaoli who, with her partner Kurt, a former Swiss sea captain, ran a ramshackle import business out of Phnom Penh for which they maintained a stable of elderly single-engined aircraft and a colourful team of pilots to hop from town to town over hostile jungle held by Pol Pot, delivering food and medical supplies and airlifting sick children to what was still the relative safety of Phnom Penh.

With the Khmer Rouge drawing the knot ever tighter round Phnom Penh and refugee families pouring into it from every side, and random shellings and car-bombings spreading havoc, Yvette Pierpaoli had discovered her true mission: saving children in peril. Her motley collection of Asian and Chinese pilots, more used to ferrying typewriters and fax machines for her trading company, now turned their hands to salvaging children and their mothers from outlying towns about to fall to Pol Pot's Khmer Rouge.

Unsurprisingly, the pilots were only part-time saints. Some had flown for Air America, the CIA's airline. Some had flown opium. Most had done both. Ailing children might find themselves cushioned by bags of opium base or semi-precious gems, bought for hard dollars in Pailin. One pilot I flew with entertained himself by instructing me how to land the plane if he was too high on morphine to do it for himself. In the novel I was researching, later titled *The Honourable Schoolboy*, I called him Charlie Marshall.

Back in Phnom Penh, Yvette was fearless in her efforts to provide shelter and hope to children who had neither. It was with Yvette that I saw my first casualties of war: dead and bloodied Cambodian soldiers, stacked head to head in an open lorry with their feet bare. Somebody had stolen their boots, along no doubt with their pay-books, wristwatches and any spare money they had taken into battle with them. The lorry was parked beside an artillery battery that was firing with seeming aimlessness into the jungle. Around the guns, small children, deaf from the blasts, drifted in bewilderment. Around the children sat young mothers whose men were fighting in the jungle. They were waiting for them to come back in the knowledge that if they didn't their commanders would not report them missing but go on collecting their pay.

Bowing, smiling, making her *wais*, Yvette sat among the women and gathered the children to herself. What she could possibly have said to them over the thunder of the guns I'll never know, but the next minute they were laughing, mothers and children both. Even the men at the guns were sharing the joke. Back in the city, small boys and girls sat cross-legged in the dust of the pavement beside litre bottles filled with the petrol they had filched from the fuel tanks of wrecked cars. If a bomb went off, the petrol ignited and the children got burned. And Yvette, hearing the explosion from the balcony of her house, would leap into the dreadful little car that she drove like a tank, and comb the streets in search of survivors.

*

I made a couple more journeys to Phnom Penh before the city finally fell. By the time I left for the last time, the Indian shopkeepers and the girls in their rickshaws were shaping to be the last to get out: the traders because the greater the shortages, the higher the prices; the girls because in their innocence they believed their services would be in demand whoever won. In the event, they were recruited to the Khmer Rouge, or died of deprivation in the killing fields. From Saigon, as it still was, I had written to Graham Greene to tell him that I had reread *The Quiet American*, and that it stood up wonderfully. Improbably the letter reached him, and he wrote back urging me to visit the museum in Phnom Penh and admire the bowler hat with ostrich feathers with which Khmer kings had been crowned. I had to tell him that not only was there no bowler hat; there was no museum any more.

Yvette has become the subject of many wild tales, some apocryphal but many, despite their improbability, true. My favourite, which I heard from her own mouth – not always a guarantee of veracity – tells how in Phnom Penh's final days she marched a troop of orphaned Khmer children into the French Consulate and demanded passports, one for each child.

'But whose children are they?' the besieged consular official protested.

'They are mine. I am their mother.'

'But they're all the same age!'

'And I had many quadruplets, you idiot!'

Defeated, perhaps complicit, the Consul demanded to know their names. Yvette reeled them off: 'Lundi, Mardi, Mercredi, Jeudi, Vendredi . . .'

*

In April 1999, while on a mission to the refugees of Kosovo, Yvette Pierpaoli was killed, along with David and Penny McCall of Refugees International, when their Albanian driver skidded off a mountain road and their car crashed hundreds of feet into a ravine. By then, with much help from my wife, she had written her own book,* which was translated into several languages. The title in English was *Woman of a Thousand Children*. She was sixty-one. I was in Nairobi at the time, researching my novel *The Constant Gardener*, which had as its central character a woman who was prepared to go to any lengths to help people unable to help themselves: in this case, African tribal women who were being used as human guinea pigs in clinical trials. Yvette had by then worked extensively in Africa, as well as in Guatemala and – her nemesis – Kosovo. In my novel, the

* Published by Robert Laffont, Paris, in 1992.

female character, whose name is Tessa, dies. I had always intended her to die, and I suppose that, after my travels with Yvette, I had known that her luck too couldn't last. As a child Yvette had been raped, abused and discarded. As a young woman she had taken refuge in Paris, and in penury resorted to prostitution. When she discovered she was pregnant by a Cambodian man, she went to Phnom Penh to find him, only to discover he had another life. In a bar she met Kurt and they became partners in business as in life.

I met her for the first time in the house of a German diplomat in the besieged city of Phnom Penh, over a dinner served to the clatter of outgoing gunfire from Lon Nol's palace a hundred yards down the road. She was accompanied by Kurt. Their trading company was called Suisindo, and operated from an old wooden house in the centre of town. She was sparky, tough, brown-eyed and in her late thirties, by turns vulnerable and raucous, never the one thing for long. She could spread her elbows and upbraid you like a bargee. She could tip you a smile to melt your heart. She could cajole, flatter and win you in any way you needed to be won. But it was all for a cause.

And the cause, you quickly learned, was to get food and money to the starving by any method and at any price: medicines to the sick, shelter for the homeless, papers for the stateless and, in the most secular, businesslike, down-to-earth way, perform miracles. This did not in the least prevent her from being a resourceful and frequently shameless businesswoman, particularly when she was pitched against people whose cash, in her unshakeable opinion, would be better in the pockets of the needy. Suisindo made good profits, as it had to, since much of the money that came through the front door flowed straight out of the back, earmarked for whatever good purpose Yvette had set her heart on. And Kurt, the wisest and most long-suffering of men, smiled and nodded it on its way.

A Swedish aid official, enamoured of her, invited Yvette to his private island off the coast of Sweden. Phnom Penh had fallen. Kurt and Yvette, having relocated to Bangkok, were on their financial uppers. A contract was at stake: would they or would they not win the

Swedish aid agency's commission to buy and deliver several million dollars' worth of rice to starving Cambodian refugees on the Thai border? Their nearest competitor was a ruthless Chinese merchant who Yvette was convinced, probably on no greater evidence than her intuition, was plotting to short-change both the aid agency and the refugees.

Under Kurt's urging, she set off for the Swedish island. The beach house was a love-nest prepared for her arrival. Scented candles, she swore, were burning in the bedroom. Her lover-to-be was ardent, but she entreated patience. Might they not first take a romantic walk on the beach? Of course! For you, anything! It's freezing cold, so they must wrap up warm. As they stumble over the sand dunes in the darkness, Yvette proposes a childhood game:

'*Stand still. So. Now you place yourself close behind me. Closer. So. That is very nice. Now I close my eyes and you put your hands over them. You are comfortable? I too. Now you may ask me one question, any question in the world, one only, and I must answer the absolute truth. If I do not, I am not worthy of you. You will play this game? Good. I too. So what is your question?*'

His question, predictably, concerns her most intimate desires. She describes them, I am sure with brazen falsehood: she dreams, she says, of a certain handsome, virile Swede making love to her in a perfumed bedroom on a lonely island in the midst of a turbulent sea. Then it's her turn. She spins him round, and perhaps with less tenderness than the poor fellow might have expected, claps her hands over his eyes and yells in his ear:

'*What is the nearest competitive tender to Suisindo's for the delivery of one thousand tons of rice to the refugees on the Thai–Cambodian border?*'

It was Yvette's work, I now realize, that I wished to celebrate when I embarked on *The Constant Gardener*. Probably I realized it from the start, whenever the start was. Probably she did. And it was Yvette's presence that, before and after the moment of her death, steered me through the book. To all of which, she would say: of course.

11

Bumping into Jerry Westerby

In a ground-floor cellar in Fleet Street that is full of wine barrels, George Smiley sits with Jerry Westerby over a very large pink gin. I am quoting from my novel *Tinker Tailor Soldier Spy*. Whose pink gin it is we're not told, but we assume it's Jerry's. A page later, Jerry orders a Bloody Mary, we assume for Smiley. He is a sports correspondent of the old school. He is built large and is a former wicket keeper for a county cricket team. He has 'enormous' hands cushioned with muscle, a mop of sandy grey hair, and a red face that in embarrassment turns scarlet. He wears a famous cricketing tie – which one, the text does not reveal – over a cream silk shirt.

In addition to being a seasoned sports correspondent, Jerry Westerby is a British intelligence agent and worships the ground Smiley walks on. He is also a perfect witness. He has no malice, no axe to grind. He does what the best secret agents do. He gives you chapter and verse, and leaves the theorizing to the Secret Service's analysts – or, as he fondly calls them, the *owls*.

While being gently debriefed by Smiley in an Indian restaurant of Jerry's choice, he orders himself the hottest curry on the menu, shatters a poppadom over it – again with his 'enormous' hands, repeated – then spreads a crimson sauce on it, we assume a lethally hot chilli, to give it bite. It is Jerry's little joke that the restaurant manager keeps the sauce in his deep shelter. In sum then, Jerry comes over as a shy, lumbering, puppyish, endearing fellow who, in his shyness, has a tic of resorting to what he would call Red Indian-speak, even to the point of saluting Smiley with *How!* before 'padding off into his own reserves'.

End of scene. And end of Jerry Westerby's cameo part in the novel. His job is to give Smiley disturbing intelligence about one of the suspected moles inside the Circus: Toby Esterhase. He hates doing it, but knows it's his duty. And that's all we learn about Jerry Westerby from *Tinker Tailor Soldier Spy*, and it's all I knew about him too, until I set off for South Asia to research *The Honourable Schoolboy*, and took Jerry along with me as my secret sharer.

If the Jerry of my novel was loosely descended from anyone in my real life, then it was probably one Gordon, an upper-class drifter of vaguely aristocratic origin whom my father had relieved of his family fortune. Later, in despair, he took his own life, which I suppose is why the detail of him remains so clearly imprinted on my memory. His aristocratic origins entitled him to put the absurd 'Honourable' before his name, and this was the 'Honourable' that I had awarded to my Jerry in *Tinker Tailor Soldier Spy* – although nothing on God's earth would ever persuade him to use it, old boy. As to the 'Schoolboy' part – well, Jerry might be a case-hardened front-line reporter and British secret agent, but when it came to matters of the heart he was forty going on fourteen.

So that was the Jerry of my imagining, and that – in surely one of the eeriest encounters of my writing life – was the Jerry I bumped into at Raffles Hotel in Singapore: not a pen-portrait, but the man himself, right down to the huge cushioned hands and 'enormous' shoulders. His name wasn't Westerby, but by then it wouldn't have surprised me if it had been. It was Peter Simms. He was a veteran British foreign correspondent and also, as is now generally known, though at the time I knew it no better than anyone else, a veteran British secret agent. He was six foot three with sandy hair and a schoolboy grin, and a habit of barking *Supah!* when he fervently shook your hand in greeting.

Nobody who met him could forget that first instantaneous surge of sheer good fellowship that swept you off your feet. And I shall never forget my sense of awed disbelief tinged with guilt that I was standing face to face with a man I had created out of adolescent memories and thin air, and here he was in the flesh, all six foot three of him.

Here's what I didn't know about Peter at the time, but picked up along the way – some of it, sadly, too late. In the Second World War, Simms serves in India with the Bombay Sappers and Miners. I had always assumed there was a bit of empire in Westerby's early life. Here it was. Afterwards, at Cambridge University, Simms studies Sanskrit and falls in love with Sanda, a beautiful princess from the Shan States who in childhood has sailed the Burmese lakes in a ceremonial boat shaped like a golden bird. Westerby would have fallen just as hard. Already in love with Asia, Simms converts to Buddhism. He and Sanda marry in Bangkok. They remain fiercely and triumphantly together all their lives, sharing all manner of adventures, either by their own choice or on Her Majesty's Secret Service. Peter teaches at Rangoon University, works for *Time* magazine in Bangkok and Singapore and later for the Sultan of Oman, and finally for the intelligence branch of the Hong Kong police while Hong Kong was still a colony. At each stage of his life, Sanda is at his side.

In a word, there was not one detail of Simms' life that I would not have awarded to Jerry Westerby, save perhaps the happy marriage, because I needed him to be a loner, still in search of love. But all this only in retrospect. When I bumped into Peter Simms at the Raffles Hotel in Singapore – where else? – I knew none of it. I knew that here was my Jerry Westerby incarnate, so full of energy and dreams, so ardently British, yet so identified with Asian culture, that if he wasn't already working for British Intelligence, it was sheer carelessness on their part.

We met again in Hong Kong, again in Bangkok and again in Saigon. Finally I popped the question: might Peter by any chance be willing to accompany me around the stickier corners of South-east Asia? I need not have been so hesitant. Nothing would please him better, old boy. Then might he also, I asked, stoop to accepting a professional fee as my researcher and guide? You jolly well bet he would! His job with the Hong Kong police was running down, and the old cashflow could do with a spot of topping up, no question. We set off on our journeyings. With Peter's unquenchable energy, Asian erudition and Asian soul, how could I not complete the full-colour version of the Westerby that I had lightly sketched in *Tinker Tailor Soldier Spy*?

In 2002, Peter died in France. An elegant obituary headed 'Journalist, Adventurer, Spy & Friend', written by David Greenway – I lifted his cry of *Supah!* from it – rightly describes him as the model of Jerry Westerby in *The Honourable Schoolboy*. But my Westerby was there ahead of Peter Simms. What Peter did, incurable romantic, generous to the last, was seize hold of Jerry with both enormous hands, and make him boisterously his own.

12

Lonely in Vientiane

We lay side by side in an upstairs opium den in Vientiane, on rush beach mats and wooden neck pillows that made you look straight up at the ceiling. A wizened coolie in a Hakka hat crouched between us in the half-darkness, replenishing our pipes or, in my case, rather irritably relighting it when it went out. If a movie script had read, INTERIOR. OPIUM DEN. LAOS. LATE SEVENTIES. NIGHT., this was the scene the set designer would have come up with, and we smokers were exactly the mix that the time and place would have required: an old French colonial planter called Monsieur Edouard, now dispossessed by the secret war that was raging away in the north, a brace of Air America pilots, a quartet of war correspondents, a Lebanese arms trader and his lady companion, and the reluctant war tourist who was myself. And Sam, my recumbent neighbour, who had kept up a soporific monologue ever since I had lain down beside him. The *fumerie* had a certain prickly nervousness about it because the Laotian authorities officially disapproved of opium, and we had been warned by an over-earnest correspondent that at any moment we might be required to find our way over the rooftops, down a ladder, into a side street. But Sam who lay beside me said don't give it a second thought, it's all bullshit. Who Sam was or is, I'll never know. My guess would be, he was some kind of English remittance man who had come East to find his soul and, after five years of kicking around the war fronts of Cambodia and Vietnam and now Laos, was still searching for it. That at least was what his amiable stream-of-consciousness seemed to be telling me.

I hadn't smoked opium before and haven't afterwards, but ever since that night I have cherished the irresponsible belief that opium is one of those proscribed drugs with a dire reputation that, smoked by sensible people in sensible proportions, does you nothing but good. You stretch out on the rush mat, you feel apprehensive and a bit of a fool. It's your first time. You take a puff under instruction, mess it up, the coolie shakes his head and you feel an even bigger fool. But once you've got the hang of it, which is about breathing in, long and slow, and at the right moment, your benign self takes over, you're not drunk or silly or aggressive, and you're not impelled by sudden sexual urges. You're just the contented, free-associating fellow you always knew you were. And best of all, come morning, there's no hangover, no remorse, no anguished coming-down, just a good night's sleep behind you and welcome to the day. Or so Sam assured me when he discovered I was a novice, and so I have believed ever since.

Sam's early life, I gathered from his meanderings, had run a pretty conventional course – nice English country house, boarding schools, Oxbridge, marriage, children: until the balloon went up. What or whose balloon, I never fathomed. Either Sam expected me to know, or he preferred I didn't, and I wasn't going to be so ill-mannered as to ask. It went up. And it must have been a pretty drastic balloon because Sam shook the dust of England from his feet that same day and, vowing never to return, went to ground in Paris, which he loved until he lost his heart to a French woman who refused him. So up went the balloon again.

Sam's first thought is to join the Foreign Legion, but either they're not recruiting that day or he sleeps late or goes to the wrong address, because by now I'm beginning to suspect that what's easy for most of us isn't necessarily easy for Sam. There's a disconnect about him that makes you wary of assuming that one thing will follow naturally on another. So instead of the Foreign Legion, he signs up with a French-based South-east Asia news agency. They don't pay your travel or expenses or anything like that, Sam explains, but if you happen to file anything faintly useful they pay you a pittance. And since

Sam still has this little bit of his own, as he puts it, he reckons this is a pretty fair deal.

So for the last five years he has been trailing round the war zones, and here and there he's got lucky and even earned himself a byline or two in the big French rags, either because he's had a tip-off from one of the real journalists, or because he's made the stuff up. He's always rather fancied his chances at fiction, what with the life he's led, and he'd like to make a thing of it: short stories, the novel, the whole bit. It's just the loneliness that holds him back, he explains: the thought of sitting down at a desk in the jungle and bashing away for days on end, with no editor to chivvy you and no deadline.

But he's getting there. And looking over his output recently, there's absolutely no question in his mind that the stories he's made up out of thin air for his French-based news agency are streets better than anything that's strictly what you'd call fact-based. And come a day not too far off, he's going to sit down at that desk in the jungle and, regardless of the loneliness involved and the absence of a deadline or an editor to chivvy him, he's going to let rip, believe him. It's just the loneliness that puts him off, he repeats, in case I haven't got his point by now. It eats into him, especially in Vientiane where there's nothing to do but smoke, get laid and listen to drunk Mexican Air America pilots boasting about their kills while they get a blow-job at the White Rose.

Then he tells me how he deals with this loneliness, which is no longer strictly related to his writing ambitions, he confesses, but embraces his entire lifestyle. What he misses most in the world is Paris. Ever since his great love turned him down and the balloon went up again, Paris has been a no-go area for him, and it always will be. He'll never go back there, not after the girl, he couldn't. Every street, every building, every bend in the river shouts of her, he explains earnestly in a rare, if somnolent, literary flourish. Or is he remembering a song by Maurice Chevalier? All the same, Paris is where his soul is. His heart too, he adds after due consideration. Hear me? I hear you, Sam.

So what he likes to do when he's had a pipe or two, he goes on – deciding to admit me to his great secret because I'm by now his closest friend and the only person in the world who gives a fuck about him, as he adds in parenthesis – what he's going to do just as soon as he feels the need on him, which could be any minute now that he's got his head straight, he's going to go down to the White Rose where they know him, and he's going to slip Madame Lulu a twenty-dollar bill and have himself a three-minute phone call to the Café de Flore in Paris. And when the waiter at the Flore picks up the phone, he's going to ask to speak to Mademoiselle Julie Delassus, which is a made-up name so far as he knows, not one he's used before. Then he's going to listen to them yelling for her all across the tables and out on to the boulevard: *Mademoiselle Delassus . . . Mademoiselle Julie Delassus . . . au téléphone s'il vous plaît!*

And while they call her name, over and over till it fades into the ether, or his time is up, whichever is the later, he'll be listening to twenty dollars' worth of Paris.

13

Theatre of the Real: dances with Arafat

This is the first of four joined-up stories about my journeyings for *The Little Drummer Girl*, between 1981 and 1983. My subject was the Palestine–Israel conflict. The drummer girl in question was Charlie, a character inspired by my half-sister Charlotte Cornwell, who is fourteen years my junior. 'Drummer' because in my story Charlie roused the combative emotions of protagonists on both sides to the conflict. At the time of writing, Charlotte was a well-known stage and television actress (the Royal Shakespeare Company, the TV series *Rock Follies*), but also a militant advocate of the political far left.

In my novel, Charlie, also an actress, is recruited by a charismatic Israeli counter-terrorist agent named Joseph to play the leading role in what he calls the Theatre of the Real. By representing herself as the radical freedom fighter she has so far *imagined* herself to be – thus Joseph – by playing herself for *real*, in other words, and raising her acting skills to new heights under Joseph's direction, she will make herself attractive to a nest of Palestinian and West German terrorists, and by so doing, save *real*, innocent lives. Torn between her compassion for the plight of the Palestinians that she has been sent to betray, her recognition of the Jewish right to a homeland, not to mention her attraction to Joseph, Charlie becomes the twice-promised woman in the twice-promised land.

The task I set myself was to share the journey with her; to be swayed, as Charlie is swayed, by the arguments hurled at her by each side, and to undergo, as best I could, her contradictory surges of loyalty, hope and despair. And that was how, on New Year's Eve 1982, at

86

a mountainside school for the orphans of those who had died in the struggle for Palestinian liberation, otherwise called the martyrs, I came to be dancing the *dabke* with Yasser Arafat and his high command.

*

My journey to Arafat had been frustrating, but he was at that time a man so luridly portrayed as the elusive, wily, terrorist-turned-statesman that anything more comfortable would have been a disappointment. My first stop was the late Patrick Seale, the Belfast-born, Oxford-educated British journalist, Arabist and alleged British spy who had succeeded Kim Philby as the *Observer* newspaper's correspondent in Beirut. My second stop, on Seale's advice, was a Palestinian military commander loyal to Arafat named Salah Tamari, whom I first met on one of his regular visits to Britain. In Odin's restaurant in Devonshire Street, while Palestinian waiters gazed on him in breathless awe, Salah confirmed to me what I had been told by everyone I consulted: if you want to go deep among the Palestinians, you have to have the Chairman's blessing.

Tamari said he would put in a word for me, but I must go through official channels. I was trying to. Equipped with introductions from both Tamari and Seale, I had twice made an appointment to see the Representative of the Palestine Liberation Organization at the League of Arab States office in Green Street in Mayfair, twice endured the scrutiny of dark-suited men on the pavement, twice stood in a glass coffin in the doorway while I was scanned for secret weapons, and twice been politely turned away for reasons beyond the Representative's control. And the reasons very probably *were* beyond his control. A month earlier his predecessor had been shot dead in Belgium.

In the end I flew to Beirut anyway, and booked myself into the Commodore Hotel because it was owned by Palestinians, and because it was known for its indulgence towards journalists, spies and similar fauna. Until now, my researches had been confined to

Israel. I had spent days with Israeli Special Forces, sat in nice offices and talked to present and past chiefs of Israeli Intelligence. But the Palestine Liberation Organization's public relations office in Beirut lay in a devastated street behind a ring of corrugated-iron barrels filled with cement. Armed men with forefingers on their trigger guards scowled at my approach. In the half-darkness of the waiting room you were greeted by yellowing propaganda magazines printed in Russian and, in cracked glass cases, displays of shrapnel and unexploded antipersonnel bomblets recovered from Palestinian refugee camps. Curling photographs of slaughtered women and children were drawing-pinned to the weeping walls.

The private sanctum of Mr Lapadi, the Representative, is no more cheerful. Seated behind a desk with a pistol at his left hand and a Kalashnikov at his side, he has a pallid, exhausted glower.

'You write for newspaper?'

Partly. Partly I'm writing a book.

'You are human zoologist?'

I'm a novelist.

'You are here to make profit from us?'

To understand your cause at first hand.

'You will wait.'

And keep waiting, day after day, night after night. I lie in my hotel room counting bullet holes in the curtains as the morning light comes up. I crouch in the Commodore's cellar bar in the small hours, listening to the musings of the exhausted war correspondents who have forgotten how to sleep. A night comes when I am eating a ten-inch-long spring roll in the Commodore's cavernous, airless dining room. A waiter whispers excitedly in my ear:

'Our Chairman will see you now.'

My first thought is chairman of the hotel group. He is going to throw me out, I haven't paid my bill, I have insulted someone in the bar or he wants me to sign a book. Then slowly the penny drops. I follow the waiter to the lobby and step into pouring rain. Armed fighters in jeans hover around a sand-coloured Volvo estate car with its rear door open. Nobody speaks, so I don't. I climb into the back of the Volvo, fighters leap in either side of me, another sits himself in the front seat next to the driver.

We are racing through a smashed city in pouring rain with a chase Jeep on our tail. We are changing lanes. We are changing cars, we are darting down side streets, bumping over the central reservation of a busy dual carriageway. Oncoming traffic is scurrying for the kerb. We are switching cars again. I am being patted down for the fourth or sixth time. I am standing on a rain-swept pavement somewhere in Beirut, surrounded by armed men in streaming capes. Our cars have vanished. A street door opens, a man beckons us into a bullet-pocked apartment house with empty windows and no lights. He gestures us up a tiled staircase lined by ghostly armed men. After two flights we reach a carpeted landing and are ushered into an open lift that stinks of disinfectant. It jerks upwards and stops with a huge jolt. We have arrived in an L-shaped living room. Fighters of both sexes are propped against the walls. Surprisingly, no one is smoking. I remember that Arafat doesn't like cigarette smoke. A fighter starts to pat me down for the umpteenth time. The unreason of fear overtakes me.

'Please. I've been searched enough.'

Opening his hands as if to show there's nothing in them, he smiles and backs away.

At a desk in the smaller part of the L sits Chairman Arafat, waiting to be discovered. He wears a white keffiyeh and khaki shirt with crisp box-creases, and totes a silver pistol in a holster of plaited brown plastic. He doesn't look up at his guest. He's too busy signing papers. Even when I am led to a carved-wood throne at his left side, he's too busy to notice me. Eventually his head lifts. He smiles ahead of him as if remembering something happy. He turns to me and at the same time leaps to his feet in surprised delight. I leap to mine. Like complicit actors we're gazing into each other's eyes. Arafat is always on stage, I've been warned. And I'm telling myself that I'm on stage too. I'm a fellow performer, and we have a live audience out there, maybe thirty strong. He leans back and reaches out both hands to me in greeting. I take hold of them and they're soft as a child's. His bulging brown eyes are fervent and imploring.

'Mr David!' he cries. 'Why have you come to see me?'

'Mr Chairman,' I reply in the same high tone. 'I have come to put my hand on the Palestinian heart!'

Have we been rehearsing this stuff? He is already guiding my right hand to the left breast of his khaki shirt. It has a button-down pocket, perfectly ironed.

'Mr David, it is *here*!' he cries fervently. 'It is *here*!' he repeats for the benefit of our audience.

The house is on its feet. We're an instant hit. We enter an Arab embrace, left, right, left. The beard is not bristle, it's silky fluff. It smells of Johnson's Baby Powder. Releasing me, he keeps a hand possessively on my shoulder as he addresses our audience. I may walk freely among his Palestinians, he declaims – he who never sleeps in the same bed twice, handles his own security and insists he is married to nobody but Palestine. I may see and hear whatever I wish to see and hear. He asks me only that I write and speak the truth, because only the truth will set Palestine free. He will entrust me to the same chief of fighters that I met in London – Salah Tamari. Salah will provide me with a hand-picked bodyguard of young fighters. Salah will take me to South Lebanon, Salah will instruct me in the great struggle against the Zionists, he will introduce me to his commanders and their troops. All Palestinians I encounter will speak to me with total frankness. He asks me to be photographed with him. I decline. He asks me why. His expression is so radiant and teasing that I risk a truthful answer:

'Because I expect to be in Jerusalem a little before you are, Mr Chairman.'

He laughs heartily, so our audience laughs too. But it's a truth too far, and I'm already regretting it.

*

After Arafat, anything else feels normal. All the young fighters of Fatah were under Salah's military command, and I had eight of them as my personal bodyguard. Their average age was seventeen at most, and they slept or didn't sleep in a ring round my bed on the top floor with orders to keep watch from my window for the first sign of enemy attack from land, air or sea. When boredom overcame them, which it easily did, they would take a pot shot with their pistols at any passing cat lurking in the bushes. But most of the time they spent murmuring among themselves in Arabic, or practising their English on me whenever I was about to fall asleep. At the age of eight they had joined the Palestinian boy scouts, the Ashbal. At fourteen they were reckoned fully fledged fighting men. According to Salah, there was no one to touch them when it came to aiming a hand-held rocket down the barrel of an Israeli tank. And my poor Charlie, star actress in the Theatre of the Real, will love them all, I am thinking, as I scribble down her thoughts in my battered notebook.

With Salah to guide me and Charlie as my familiar, I visit Palestinian outposts on the Israeli border and, to the putter of Israeli spotter planes and bursts of occasional gunfire, listen to fighters' tales – real or imagined, I don't know – of night raids by rubber boat across the Galilee. It isn't their derring-do that they boast of. *To be there* is already enough, they insist: to live the dream, even for a few hours, at the risk of death or capture; to pause your stealth boat in mid-crossing, breathe the scent of the flowers and olive trees and farmlands of your own homeland, to listen to the bleating of the sheep on your own hillsides – *that* is the real victory.

With Salah at my side, I walk the wards of the children's hospital in Sidon. A seven-year-old boy with his legs blown off gives us the thumbs-up. Charlie has never been more present. Of the refugee camps, I remember Rashidieh and Nabatieh, townships in their own right. Rashidieh is famous for its football team. The pitch, which is of dust, has been bombed so often that matches can be arranged only at short notice. Several of its best footballers are martyrs to the cause. Their photographs are propped among the silver cups they won. In Nabatieh, an old Arab man in a white robe notices my brown English shoes, and something colonial about my walk.

'You are British, sir?'

'I am British.'

'Read.'

He has the document in his pocket. It is a certificate, printed in English and stamped and signed by a British officer of the Mandate, confirming that the bearer is the rightful owner of the following smallholding and olive grove outside Bethany. The date is 1938.

'I am the bearer, sir. Now look at us, who we have become.'

My useless rush of shame is Charlie's outrage.

Evening meals in Salah's house in Sidon gave an illusion of magical calm after the travails of the day. The house might be bullet-pocked; an Israeli rocket fired from the sea had passed clean through one wall without exploding. But there were lazy dogs and flowers in the garden, and a log fire burning in the hearth and lamb cutlets on the table. Salah's wife, Dina, is a Hashemite princess who was once married to King Hussein of Jordan. She was educated at a British private school and read English at Girton College, Cambridge.

With literacy and tact and a lot of humour, Dina and Salah educate me in the Palestinian cause. Charlie is seated close beside me. The last time there was a pitched battle in Sidon, Salah tells me proudly, Dina, a slight woman of renowned beauty and force of character, drove their ancient Jaguar into town, picked up a stack of pizzas from the baker, drove to the front line and insisted on delivering them personally to the fighters.

*

It is a November evening. Chairman Arafat and his entourage have descended on Sidon to celebrate the seventeenth anniversary of the Palestinian Revolution. The sky is blue-black, rain threatens. All but one of my bodyguards have vanished as we cram ourselves by the hundred into the narrow street where the procession will take place – all, that is, but the inscrutable Mahmoud, a member of my bodyguard, who carries no gun, shoots no cats from Salah's window, speaks the best English and wears an air of mysterious apartness. For the last three nights Mahmoud has disappeared completely, not returning to Salah's house till dawn. Now, in this palpitating, densely crowded street hung with banners and balloons, he stands possessively at my side, a diminutive, tubby eighteen-year-old boy in glasses.

The parade begins. First the pipers and flag-bearers; after them a loudspeaker van bellowing slogans. Burly military men in uniform, official dignitaries in dark suits, assemble on a makeshift podium. Arafat's white keffiyeh is spotted among them. The street explodes in celebration, green smoke belches over our heads and turns to red. A firework display, assisted by live ammunition, gets under way despite the falling rain, as our leader stands motionless at front of stage, acting his own effigy in the flickering light of the fireworks, fingers raised in a victory sign. Now it's hospital nurses with green crescent badges, now it's war-crippled kids in wheelchairs, now it's girl guides and boy scouts of the Ashbal, swinging their arms and marching out of step, now a Jeep towing a float with fighters wrapped in the Palestinian flag, pointing their Kalashnikovs at the rain-black heavens. And Mahmoud, close beside me, waves wildly at them, and to my surprise they turn as one and wave back at him. The boys on the float are the rest of my bodyguard.

'Mahmoud,' I shout at him through cupped hands. 'Why are you not with our friends, pointing your gun at the sky?'

'I have no gun, Mr David!'

'Why not, Mahmoud?'

'I do night work!'

'But what do you *do* at night, Mahmoud? Are you a *spy*?' – lowering my voice as best I can amid the din.

'Mr David, I am not spy.'

Even in the clamour Mahmoud remains undecided whether to impart his great secret.

'You have seen on the breasts of the uniform of the Ashbal the photograph of Abu Amar, our Chairman Arafat?'

I have, Mahmoud.

'I personally, all night, in a secret place, with a hot iron, have impressed upon the breasts of the Ashbal the photograph of Abu Amar, Chairman Arafat.'

And Charlie will love you best of all of them, I think.

*

Arafat has invited me to spend New Year's Eve with him at a school for the orphans of Palestine's martyrs. He will send a Jeep to pick me up from my hotel. The hotel was still the Commodore, and the Jeep was part of a convoy that drove bumper to bumper up a winding mountain road at breakneck speed through Lebanese, Syrian and Palestinian checkpoints in the same pouring rain that always seemed to bedevil my encounters with Arafat.

The road was single-track, unmade and falling apart in the deluge. Loose stones kept flying at us from the Jeep in front. Valleys opened up inches from the kerbside, revealing small carpets of light thousands of feet below. Our lead vehicle was an armoured red Land Rover. Word was, it contained our Chairman. But when we drew up at the school the guards told us they had fooled us. The Land Rover was a decoy. Arafat was safe downstairs in the concert hall, greeting his New Year's guests.

From outside, the school looked like any modest two-storey house. Once inside, you realized you were on the top floor and the rest of the building went in steps down the hill. The usual armed men in keffiyehs and young women with ammunition belts across their chests watched over our descent. The concert hall was a huge, tightly packed amphitheatre with a raised wooden stage, and Arafat was standing in the front row beneath it, embracing his guests while the packed hall boomed to the rhythmic thunder of clapping hands. New Year's streamers dangled from the ceiling. Slogans of the

Revolution decked the walls. I was prodded towards him and he once more received me in a ritual embrace, while grizzle-haired men in khaki drills and gun-belts clasped my hand and bellowed New Year's greetings over the handclapping. Some had names. Some, like Arafat's deputy, Abu Jihad, had *noms de guerre*. Others had no names at all. The show began. First, the parentless girls of Palestine, dancing in a ring, singing. Then the parentless boys. Then all the children together dancing the *dabke* and trading wooden Kalashnikovs to the beat-beat of the crowd. To the right of me, Arafat was standing, holding out his arms. On a nod from the grim-faced warrior on his other side, I grabbed Arafat's left elbow and between us we manhandled him bodily on to the stage and went scrambling after him.

Pirouetting among his beloved orphans, Arafat seems to lose himself in their scent. He has taken hold of the tail end of his keffiyeh and is whirling it like Alec Guinness playing Fagin in the movie of *Oliver Twist*. His expression is of a man transported. Is he laughing or weeping? Either way, the emotion in him is so evident that it barely matters. Now he is signalling to me to grab hold of his waist. Somebody grabs hold of mine. Now the whole lot of us – high command, camp followers, ecstatic children – and no doubt an entire convocation of the world's spies, since probably nobody in history has been more thoroughly spied on than Arafat – have formed a crocodile with our leader at its head.

Down the concrete corridor, up a flight of steps, across a gallery, down another flight. The stamp-stamp of our feet replaces the handclapping. Behind or above us, thunderous voices strike up Palestine's national anthem. Somehow we tramp and shuffle our way back to the stage. Arafat walks to the front, pauses. To the roars of the crowd, he does a swallow dive into the arms of his fighters.

And in my imagination my ecstatic Charlie is cheering him to the rooftops.

Eight months later, on 30 August 1982, following the Israeli invasion, Arafat and his high command were expelled from Lebanon.

From the docks of Beirut, firing their guns defiantly into the air, Arafat and his fighters sailed to the docks of Tunis, where President Bourguiba and his cabinet were waiting to receive them. A luxury hotel outside the town had been hastily fitted out as Arafat's new headquarters.

A few weeks later, I went to see him there.

A long drive led up to the elegant white house nestling among dunes. Two young fighters demanded to know my business. There were no dashing smiles, no customary gestures of Arab courtesy. Was I American? I showed them my British passport. With savage sarcasm, one asked me whether by any chance I had heard of the massacres of Sabra and Chatilla. I told him I had visited Chatilla only days before, and I was deeply grieved by all that I had seen and heard while I was there. I told him I had come to see Abu Amar, a term of familiarity, and offer him my condolences. I said we had met a few times in Beirut and again in Sidon, and I had spent New Year's Eve with him at the school for the orphans of the martyrs. One of the boys picked up a telephone. I didn't hear my name spoken, although he was holding my passport in his hand. He put down the phone, snapped 'Come', drew a pistol from his belt, jammed it into my temple and frogmarched me down a long passage to a green door. He unlocked it, gave me back my passport and shoved me through the doorway into the open air. In front of me lay an equestrian ring of beaten sand. Yasser Arafat, in white keffiyeh, was riding round it on a pretty Arab horse. I watched him complete a circuit, then another, then a third. But either he didn't see me, or he didn't want to.

*

Meanwhile, Salah Tamari, my host and the commander of Palestinian militias in South Lebanon, was receiving the treatment due to the highest-ranking Palestinian combatant ever to fall into Israeli hands. He was in solitary confinement in Israel's notorious Ansar jail, subjected to what these days we are pleased to call *enhanced interrogation*. Intermittently, he was also forming a close friendship with a distinguished visiting Israeli journalist named Aharon Barnea, which led to the publication of Barnea's *Mine Enemy*, and affirmed, among other points of mutual agreement, Salah's Israeli-Palestinian commitment to coexistence, rather than the everlasting, and hopeless, military struggle.

14

Theatre of the Real: the Villa Brigitte

The prison was a discreet cluster of green military huts set in a fold of the Negev desert and surrounded by barbed wire. A watchtower stood at each corner. To insiders of the Israeli intelligence community it was known as the Villa Brigitte; to the rest of the world, not at all. Brigitte, as the young English-speaking colonel of Shin Bet, Israel's security service, explained to me as he drove our Jeep over billows of sand, was a radicalized German activist who had thrown in her lot with a group of Palestinian terrorists. Their plan was to shoot down an El Al plane as it approached Nairobi's Kenyatta airport, to which end they had provided themselves with a rocket launcher, a rooftop on the plane's flight path, and Brigitte.

All she had to do, with her Nordic looks and blonde hair, was stand in a phone booth inside the airport and, with a shortwave radio to one ear and a phone to the other, relay the control tower's flight instructions to the boys on the roof. She was in the process of doing this when she was joined by a team of Israeli agents, at which point her contribution to the operation ended. The El Al plane, forewarned, had already arrived – empty save for her captors. It returned to Tel Aviv with Brigitte manacled to the floor. The fate of the boys on the roof remained vague. They had been taken care of, my Shin Bet colonel assured me, but did not specify how, and I did not feel it proper to ask. I had been given to understand I was being granted a rare privilege, thanks to the good offices of General Shlomo Gazit, until recently the head of Israeli military intelligence, and a valued acquaintance.

Brigitte was now a prisoner in Israeli hands, but the secrecy of the operation remained essential, I had been warned. The Kenyan authorities had collaborated with the Israelis but had no wish to inflame domestic Muslim feeling. The Israelis had no wish to compromise their sources or embarrass a valued ally. I was being taken to visit her on the understanding that I wouldn't write about her until I had the Israelis' permission. And since they told me that they had so far not admitted either to her parents or to the German government that they knew of her whereabouts, I might have to wait a while. But that didn't trouble me too much. I was about to introduce my fictional Charlie to the kind of company she would be keeping if she succeeded in penetrating the West German–Palestinian terrorist cell that she was being groomed for. At Brigitte's hands, if I was lucky, Charlie would be taking her first lessons in the theory and practice of terror.

'Does Brigitte talk?' I ask the young colonel.

'Maybe.'

'About her motives?'

'Maybe.'

Better I ask her myself. Fine. I feel I can do that. I have a notion that I'm going to strike up a relationship with Brigitte, however false and fleeting. Although I left Germany six years before the flowering of Ulrike Meinhof's Red Army Faction, I have no problem understanding its origins, or even sympathizing with some of its arguments: just not its methods. In this, and this alone, I am no different from large sections of Germany's middle classes, who are secretly providing the Baader–Meinhof Group with money and comfort. I too am disgusted by the presence of former high-ranking Nazis in politics, the judiciary, the police, industry, banking and the Churches; by the refusal of German parents to discuss the Nazi experience with their own children; and by the West German government's subservience to America's Cold War policy in its ugliest manifestations. And have I not, if Brigitte requires further proof of my credentials, visited Palestinian camps and hospitals, witnessed the misery and heard the cry? Surely all of this added together will buy me some sort of ticket of entry, however short lived, to the mind of a radical German woman in her twenties?

Prisons have an unpleasant hold on me. It's the abiding image of my incarcerated father that won't let me go. In my imagination, I have seen him in more prisons than he ever inhabited, always the same burly, powerful, restlessly active man with his Einstein brow, prowling his cage and protesting his innocence. In an earlier life, whenever I was sent to interrogate men in prison, I had to take myself in hand for fear of earning the jeers of the inmates I had come to question when the iron door slammed behind me.

There was no courtyard to the Villa Brigitte, or none I remember. We were stopped at the gates, scrutinized and allowed to pass. The young colonel led me up an outdoor staircase and called out a greeting in Hebrew. Major Kaufmann was the prison governor. I don't know whether she was really called Kaufmann, or whether that was the name I have since awarded her. When I was an army intelligence officer in Austria, a Sergeant Kaufmann was the keeper of Graz's town jail, where we locked up our suspects. What is certain to me is that she wore a white name-tag above the left breast pocket of her untypically immaculate uniform, that she was an army major aged fifty or so, sturdy but not plump, with bright brown eyes and a pained but kindly smile.

*

And we speak English, Major Kaufmann and I. I have been speaking English with the colonel, and since I have no Hebrew it is only natural that we go on speaking English. So you've come to see Brigitte, she says, and I say, yes, it's a privilege, I'm very sensible to it, very grateful, and is there anything I should be saying or not saying to her? I go on to explain what I haven't explained to the colonel: that I'm not a journalist but a novelist, here to collect deep background, and pledged not to write or speak about today's encounter without the consent of my hosts. To all of which she smiles politely and says, of course, and would I prefer tea or coffee, and I say coffee.

'Brigitte has not been very *easy* recently,' she warns me in the considered tone of a doctor discussing her patient's condition. 'When she was first here, she *accepted*. Now, in these last weeks, she has been' – a little sigh – '*not* accepting.'

Since I cannot understand how anyone accepts imprisonment, I say nothing.

'She will talk to you, maybe she won't talk to you. I don't know. First she said no, now she says yes. She is not decided. Shall I send for her?'

She sends for her in Hebrew over a radio. We wait, and go on waiting. Major Kaufmann smiles at me, so I smile back at her. I'm beginning to wonder whether Brigitte has changed her mind again when I hear multiple footsteps approach an interior door, and have a momentary sickening expectation of a young demented woman in handcuffs with her hair torn, being delivered to me against her will. The door is unlocked from the other side, and a tall, beautiful woman in a prison tunic, enhanced by a tightly drawn belt, strides in with a diminutive wardress either side of her, each lightly holding an arm. Her long blonde hair is combed freely down her back. Even her prison tunic becomes her. As her wardresses withdraw, she steps forward, drops an ironic bob and, like a well-brought-up daughter of the house, extends her hand to me.

'With whom do I have the honour?' she enquires in courtly German, to which I hear myself repeating in German what I have already told Major Kaufmann in English: that I am this novelist, here to inform myself. To which she says nothing at all, but looks at me, until Major Kaufmann, from her chair in the corner of the room, says helpfully in her excellent English:

'You may sit down now, Brigitte.'

So Brigitte sits, prim and upright like the good German schoolgirl she has evidently decided to be. I have planned to exchange a few opening banalities with her, but discover I have none to hand. So I go straight to the point with a couple of cumbersome questions such as: 'Do you in retrospect regret your actions, Brigitte?' And: 'What actually set you on the path to radicalism?' To neither of which she has anything to say, preferring instead to sit stock still with her hands flat on the table and stare at me in a mixture of puzzlement and contempt.

Major Kaufmann comes to my rescue:

'Maybe you like to tell him how you joined the group, Brigitte,' she suggests, speaking like an English schoolmistress with a foreign accent.

Brigitte seems not to hear this. She is looking me up and down, methodically, if not insolently. When she has completed her examination, her expression tells me all I need to know: I am just another unenlightened lackey of the repressive bourgeoisie, a terror tourist, half a man at best. Why should she bother with me? She bothers all the same. She will make a brief mission statement, she says, if not for my sake, then her own. Intellectually she is probably a communist, she concedes, analysing herself objectively, but not necessarily a communist in the Soviet sense. She prefers to think of herself as not confined by any single doctrine. Her mission is to the unawakened bourgeoisie of whom she considers her parents prime examples. Her father shows signs of enlightenment, her mother as yet none. West Germany is a Nazi country run by bourgeois state fascists of the Auschwitz generation. The proletariat merely follows their example.

She returns to the subject of her parents. She has hopes of converting them, her father especially. She has given much thought to how she will break down the subconscious barriers in them, left behind by Nazism. Is this a coded way of saying she misses her parents, I wonder? Even that she loves them? That she worries herself sick about them day and night? As if to correct any such bourgeois-sentimental thoughts, she launches off on a list of her guiding prophets: Habermas, Marcuse, Frantz Fanon and a couple I haven't heard of. From there, she discourses on the evils of armed capitalism, the remilitarization of West Germany, imperialist America's support of fascist dictators such as the Shah of Iran, and other issues where I might have agreed with her were she faintly interested in my opinions, but she isn't.

'And now I would like to go back to my cell, please, Major Kaufmann.'

With another ironic bob and a handshake for me, she indicates to the wardresses that they may take her away.

*

Major Kaufmann has not left her place in the corner of the room, and I have not left mine at the table opposite Brigitte's empty chair. The silence between us is a little strange. It's as if we're both emerging from the same bad dream.

'Did you get what you came for?' Major Kaufmann asks.

'Yes, thank you. It was very interesting.'

'Brigitte is a little confused today, I would say.'

To which I reply, yes, well, to be honest, I'm a little confused myself. And it's only now, in my self-absorption, that I realize we are speaking German, and that Major Kaufmann's German has no distinguishing traces, Yiddish or other. She notices my surprise, and answers my unspoken question.

'I only ever speak English with her,' she explains. 'German, never. Not one word. When she speaks German, I cannot trust myself.' And as if further explanation were needed: 'You see, I was in Dachau.'

15

Theatre of the Real: a question of guilt

On a hot summer's night in Jerusalem, I am sitting in the house of Michael Elkins the American broadcaster, who worked first with CBS, then for seventeen years with the BBC. I had gone to him because, like millions of my generation, I'd grown up in the company of his stentorian New York growl, delivered in perfect sentences, usually from some inhospitable war front; but also, in another part of my head, because I was on the lookout for two fictional Israeli intelligence officers I had arbitrarily named Joseph and Kurtz. Joseph was the young one, Kurtz the old hand.

What precisely I hoped to find in Elkins I can't say from here with clarity, and probably I couldn't have said at the time. He was in his seventies. Was it a bit of my Kurtz that I was after? I knew that Elkins had done more than his share of *this and that*, although I had yet to learn quite how much: worked for the OSS; and, while he was about it, run illegal arms shipments into Palestine for the Jewish Haganah before the creation of Israel; which was how he came to be fired from the OSS and go to ground in a kibbutz with his wife, whom he subsequently divorced. But I hadn't read his book, which I should have done: *Forged in Fury*, published in 1971.

I knew also that Elkins, like Kurtz, was of East European stock, and had grown up in Lower East Side New York where his immigrant parents had worked in the garment trade. So yes, maybe I was looking for a bit of Kurtz in him: not for his appearance or mannerisms, because I already had a perfectly good physical image of my own Kurtz and wasn't about to let Elkins steal it, but for the odd pearl of wisdom that he might let fall as he reminisced about vanished times. In Vienna I had sat at the feet of Simon Wiesenthal, the celebrated if controversial Nazi hunter, and although he had told me nothing I didn't already know, the memory had never left me.

But, mostly, I wanted to meet him because he was Mike Elkins, owner of the toughest, most beguiling voice I had ever heard on radio. His vivid, carefully structured sentences, told in a deep-brown Bronx drawl, made you sit up, listen and believe. So when he called me at my hotel and told me he had heard I was in Jerusalem, I leapt at the chance to meet him.

*

The Jerusalem night is unusually oppressive and I'm sweating, but I don't think Mike Elkins ever sweated. He has a lank, powerful body and a physical presence as strong as his voice. He is large-eyed and hollow-cheeked and long-limbed, and he sits in silhouette to my left side, whisky glass in one hand, the other fastened over the arm of his deckchair, and a huge moon behind his head. The radio-perfect voice is as reassuring and carefully phrased as it always was, even if the sentences come a bit shorter. And sometimes he breaks off and considers himself, as if from afar, before taking another pull of Scotch.

He's not talking directly at me, but ahead of himself into the darkness, to a microphone that isn't there, and it's clear he still cares about syntax and cadence while he speaks. We started indoors, but the night was so beautiful that we carried our glasses on to the balcony. I'm not sure when or how we began talking about Nazi hunting. Perhaps I had mentioned my visit to Wiesenthal. But Mike is talking about it now. And he's not talking about the hunting, but about the killings.

Sometimes we didn't have the time to explain our business, he says. We just killed them and walked away. Other times we'd take them somewhere and then we'd explain. A field, a warehouse. Some wept and confessed. Some blustered. Some implored us. Some couldn't come out with anything much. If a man had a garage, maybe we'd take him to his garage. Noose round his neck, fix it to the rafters. Stand him on the top of his car, drive it out of the garage. Then we'd go back in and make sure he's dead.

We, I am hearing? What kind of *we* is this exactly? Are you telling me that you, Mike, personally, were one of the avengers? Or is this a general sort of *we*, like *we Jews,* and you're just counting yourself among them?

He describes other ways of killing, still using the *we* that I'm not entirely understanding, until his thoughts wander to the moral justification of killing Nazi war criminals who, because they have concealed their identities and gone to ground – for instance in South America – would not otherwise face justice in this life. From there he drifts to guilt in general: no longer the guilt of the men who were killed, but the guilt, if any, of the men who killed them.

*

Too late, I dig out Mike's book. Its publication caused quite a stir, particularly among the Jews themselves. In tone and content it is as fearsome as the title suggests. Mike was exhorted to write it, he says, by one Malachi Wald, in a kibbutz in Galilee. He describes his own Jewish awakening, prompted by American anti-Semitism in his childhood, and then made absolute by the monstrosities of the Holocaust and his own experiences as a member of the OSS in occupied Germany. The style of writing is one minute intensely personal, the next scathingly ironic. In meticulous detail, he describes unthinkable acts of Nazi savagery perpetrated against Jews in the ghettos, and in the camps: and just as vividly the heroism of the martyrs of the Jewish resistance.

But most significantly – and controversially – he reveals for us the existence of a Jewish organization named DIN, Hebrew for judgement, of which the founder was the same Malachi Wald who, in the kibbutz in Galilee, had urged him to write the book in the first place.

In the years 1945 and 1946 alone, he tells us, DIN hunted down and killed no fewer than a thousand Nazi war criminals. Its work, which continued into the seventies, included a plan, mercifully never completed, to poison the water supply of 250,000 German households with the aim of killing a million German men, women and children in recompense for the six million murdered Jews. DIN, Mike tells us, enjoyed the support of Jews across the world. Its original membership of fifty came from all walks of life: businessmen, men of religion, poets.

But also, Mike adds without comment, journalists.

16

Theatre of the Real: terms of endearment

The Commodore Hotel in those tense days – and it's hard to remember a time when days in Beirut were not tense – was the favoured watering hole of every real or pretended war correspondent, arms dealer, drug merchant and bogus or real aid worker in the hemisphere. Its aficionados liked to compare it with Rick's joint in *Casablanca*, but I never saw the comparison. Casablanca wasn't an urban battlefield, it was just a clearing station, whereas people came to Beirut to make money, or trouble, or even peace, but not because they wanted to escape.

The Commodore was no great looker. Or it wasn't in 1981, and today it doesn't exist. It was a boring, straight-up-and-down building of no architectural merit, unless you included the four-foot-thick welcome desk of hardened concrete in the entrance lobby, which in troubled times doubled as a gun emplacement. Its most revered resident was an elderly parrot named Coco that ruled over the cellar bar with a rod of iron. As the techniques of urban warfare became ever more sophisticated – from semi-automatic to rocket-propelled, from light to medium, or whatever the correct vocabulary is – so Coco updated his repertoire of battle sounds to a point where the uninitiated guest grazing at the bar would be roused by the *whoosh* of an incoming missile and a shriek of 'Hit the deck, dumb bastard, get your ass down *now!*' And nothing better pleased the war-weary hacks returning from another hellish day in paradise than the sight of some poor neophyte disappearing under a table while they go on sipping nonchalantly at their mahogany whiskies.

Coco is also credited with the first bars of the Marseillaise and the opening chords of Beethoven's Fifth. His leaving is shrouded in mystery: he was smuggled to a safe haven where he sings to this day; he was shot by Syrian militia; he finally succumbed to the alcohol in his feed.

I made several trips to Beirut and South Lebanon that year, partly for my novel, partly for the ill-starred film that resulted from it. In my memory they form a single, unbroken chain of surreal experiences. For the timid, Beirut did fear round the clock, whether you were dining on the Corniche to the clatter of gunfire, or listening carefully to the words of a Palestinian teenager who is holding a Kalashnikov to your head and describing his dream of getting himself to university in Havana to study international relations, and can you help?

*

As a new boy to the Commodore, I had been drawn to Mo on sight. He had seen more death and dying in an afternoon than I had in a lifetime. He had filed scoops from the worst hearts of darkness the world has to offer. You had only to glimpse him at the end of yet another day at the battlefront, with a tattered khaki carry-bag slung over his shoulder, loping across the crowded lobby on his way to the press office, to recognize his apartness. Mo has the brownest knees in town, they said. Seen it all, done it all, no bullshit, and nobody better in a tight corner, that was Mo, ask anyone who knew him. A little depressed sometimes, a little droll, maybe. And given to locking himself in his room with a bottle for a day or two, why not? And the only known companion of his recent life, a cat, which according to Commodore folklore had hurled itself in despair from a top-floor window.

So when Mo casually suggested, on the second or third day of my very first Beirut visit, that I might care to join him on a little road trip he had in mind, I jumped at the chance. I had been picking the brains of all the other journalists, but Mo had kept himself aloof. I was flattered.

'Take a ride out to the sands? Say hullo to a coupla crazies I know?'

I said I could wish for nothing better.

'Lookin' for colour, right?'

I was looking for colour.

'Driver's a Druze. Druze ass'ls don't give a rat's fart for any ass'l 'cept themselves. Right?'

Very right indeed, Mo, thank you.

'Other ass'ls – Shia, Sunni, Christian – they go lookin' for trouble. Druze ass'ls don't go lookin' for trouble.'

Sounds really good.

It's a checkpoint trip. I hate airports, lifts, crematoria, national borders and frontier guards. But checkpoints are in a league of their own. It's not your passport they're checking, it's your hands. Then it's your face. Then it's your charisma or lack of it. And even if one checkpoint decides you're okay, the last thing it's going to do is pass on the happy news to the next one, because no checkpoint is going to let itself be sold short on its own suspicions. We have stopped at a barber's pole balanced between two oil drums. The boy pointing his Kalashnikov at us wears yellow Wellingtons and frayed jeans cut short at the knee, and has a Manchester United supporters' club badge stitched to his breast pocket.

'Ass'l Mo!' this apparition cries delightedly in welcome. 'Hullo indeed, sir! And how are you today?' – in studiously practised English.

'I'm just fine, thank you, Ass'l Anwar, just fine,' Mo drawls easily. 'Is Ass'l Abdullah receiving today? Proud to introduce my good friend, Ass'l David.'

'Ass'l David, you are most extremely welcome, sir.'

We wait while he bawls joyously into his Russian walkie-talkie. The rickety red-and-white pole lifts. I have only a hazy picture of our conference with Ass'l Abdullah. His headquarters was a pile of brick and rock, pitted by gunfire and daubed with slogans. He sat behind a gigantic mahogany desk. Fellow ass'ls lolled around him, fingering their semi-automatics. Above his head hung a framed photograph of a Swissair Douglas DC-8 being blown apart on an airstrip. I remember knowing exactly that the airstrip was called Dawson's Field, and that the DC-8 had been hijacked by Palestinian fighters with the assistance of the Baader–Meinhof Group. In those days, I flew Swissair a lot. I remember wondering who had gone to the trouble of taking the photograph to the framer and choosing the frame. But most of all I remember thanking my maker that our exchanges were being conducted through an interpreter whose grasp of English was at best uneven, and praying it would remain uneven long enough for our Druze driver who didn't go looking for trouble to return us to the sweet sanity of the Commodore Hotel. And I remember the happy smile on Abdullah's bearded face as he laid his hand over his heart and cordially thanked Ass'l Mo and Ass'l David for their visit.

'Mo likes to take guys to the edge,' a kind person warned me when it was too late. But the subtext was clear: in Mo's world, war tourists get what they deserve.

*

Did the phone call from outer space happen to me that same night? If it didn't, it should have done. And certainly it happened at the outset of my Beirut period, because only a first-time guest could have been fool enough to accept a complimentary upgrade to a bridal suite on the Commodore's mysteriously empty top floor. The Beirut nocturnal orchestra in 1981 was not up to the quality of later years, but it was coming on. A standard performance would start around 10 p.m. and hit its climax in the small hours. Guests upgraded to the top floor would be treated to the entire spectacle: flashes like a false dawn, the clatter of incoming and outgoing artillery fire – but which is which? – and the rattle of small-arms fire followed by eloquent silence. And all of it, to the untrained ear, happening in the next-door room.

My hotel phone was ringing. I had been considering lying underneath the bed, but now I was sitting upright on it with the receiver to my ear.

111

'John?'

John? Me? Well, a few people, mainly journalists who don't know me, do sometimes call me John. So I say, yes, and who's this? – and in return receive a blast of abuse. My caller is a woman, she's American, and she's cross about something.

'What the *fuck* d'you mean, who's this? Don't pretend you don't recognize my fucking voice! You are one *slimy* British bastard, okay? You are an utter weak, cheating – just don't fucking interrupt, all right?' – now furiously shouting down my protestations. 'Just don't give me that blasé British shit like we're taking tea in Buckingham fucking Palace! I *counted on* you, okay? It's called trust. Just fucking listen. I go to the fucking hairdresser. I pack my shit in a nice little bag. I stand on the sidewalk like a hooker for like *two fucking hours*. I eat my heart out thinking you're lying dead in a ditch, and where are you? In fucking bed!' – her voice drops as a sudden thought strikes her – 'Are you fucking some woman up there? Because if – *stop!* – just don't give me that fucking *voice*, you British bastard!'

Slowly, but only slowly, I disabuse her. I explain that she has the wrong John; that I'm not actually a John at all, I'm a David – pause for a lively exchange of gunfire – and that John, the real John, whoever he may be, must have checked out – boom-boom again – because the hotel made me a gift of this fine suite earlier in the day. And I'm sorry, I say, I'm *really* sorry, that she has suffered the humiliation of blasting off at the wrong man. And I *really* appreciate her distress – because by now I'm grateful to be talking to a fellow human being instead of dying alone under the bed in a complimentary hotel suite. And how rotten to be stood up like that, I go on chivalrously – because by now her problem is my problem and I really want us to be friends. And perhaps the real John has a perfectly sound reason for not appearing, I suggest, because after all, in this town anything can happen at any moment, can't it? – boom-boom again.

And she says, it sure as hell can, David, and why had I got two names anyway? So I tell her that too, and ask where she's calling from, to which she says the bar in the basement, and her John's a

British writer too, isn't that really *weird*, and *her* name is Jenny – or maybe it's Ginny, or Penny, because I'm not hearing everything rationally amid the boom-booms. And why don't I come on down to the bar and we can have a drink together?

To which, prevaricating, I say, what about the real John?

And she says, oh fuck John, he'll be all right, he always is.

Anything is better than lying on or under my bed and being bombarded. Because her voice, once calmed, is quite agreeable. Because I'm lonely and scared. And after that I have only bad excuses to offer. I put on some clothes and go downstairs. And because I hate lifts, and because by now I'm feeling shifty about my true motives, I dawdle and take the staircase. And by the time I reach the bar in the basement, it's empty apart from two drunk French arms dealers, the barman and that old parrot who I think must be male – but who knows? – working on his repertoire of ballistic effects.

*

Back in England, I am more than ever determined that *The Little Drummer Girl* is to be a movie. My sister Charlotte must play the part of Charlie she inspired. Warner Brothers buy the rights and sign up George Roy Hill of *Butch Cassidy* fame. I put her name forward. Hill expresses enthusiasm, meets her, likes her. He will talk to the studio. The part goes to Diane Keaton, which may be as well. As George himself, not a man known to mince his words, later put it:

'David, I fucked up your movie.'

17

The Soviet knight is dying inside his armour

I have been to Russia twice only: first in 1987, when thanks to Mikhail Gorbachev the life of the Soviet Union was ebbing away, and everyone except the CIA knew it; the second, six years later in 1993, by which time criminalized capitalism had seized hold of the failed state like a frenzy and turned it into the Wild East. I was keen to take a look at that new, windy Russia too. It therefore happened that my two trips straddled the greatest social upheaval in Russian history since the Bolshevik Revolution. And uniquely – if you set aside a coup or two, a few thousand victims of contract killings, gang shootouts, political assassinations, extortion and torture – the transition was, by Russian standards, bloodless.

Over the twenty-five years leading up to my first trip, my relations with Russia had been less than friendly. Ever since *The Spy Who Came in from the Cold*, I had been the target of Soviet literary invective, one moment – as my critics put it – for elevating the spy to heroic status, as if they themselves had not made an art form of doing exactly that, and the next for making the right perceptions about the Cold War but drawing erroneous conclusions, a charge to which there is no logical response. But then we were not talking logic, we were talking propaganda. From the trenches of the *Soviet Literary Gazette*, controlled by the KGB, and *Encounter* magazine, controlled by the CIA, we dutifully lobbed our bombs at each other, aware that in the sterile ideological war of words, neither side was going to win. Hardly surprising then, when in 1987 I paid my obligatory call on the Soviet Cultural Attaché at his Embassy in Kensington

Palace Gardens to secure my visa, that he should observe not very nicely that if they'd have me they'd have anyone.

Not surprising either, when a month later I arrived at Moscow's Sheremetyevo airport as the guest of the Union of Soviet Writers – an invitation apparently brokered by our Ambassador and Mikhail Gorbachev's wife, Raisa, over the heads of the KGB – that the rock-faced boy in magenta shoulder boards behind his glass cage should dispute the authenticity of my passport; or that my luggage should go mysteriously missing for forty-eight hours, only to reappear unexplained in my hotel room with my suits rolled into a ball; or that my room at the dismal Hotel Minsk was ostentatiously shaken out every time I left it for a couple of hours – wardrobe rummaged, papers strewn in a mishmash across my desk – or that the same pair of overweight middle-aged male KGB watchers – I dubbed them Muttski and Jeffski – was assigned to trail me at a distance of two yards whenever I ventured out alone.

And thank goodness for them. After a rousing evening spent at the house of the dissident journalist Arkadi Vaksberg, who has passed out on the floor of his own living room, I find myself standing utterly alone in an unidentifiable street with nothing but the black night round me, no moon, no sign of dawn, and not a glimmer of light from the city centre to tell me which way to walk. And no spoken Russian with which to ask the advice of a passerby even if there'd been one, which there wasn't. Then to my relief I identify the silhouettes of my faithful watchers slumped side by side on a park bench, where I guess they have been taking it in turns to nap.

'You speak English?'

Niet.

'Français?'

Niet.

'Deutsch?'

Niet.

'I-am-*very*-drunk' – idiot smile, slow rotation of right hand round right ear – 'Hotel *Minsk* – okay? You know *Minsk*? We go together?' Extend both elbows, indicating fraternity and passivity.

Three abreast, we process at a slow march down a tree-lined boulevard through deserted streets to the awful Hotel Minsk. As a man who likes his creature comforts, I had tried to stay in one of Moscow's few dollar-hotels, but my hosts would have none of that. I must stay in the Minsk, in the VIP suite on the top floor, where ageing microphones were permanently in place and a redoubtable female concierge kept guard over the corridor.

But watchers are people too. And with time there was something so resigned, so enduring, I would almost say endearing, about Muttski and Jeffski that, contrary to convention, I would have wished to draw closer to them, rather than further away. One evening I dined with my younger brother Rupert, in those torrid days the Moscow bureau chief of the *Independent* newspaper, at an early cooperative – privately owned – restaurant. There is a score of years between Rupert and me, but in poor light we do look vaguely alike, particularly if you're drunk. Rupert had invited other Moscow correspondents. While we chatted and drank together, my two watchers sat inconsolably at their corner table. Moved by their plight, I asked a waiter to take them over a bottle of vodka while keeping my gaze elsewhere. When I turned my head, the bottle was nowhere to be seen, but when we broke up they followed the wrong brother home.

*

Try to describe Russia without vodka in those days, you might as well describe a horse race without horses. In the same week I pay a visit to my Moscow publisher. It is eleven in the morning. His cramped attic office is littered with dusty Dickensian files, stacks of mysterious cardboard boxes and yellowing typescripts bound in harvest twine. Seeing me enter, he springs from his desk and, with a roar of delight, hugs me to his bosom.

'We have *glasnost*!' he cries. 'We have *perestroika*! Censorship is over, my friend! Henceforth I publish *all* your books for ever: old books, new books, lousy books, I don't give a shit! You write telephone directory? I *publish* it! I publish anything except the books those lousy bastards in Party censorship office want me to publish!'

Blissfully indifferent to Gorbachev's recently enacted laws on the consumption of alcohol, he yanks a bottle of vodka from a drawer, tears off the cap and, to my sinking heart, tosses it joyously into the wastepaper basket.

*

It appeared entirely logical to me, in the looking-glass world I had entered, that while I was being watched, followed and regarded with the heaviest suspicion, I should also be treated as an honoured guest of the Soviet government. My photograph was featured in *Izvestia* over a pleasant enough caption, I was royally entertained by my hosts, the Union of Writers, whose literary qualifications were for the most part obscure, and in some cases downright mythical.

There was the great poet whose oeuvre consisted of a volume of poems published thirty years ago, but they were rumoured to be the work of a different poet whom Stalin had shot for insurrection. There was the old, old man with white beard and red eyes flooded with tears, who had spent half a century in the Gulag labour camps before being rehabilitated as part of the *glasnost*, or openness. Somehow he had kept and published a doorstep-sized diary of his life's ordeal. It is in my library now, in Russian, which I can't read. There were the literary acrobats who for years had walked the tightrope of official censorship, with allegories conveying coded messages to those with the insight to interpret them. Whatever will they write, I wondered, when they are let into the wild? Will they be the Tolstoys and Lermontovs of tomorrow? Or have they been thinking round corners for so long that they can't write in straight lines?

At an outdoor party at the writers' colony in the leafy suburb of Peredelkino, those who were reckoned to have conformed too zealously with the Party line were – thanks to the advent of the *perestroika*, Gorbachev's policy of political and economic reform – already looking a trifle hangdog beside those who had earned themselves a name for indiscipline. One of this latter group, he informed me, was Igor, a drunken playwright who insisted on keeping his arm round my neck while he murmured conspiratorially into my ear.

By now Igor and I had discussed Pushkin, Chekhov and Dosto-evsky. That is to say, Igor had discussed them and I had listened. We had admired Jack London. Or Igor had. Now he was telling me that if I *really* wanted to know what a total fuck-up the real communist Russia was, I should try sending a second-hand refrigerator from my house in Leningrad to my grandmother in Novosibirsk and see how far I got. We agreed that this was a fine measure for the state of the disintegrating Soviet Union, and had a good laugh about it.

Next morning Igor called me at the Hotel Minsk.

'Don't say my name. You recognize my voice. Yes?'

Yes.

'Last night I told you shit joke about my grandmother, okay?'

Okay.

'You remember?'

I do.

'I never told you shit joke. Okay?'

Okay again.

'Swear me.'

I swear him.

The one artist I met who would indubitably survive whatever restraints had been imposed upon him, even relish them, was Ilya Kabakov, who over the decades had flitted in and out of official Soviet favour to the point of being obliged to sign his own illustrations under another name. To reach Kabakov's studio you had to be trusted, you had to know somebody, and your way had to be lit for you by a boy with a hand torch across a long rickety pathway of loose planks laid on the rafters of several adjoining attics.

When you at last arrived, there was Kabakov, exuberant hermit and painter extraordinary, with an entourage of smiling womenfolk and admirers. And there on canvas was the wonderful world of his self-imprisonment: mocked, forgiven, made beautiful and given universality by the loving eye of its unconquerable creator.

In the St Sergius cathedral in Zagorsk, often called the Russian Vatican, I watched old Russian women in black prostrate themselves on the flagstone floor and kiss the thick, misted glass covers of tombs containing relics of the saints. In a modern office fitted out with slick Scandinavian furniture, the exquisitely robed Archimandrite's representative explained to me how the Christian God worked his wonders through the agency of the state.

'Is this only the *communist* state we're talking about?' I ask him when his set-piece has ground to its appointed end. 'Or does He work them through *any* state?'

For answer, I get the torturer's broad, forgiving smile.

To visit the writer Chingiz Aitmatov, of whom to my shame I had never heard, my British interpreter and I take an Aeroflot flight to the military city of Frunze, now Bishkek, in Kyrgyzstan. We are accommodated not in Frunze's answer to the Hotel Minsk, but in the five-star luxury of a Central Committee rest home.

The wire perimeter is patrolled by armed KGB guards with dogs. They are there, we are told, to protect us from rustlers from the mountains. No suggestion then of dissident Muslim tribesmen. We are the rest home's only guests. In the basement we have an excellently equipped swimming pool and sauna. Lockers, towels and beach robes are embroidered with fluffy animals. I choose moose. The pool is heated to stockbroker temperature. In return for a few American dollars, the manager offers us forbidden vodka of various flavours, and ladies of the town. We take the first, pass on the second.

Back in Moscow, Red Square is mysteriously off-limits. Our pilgrimage to Lenin's tomb has been postponed until another day. It takes us another twelve hours to discover what the rest of the world knows: that a young German aviator named Mathias Rust, defying Soviet ground and air defences, has landed his little aeroplane on the Kremlin's doorstep, and incidentally provided Gorbachev with the excuse to sack his Defence Minister and a nest of generals opposed to his reforms. I remember no raucous celebration of this feat of aviation, no hoots of laughter as the word was passed around the literati of Peredelkino: rather a stiffening and a quieting, as the familiar fear gathered that some unforeseeable and violent consequence could result. Will it be a political coup, a military putsch, or – even today – a purge of undesirable intellectuals like us?

In the city that is still Leningrad I meet the most distinguished Russian dissident of his generation and one of its greatest men: the physicist and Nobel Peace Laureate Andrei Sakharov, with his wife Elena Bonner, newly released by Gorbachev in the spirit of *glasnost* after their six years of internal exile in Gorky, to assist in the *perestroika*.

It was Sakharov the physicist who through his exertions provided the Kremlin with its first hydrogen bomb; and it was Sakharov the dissident who woke one morning to the realization that he had given his bomb to a bunch of gangsters, and had the courage to tell them as much out loud. As we sit talking at a round table in the city's only cooperative restaurant, with Elena Bonner at Sakharov's side, a troupe of young KGB apparatchiks circle our table, incessantly firing 1930s flash-bulb cameras at us. This gesture is all the more surreal because, either in the restaurant or on the streets of Russia, no head turns to stare at Andrei Sakharov, nobody surreptitiously steps forward to shake the great man's hand, for the good reason that ever since his fall his face has been forbidden. Our un-photographers are photographing an un-face.

Sakharov asks me whether I ever met Klaus Fuchs, the British atom scientist and Soviet spy, by then released from a British jail and living in East Germany.

No, I never did.

Then do I happen to know by any chance how Fuchs was caught?

I knew the man who interrogated him, I reply, but not how he was caught. A spy's worst enemy is another spy, I suggest, with a nod for our rotating ring of fake photographers. Maybe one of *your* spies told one of *our* spies about Klaus Fuchs. He smiles. Unlike Bonner, he smiles a lot. I wonder whether that was always natural to him, or whether smiling was something he taught himself to do as a way of disarming his interrogators. But why does he ask me about Fuchs? I wonder, though not aloud. Maybe because Fuchs, in the relatively open society of the West, chose the path of secret betrayal in preference to standing up and openly proclaiming his beliefs. Whereas Sakharov, in the police state that was now entering its death throes, suffered torture and imprisonment for his right to speak out.

*

Sakharov describes how the uniformed KGB guard who stood daily outside their quarters in Gorky was forbidden to make eye contact with his prisoners, and accordingly handed them their daily copy of *Pravda* over his shoulder: take this, but don't look into my eyes. He describes reading the works of Shakespeare from end to end. Bonner puts in that Andrei has committed swathes of the Bard to memory, but he doesn't know how to say the words because in exile he has heard no spoken English. He describes a night when, after six years of exile, there came a thunderous knock on the door of their quarters, and Bonner said, 'Don't open it,' but he did.

'I told Elena there was nothing they could do to us that they hadn't done already,' he explains.

So he opened the door nonetheless and saw two men, one in KGB officer's uniform and one in workman's overalls.

'We've come to install a telephone,' said the KGB officer.

Sakharov allows himself one of his mischievous smiles. He's not a drinking man, he says – in truth he is a teetotaller – but being offered a telephone in a Russian closed city is about as improbable as being offered a glass of iced vodka in the Sahara desert.

'We don't want a telephone, take it away,' Bonner told the KGB officer.

But again Sakharov overrode her: let them install a telephone, what have we to lose? So they installed the telephone, not to Bonner's pleasure.

'Expect a call tomorrow at midday,' the departing KGB officer said, and slammed the door.

Sakharov speaks carefully, as scientists do. The truth is in the detail. Midday came and went, one o'clock, then two o'clock. They decided they were both hungry. They had slept badly and eaten no breakfast. He told the back of the guard's head that he was going down to the shop to buy bread. As he set off, Bonner called after him.

'It's for you.'

He returned to their quarters and picked up the receiver. After being passed through a succession of intermediaries of varying rudeness, he was connected with Mikhail Gorbachev, General Secretary of the Soviet Communist Party. The past is the past, Gorbachev says. The Central Committee has considered your case and you are free to come back to Moscow. Your old apartment is waiting for you, you will be immediately readmitted to the Academy of Sciences, everything is clear for you to take up your rightful place as a responsible citizen in the new Russia of the *perestroika*.

The words 'responsible citizen' got Sakharov's goat. His idea of a responsible citizen, he informed Gorbachev – I imagine with some heat, although Sakharov as so often is smiling – was somebody who obeyed the law of his country. In this one closed city alone, he said, there were inmates walking around who had never even been near a law court, and some barely knew why they were here at all.

'I sent you letters to this effect, and received not a murmur of a reply.'

'We've got your letters,' Gorbachev replied soothingly. 'The Central Committee is considering them. Come back to Moscow. The past is over. Help with the reconstruction.'

By now the wind seems really to have got into Sakharov's nostrils, because he is reeling off to Gorbachev a list of the Central Committee's other derelictions, past and present, that he has written to him about, also to no effect. But somewhere in midstream, he says, he caught Bonner's eye. And he realized that if he went on like this much longer, Gorbachev was going to tell him: 'Well, if that's the way you feel, Comrade, you can stay where you are.'

So Sakharov rang off. Like that. Without even a 'Goodbye, Mikhail Sergeyevich.'

And then it occurred to him – the mischievous smile broad now, and even Bonner is giving way to an impish twinkle:

'And then it occurred to me,' he repeats in bemusement, 'that in my first telephone conversation for six years, I had managed to hang up on the General Secretary of the Soviet Communist Party.'

*

It is a couple of days later. I am billed to address an assembly of students at Moscow State University. On the podium we have John Roberts, my intrepid British guide and interpreter; Volodya, my Russian guide, supplied by PEN or the Union of Writers, I was never sure which; and a wan professor who has introduced me to the audience, rather disobligingly in my opinion, as a product of the new *glasnost*. My impression is that he feels *glasnost* would be a lot better without me. Now, without enthusiasm, he is inviting questions from the audience.

The first questions come in Russian, but the wan professor filters them so patently that the students, already restive, decide to yell their questions in English instead. We do writers I admire, and writers I don't. We do the spy as a product of the Cold War. We debate – saucily – the morality or otherwise of reporting on your colleagues. By now the wan professor has heard enough. He will take one last question. A woman student's arm is up. Yes, you.

Woman student: Sir. Please. Mr le Carré. What do you think of Marx and Lenin, please?

Howls of laughter.

Self: I love them both.

It doesn't strike me as my best line, but the audience treats it with prolonged applause and shouts of merriment. The wan professor calls it a day and I am quickly commandeered by the students and ushered down a staircase to some kind of common room, where they interrogate me intently about a novel of mine that I know for certain has been banned here for the last twenty-five years. Where on earth have they managed to read it? I ask.

'In our private book club, of course,' a woman student retorts proudly in fractured Jane Austen English, pointing to a cumbersome computer screen. 'Our team has typed out text of your book from illicit copy given us by one of your countrymen. We have read this book together at night-time many times. We have read many forbidden books in this manner.'

'And if you're caught?' I ask.

They laugh.

Paying a farewell visit to Volodya, my ever helpful Russian guide, and his wife Irena in their tiny apartment, I play Santa Claus, although it's nowhere close to Christmas. They are a couple of gifted university graduates, living on the breadline. They have two smart little girls. For Volodya, I have brought Scotch whisky, ballpoint pens, a silk tie and other unobtainable treasures I picked up at the duty-free in Heathrow; for Irena, bars of English soap, toothpaste, tights, headscarves, whatever my wife advised. And for their two little girls, chocolate and tartan skirts. Their gratitude embarrasses me. I don't want to be this person. And they don't want to be those people.

*

Piecing together now the encounters crammed into those two short weeks in the Russia of 1987, I am moved again by the pity of it, by the striving and endurance of so-called ordinary people who weren't ordinary at all; and by the humiliations they were forced to share, whether standing in line for life's essentials, servicing their own bodies and those of their children, or guarding their tongues against a fatal slip. Strolling in Red Square with an elderly lady of letters in the aftermath of Mathias Rust's unscripted arrival, I took a snapshot of the sentries guarding Lenin's tomb, only to see her face turn white as she hissed at me to put my camera out of sight.

What the collective Russian psyche most fears is chaos; what it most dreams of is stability; and what it dreads is the unknowable future. And who wouldn't, in a nation that gave twenty million of its souls to Stalin's executioners and another thirty million to Hitler's? Was life after communism *really* going to be better for them than the one they had now? True, the artists and intellectuals, when they felt sure of you, or bold enough, spoke glowingly of the freedoms that would soon – touch wood – be theirs. But between the lines they had their reservations. What status would *they* have in whatever new society beckoned? If they had Party privileges, what was going to replace them? If they were Party-approved writers, who was going to approve them in a free market? And if they were currently out of favour, would the next system restore them?

In 1993, I returned to Russia in the hope of finding out.

18

The Wild East: Moscow 1993

The Berlin Wall is down. Mikhail Gorbachev, after a rollercoaster ride that saw him one minute under house arrest in the Crimea and the next restored to power in the Kremlin, has been supplanted by his long-time enemy Boris Yeltsin. The Soviet Communist Party is suspended, its Moscow headquarters closed. Leningrad is once more St Petersburg, Stalingrad is Volgograd. Organized crime has gone viral. Justice is nowhere. Unpaid soldiers returned from the ill-starred Soviet campaign in Afghanistan roam the country and are everywhere for hire. Civil society does not exist, and Yeltsin is unwilling or unable to impose it. All this I knew before I left for Moscow in the summer of 1993. So what possessed me to take my twenty-year-old undergraduate son along with me, I'll never know. But come along he did, and happily, and we muddled through without a mishap or a cross word.

The purpose of our journey was clear to me, or so I tell myself now. I wanted to get a taste of the new order. Were the new crime bosses the old ones in new clothes? Was the KGB really being disbanded by Yeltsin, or had it been, as so often in the past, merely reconstituted under another name? In Hamburg, our starting-out point, I solemnly set about stocking up with the same essential supplies that I had taken to the Russia of 1987: give-away soaps, shampoos, toothpaste, Cadbury's chocolate biscuits, Scotch whisky, German toys. Yet already at Sheremetyevo airport, where we passed through on the nod, there was an air of garish materialism. Perhaps the most improbable to my unready eye: for a deposit of fifty dollars you could rent a cellphone from the kiosk at the exit.

As to our hotel: forget the Minsk. This was a glittering, marbled palace with wide, curling staircases, chandeliers big enough to light an opera house and a bevy of smart, conspicuously unattached girls dawdling in the lobby. Our bedrooms reeked of fresh paint, air purifier and plumbing. One glance at the shop fronts as we drove through the city had said it all: gone was the fabled state-run shopping emporium GUM, and in its place, Estée Lauder.

*

This time my Russian publisher does not embrace me. He does not joyously whisk a bottle of vodka from his desk drawer and toss the cap into the wastepaper basket. First he eyes me through the peephole in his steel door, unfastens a battery of locks, shuffles me through and fastens them again. In a low voice he apologizes for being the only one in the office to greet me. Since the insurance company came, he says, his staff won't come in.

Insurance company?

Men in suits with briefcases. Selling insurance against fire, theft and flooding, mostly fire. The neighbourhood is very high-risk following a spate of arson attacks. So the premiums have to be high too, which is only natural. A fire could break out any time. Better sign up straight away, and here's a pen. Because otherwise certain people they know will firebomb the place, then what will happen to all those old files and manuscripts we see lying about?

And the police, I ask?

Advise you to pay up and shut up. They're part of the racket.

So will you pay?

Maybe. He'll see. He won't give up without a fight. He used to know influential people. But they're not influential any more.

I ask a former KGB friend how I can meet a top mafia chief. He calls me back. Be at the so-and-so nightclub at 1.00 on Thursday morning, and Dima will receive you. Your son? Bring him along, he'll be welcome, and if he's got a girl, bring her too. It's Dima's nightclub. He owns it. Nice customers, good music. Very safe. Our indispensable bodyguard is Pusya, the all-Abkhazia wrestling champion and adviser on all matters relating to his people's struggle for liberation. He is as squat and broad as the Michelin Man, a polymath, linguist, scholar and paradoxically the most peaceable fellow you are likely to meet. He is also by way of being a national celebrity, which is a kind of protection in itself.

Fit young men with submachine guns line the way to the nightclub entrance. While Pusya looks on benignly, they frisk us. Benches of scarlet plush surround a circular dance floor. Couples dance sedately to sixties music. Mr Dima will be with you shortly, the manager informs Pusya as he ushers us to a banquette. Driving us here in his car, Pusya has already provided us with an example of his powers of peaceful intervention. The street is blocked. A small car and a large car are intertwined. The drivers are about to come to blows. An eager crowd is taking sides. Pusya opens his door and strolls over to the belligerents, I assume with the intention of separating or quelling them. Instead he takes hold of the smaller car by its rear bumper, disentangles it from the larger car and, to the raucous applause of the crowd, delicately parks it at the side of the road.

We drink our soft drinks. Mr Dima may be late, the manager warns us. Mr Dima may have *business* to attend to, *business* being the new Russian catchword for impenetrable transactions. Sounds of circumstance in the corridor alert us to a royal arrival. The music swells in greeting, then stops dead. First to enter are two fit young men with close-cropped hair and tight, blue-black Italian suits. Spetsnaz, Pusya tells me in a murmur. For Moscow's new rich, former Special Forces soldiers are the bodyguard of choice. With bird-like jerks of the head, the two men case the room by sections. Spotting Pusya, they hold the stare. Pusya smiles benignly in return. They take a step backwards, one to each side of the entrance. A pause, then enter – as if by popular demand – Kojak of the New York Police Department, alias Dima, followed by a retinue of pretty girls and more young men.

If you have seen the *Kojak* television series the comparison is ridiculously apt, right down to the Ray-Ban shades: shiny bald head, very big shoulders, rolling walk, single-breasted suit, arms lifted ape-style from the sides. A bulbous, clean-shaven face, frozen in a half-sneer. *Kojak* is a big hit in the new Russia just now. Is Dima deliberately styling himself after him? He wouldn't be the first crime boss to think he's the star of his own movie.

The front row of the stalls is evidently the family pew. Dima sits himself at the centre. His people sidle in beside him. To his right, an extremely pretty girl in jewels; to his left, an expressionless, pock-faced man: think *consigliere.* The nightclub manager brings a tray of soft drinks. Dima abjures alcohol, says Pusya, who abjures it himself.

'Mr Dima will speak to you now, please.'

Pusya sits tight. With my Russian interpreter I pick my way across the dance floor. Dima extends a hand; I shake it, and it's as soft as my own. I kneel down in front of him on the dance floor. My interpreter kneels beside me. It's hardly the best of postures, but there's no space for us to do anything else. Dima and his people are peering at us over the balustrade. I have been warned that Dima has no language but Russian. I have no Russian.

'Mr Dima says, what do you want?' my interpreter bellows into my right ear. The music is so loud that I haven't heard Dima speak, but my interpreter has, which is what matters, and his mouth is four inches from my right ear. Our kneeling position seems to call for a moment of bravado, so I say I would like the music turned down, and would Dima be kind enough to remove his dark glasses because it's difficult to have a conversation with a pair of blacked-out eyes? Dima orders the music down, then testily removes his dark glasses, leaving his eyes naked and pig-like. He is still waiting to know what I want. Come to think of it, so am I.

'I understand you're a gangster,' I say. 'Is that correct?'

I can't know how my interpreter translates this question, but I have a suspicion that he has watered it down because Dima seems remarkably at ease with it.

'Mr Dima says, in this country everyone is gangster. Everything is rotten, all businessmen are gangsters, all businesses are crime syndicates.'

'Then may I enquire of Mr Dima what line of business he is actually engaged in?'

'Mr Dima is engaged in import–export,' my interpreter begs me in a don't-go-there voice.

But I have nowhere else to go.

'Please ask him what type of import and export. Just ask him.'

'It is not convenient.'

'All right, then. Ask him what he's worth. Can we say he's worth five million dollars?'

Reluctantly, my interpreter must have asked the question, or something like it, because Dima's people are sniggering and Dima has responded with a contemptuous shrug. Never mind. I think I see where I'm heading now.

'All right. It's a hundred million, it's two hundred, it's whatever. Let's agree that it's pretty easy to make a lot of money in Russia just now. And if things stay as they are, we can assume that in a couple of years Dima will be a *very* rich man indeed. Mega-rich. Just put that to him, please. It's a simple point.'

And presumably my interpreter puts it to Dima, because I get a kind of smirk of agreement from the lower part of his bald face.

'Has Dima got children?' I enquire, reckless now.

He has.

'Grandchildren?'

'It is immaterial.'

Dima has replaced his Ray-Bans, as if to say the conversation is over, but for me it isn't. I've blundered too far down the road to stop.

'Here's my point. In the United States, as I'm sure Dima knows, the great robber barons of olden days made their fortunes by what we may call *informal* methods.'

I am pleased to detect a flicker of interest from behind the Ray-Bans.

'But as the robber barons grew older and looked at their children and grandchildren, they got all idealistic and decided they needed to create a brighter, kinder world than the one they had ripped off.'

The blacked-out eyes remain fixed on me as the interpreter conveys whatever he conveys.

'So my question of Dima is this. Could he imagine, as he grows older – let's say in ten, fifteen years from now – could *Dima* see a time coming when *he* might start building hospitals and schools and art museums? As an act of philanthropy? I'm serious. Just ask him. As a way of giving something back to the Russian people he's – well – robbed, actually?'

There's a standard joke in old movie comedies when people talk to each other through an interpreter. A question is put. It is interpreted. The person for whom it is intended listens intently, then flings his arms around and orates for two long minutes of movie time, and the interpreter, after a stage pause, says: 'No.' Or 'Yes.' Or 'Maybe.' Dima doesn't fling his arms around. He speaks a measured Russian. The supporters' club starts to giggle. The shorthaired sentries at the door giggle. But Dima goes on talking. Satisfied at last, he puts his hands together and waits for our interpreter to relay his message.

'Mr David, I regret to tell you, Mr Dima says fuck off.'

*

Seated under the crystal chandelier in the lobby of our glitzy Moscow hotel, a slender, shy man of thirty in a grey suit and spectacles, sips at his orange fizz while he explains the code of conduct of the thieves' brotherhood or *vory*, of which he is a made member. I have been told he is one of Dima's soldiers. Perhaps he is one of the suited men selling fire insurance to my publisher. By his careful choice of words he puts me in mind of a Foreign Office spokesman.

'Have the *vory* changed much since the collapse of Soviet communism?'

'I would say the *vory* have *expanded*. Owing to greater freedom of movement in the post-communist era, and better communications, one may say the *vory* have extended their influence in many countries.'

'And which countries might those be, in particular?'

It is better, he would say, to speak of towns rather than countries. Warsaw, Madrid, Berlin, Rome, London, Naples, New York are all favourable to *vory* activities.

'And here in Russia?'

'I would say that social chaos in Russia has benefited many *vory* activities.'

'Such as?'

'Please?'

'Such as *what* activities?'

'I would say here in Russia, drugs are profitable. Also many new businesses cannot function without extortion. Also we have gambling houses and many clubs.'

'Whorehouses?'

'Whorehouses are not necessary to the *vory*. Better we own the women and arrange hotels for them. Sometimes we own the hotels also.'

'Is ethnicity a criterion?'

'Please?'

'Are *vory* brotherhoods drawn from specific regions?'

'I would say, today we are composed of many thieves who are not ethnic Russians.'

'Such as?'

'Abkhaz, Armenian, Slavs. Also Jews.'

'Chechen?'

'With Chechen, I would say it is different.'

'Is there racial discrimination within the *vory*?'

'If a *vor* is good thief and obeys the rules, *vory* are equal.'

'Do you have many rules?'

'We do not have many rules but they are severe.'

'Kindly give me an example of your rules.'

He seems happy to. A *vor* must not work for authority. The state is authority, therefore he must not work for the state, or fight for the state, or serve the state in any way. He must not pay taxes to the state.

'Do the *vory* love God?'

'Yes.'

'Can a *vor* go into politics?'

'If a *vor*'s purpose in going into politics is to extend the influence of the *vory* and not to assist authority, he may go into politics.'

'And if he becomes politically prominent? Popular even? Successful? He can remain a *vor* at heart?'

'It is possible.'

'Does one *vor* kill another for breaking *vory* law?'

'If it is ordered by the council.'

'You would kill your best friend?'

'If it is necessary.'

'Have you personally killed many people?'

'It is possible.'

'Have you ever thought of being a lawyer?'

'No.'

'Can a *vor* marry?'

'He must be a man above women. He may have many women, but he must not submit to them because they are not relevant.'

'So better not to marry?'

'It is a rule that a *vor* may not marry.'

'But some do?'

'It is a rule.'

'May a *vor* have children?'

'No.'

'But some do?'

'I would say it is possible. It is not desirable. Better is to help other thieves and submit to the *vory* council.'

'How about the mothers and fathers of *vory*? Are they acceptable?'

'Parents are not desirable. It is better to abandon them.'

'Because they're authority?'

'It is not permitted to show emotions and remain within the thieves' law.'

'But some *vory* love their mothers?'

'It is possible.'

'Have you abandoned your own parents?'

'A little. Maybe not enough.'

'Have you ever fallen in love with a woman?'

'It is not appropriate.'

'Not appropriate to ask the question or not appropriate to fall in love?'

'It is not appropriate,' he repeats.

But by then he is blushing and laughing like a schoolboy, and my interpreter is laughing too. Then all three of us are laughing. And I am pondering, as a humble reader of Dostoevsky, where the morality, pride and humanity are to be found in the contemporary Russian criminal soul, because I have a character in my head who needs to know.

In fact, it turns out, I have several. They are spread over the two rather unresolved novels I eventually wrote about the new Russia in the immediate post-communist aftermath, *Our Game* and *Single & Single*. Both took me to Russia, Georgia and the Western Caucasus. Both attempted to address the scale of criminal corruption in Russia and its continuing wars on its own Muslim south. A decade later, in *Our Kind of Traitor*, I wrote a third novel about what was by then arguably Russia's greatest export, second only to energy: dirty money by the billion, stolen from Russia's own coffers.

*

And always close at hand, but never too close, Pusya, our all-Abkhazia wrestling champion. Once only did I fear we might have to call on his more physical services.

This time the nightclub is in Petersburg. Like Dima's, it is owned by a rising man of *business* named Karl, who has a lawyer called Ilya who seldom leaves his side. We have been driven there in an armoured minibus with an armoured Land Rover for a chase car. At the entrance, which lies at the end of a stone footpath decked with paper lanterns, we encounter the usual platoon of armed men, who in addition to submachine guns sport hand grenades hanging from polished brass hooks on their ammunition belts. Inside the club, girls of the house dance languidly with each other to deafening rock music while they wait for the punters to show up.

But there aren't any punters, and it has gone half-past eleven.

'Petersburg wakes up late,' Karl explains with a knowing smile, guiding us to a long dining table that has been set in our honour among the plush seats. He is beaky, donnish-looking and young, with old manners. The lumbering Ilya at his side seems too crude for him. Ilya's blonde wife wears a sable coat although it is mid-summer. We are escorted to the top row of a steep ring of seats. The dance floor below us doubles as a boxing ring, says Ilya proudly, but tonight there is no boxing. Pusya sits to my left, son Nick to my right. Ilya, at his master's side, mumbles into a cellphone, one call after another in an emotionless flow.

Still no punters have arrived. With empty benches all round us, rock music blaring for attention and bored girls dutifully gyrating on the dance floor, the small talk at our table is getting less easy. It's the traffic, Karl explains, talking across Ilya's bulk. It's the new prosperity. With everyone owning a car these days, evening traffic in Petersburg is getting to be a scandal.

Another hour passes.

It's because it's Thursday, Karl explains. On Thursdays, Petersburg's glitterati go partying first and nightclubbing afterwards. I don't believe him, and I don't think Pusya does, and we exchange worried glances. Too many bad scenarios are running through my head, and I assume Pusya's also. Do the Petersburg glitterati know something we don't? Has Karl fallen foul of a business rival, and are we sitting here waiting to be blown up or shot to smithereens? Or – shades of those hand grenades hanging from their brass hooks – have we already been taken hostage, hence Ilya's mumbled negotiations on his cellphone?

Putting a finger to his lips, Pusya heads for the men's room, then veers into the darkness. A couple of minutes later he is back, smiling more benignly than ever. Our host, Karl, has made a false economy, he explains softly beneath the music. The bodyguards with grenades on their belts are Chechen. In Petersburg society, Chechen body-guards are a bridge too far. Nobody who is anybody in Petersburg, says Pusya, wants to be seen in a nightclub protected by Chechen.

*

And Dima? It took another year, but unusually for the times he was actually called to account by the Moscow police, either on orders from one of his rivals or – if he hadn't been paying his dues – the Kremlin. When last heard of, he was in prison, trying to explain why he had two very damaged fellow businessmen chained to a wall in his cellar. In my novel called *Our Kind of Traitor*, I eventually had my own Dima, but only in name. He was a hardened gangster who, unlike his original, really might have stumped up for the odd school, hospital and art museum.

19

Blood and treasure

In recent years I have acquired a childish aversion to reading anything that is written about me in the press, good, bad or other. But there are occasions when something slips through my defences, as happened one morning in the autumn of 1991 when I opened my *Times* newspaper to be greeted by my own face glowering up at me. From my sour expression I could tell at once that the text around it wasn't going to be friendly. Photographic editors know their stuff. A struggling Warsaw theatre, I read, was celebrating its post-communist freedom by putting on a stage version of *The Spy Who Came in from the Cold*. But the rapacious le Carré [see photograph] wanted a whacking £150 per performance: 'The price of freedom, we suppose.'

I took another look at the photograph and saw exactly the sort of fellow who does indeed go round preying on struggling Polish theatres. Grasping. Unsavoury appetites. Just look at those eyebrows. I had by now ceased to enjoy my breakfast.

Keep calm and call your agent. I fail on the first count, succeed on the second. My literary agent's name is Rainer. In what the novelists call a quavering voice, I read the article aloud to him. Has he, I suggest delicately – might he possibly, just this once, is it at all conceivable? – on this occasion been a tad too zealous on my behalf?

Rainer is emphatic. Quite the reverse. Since the Poles are still in the recovery ward after the collapse of communism, he has been a total pussycat. To prove it, he recites the terms he negotiated with the Polish theatre. We are not charging the theatre £150 per performance, he assures me, but a measly £26, the minimum standard rate, or have I forgotten? Well yes, actually, I have. In addition to which we've thrown in the rights for free. In short, a sweetheart deal, David, a deliberate helping hand to a Polish theatre in time of need. Great, I say, bewildered and inwardly seething.

Keep calm and fax the editor of *The Times*. He is a man whose life and writing I have since learned to admire greatly, but in 1991 I was less aware of his virtues. His response is not soothing. It is lofty. Not to put too fine an edge on it, it is infuriating. He sees no great harm in the piece, he says. He suggests that a man in my fortunate position should take the rough with the smooth. This is not advice I am prepared to accept. But who to turn to?

Why, of course: the man who owns the newspaper, Rupert Murdoch, my old buddy!

*

Well, not exactly buddy. I *had* met Murdoch socially on a couple of occasions, though I doubted whether he remembered them. The first was at Boulestin's restaurant in the mid-eighties, where I was lunching with another literary agent of the time, and in walked Murdoch. My agent made the introductions, Murdoch joined us for a dry martini. He was my age exactly. His war to the death with Fleet Street's print unions was gathering heat. We discussed it a bit, then I asked him in a casual way – maybe it was the martini talking – why he had broken with tradition. In the old days, I said lightly, needy Brits had set out for Australia to seek their fortunes. Now an Australian who wasn't needy had come to Britain to seek his. What had gone wrong? It was an asinine question at the best of times, but Murdoch leapt at it.

'*I'll* tell you why,' he retorted. 'It's because you're wood *from here up!*'

And he made a slicing gesture across his throat to show where the wood began.

At our second meeting, which took place in a private house, he had treated the table in the frankest terms to his negative views on the collapse of the Soviet Union. At the end of the evening he had generously handed me his card: phone, fax, home address. Any time, and the phone rings right on his desk.

Keep calm and fax Murdoch. I have three conditions, I say: number one, a generous apology prominently printed in *The Times*; number two, a handsome donation to the struggling Polish theatre. And number three – was that dry martini still talking? – lunch. Next morning his reply was lying on the floor beneath my fax machine:

'Your terms accepted. Rupert.'

*

The Savoy Grill in those days had a kind of upper level for moguls: red-plush, horseshoe-shaped affairs where in more colourful days gentlemen of money might have entertained their ladies. I breathe the name Murdoch to the maître d'hôtel and am shown to one of the privés. I am early. Murdoch is bang on time.

He is smaller than I remember him, but more pugnacious, and has acquired that hasty waddle and little buck of the pelvis with which great men of affairs advance on one another, hand outstretched, for the cameras. The slant of the head in relation to the body is more pronounced than I remember, and when he wrinkles up his eyes to give me his sunny smile, I have the odd feeling he's taking aim at me.

We sit down, we face each other. I notice – how can I not? – the unsettling collection of rings on his left hand. We order our food and exchange a couple of banalities. Rupert says he's sorry about that stuff they wrote about me. Brits, he says, are great penmen, but they don't always get things right. I say, not at all, and thanks for your sporting response. But enough of small talk. He is staring straight at me and the sunny smile has vanished.

'Who killed Bob Maxwell?' he demands.

Robert Maxwell, for those lucky enough not to remember him, was a Czech-born media baron, British parliamentarian and the alleged spy of several nations, including Israel, the Soviet Union and Britain. As a young Czech freedom fighter he had taken part in the Normandy landings, and later earned himself a British army commission and a gallantry medal. After the war, he worked for the Foreign Office in Berlin. He was also a flamboyant liar and rogue of gargantuan proportions and appetites who plundered the pension fund of his own companies to the tune of £440 million, owed around £4 billion that he had no way of repaying, and in November 1991 was found dead in the seas off Tenerife, having apparently fallen from the deck of a lavish private yacht named after his daughter.

Conspiracy theories abounded. To some it was a clear case of suicide by a man ensnared by his own crimes; to others, murder by one of the several intelligence agencies he had supposedly worked for. But which one? Why Murdoch should imagine I know the answer to this question any better than anyone else is beyond me, but I do my best to give satisfaction. Well, Rupert, if we're really saying it's not suicide, then probably, for my money, it was the Israelis, I suggest.

'Why?'

I've read the rumours that are flying around, as we all have. I regurgitate them: Maxwell, the long-term agent of Israeli Intelligence, blackmailing his former paymasters; Maxwell, who had traded with the Shining Path in Peru, offering Israeli weapons in exchange for strategic cobalt; Maxwell, threatening to go public unless the Israelis paid up.

But Rupert Murdoch is already on his feet, shaking my hand and saying it was great to meet me again. And maybe he's as embarrassed as I am, or just bored, because already he's powering his way out of the room, and great men don't sign bills, they leave them to their people. Estimated duration of lunch: twenty-five minutes.

But today I wish we'd had our lunch a couple of months later, because by then I would have had a much more interesting theory to offer him about why Bob Maxwell died.

*

I'm in London, writing about the new Russia, and I want to meet Western carpetbaggers who have joined the gold rush. Somebody has told me Barry is the man I am looking for, and somebody is right. Sooner or later there's a Barry, and when you find him, you best stick to him like glue. Friend A gives you an introduction to his friend B. Friend B's sorry he can't help, but maybe his friend C can. C can't, but it so happens that D's in town, so why not give old D a ring, say you're a pal of C's and here's D's number. And suddenly you're in the room with the right man.

Barry is a natural-born East Ender who's made it big in the West End: classless, fast-talking, likes the idea of meeting a writer but doesn't read a book unless he's got to, has a reputation for making effortless fortunes fast, and is indeed taking a more than academic interest in the possibility of making a serious killing in the disintegrating Soviet Union. All of which, he tells me, explains why Bob Maxwell called him up one day and told him, as only Bob could, to get his arse round to Bob's office *now*, and advise him how to make a Russian fortune inside a week, or Bob would be in serious ordure.

And, yes, it so happens that Barry *is* free for lunch today, David, so it's Julia, darling, scrub my afternoon engagements, will you dear, because me and David are slipping round to the Silver Grill, so call up Martha and tell her it's for two, and a nice quiet corner.

And what's really important to remember, David, Barry urges me sternly, first in the cab, then again over a nice fillet steak done the way he likes, is the *date* when Bob Maxwell makes that call to me. It's July 1991, so it's four months before his body is found floating in the briny. Got that? Because if you haven't, you're going to miss the whole point. All right, then. I'll begin.

*

'I *own* Mikhail Gorbachev,' Robert Maxwell announces to Barry as soon as they are sitting head to head in Maxwell's grandiose penthouse office. 'And what I want you to do, Barry, is take the yacht' – meaning the *Lady Ghislaine* from which Maxwell later fell to his death, if he wasn't dead already – 'and sit on it for three days maximum, then come back here to me with a *proposal*. Now fuck off.'

And of course there was a nice piece of change in it for Barry too, or he wouldn't have been sitting there, would he? – a consideration up front for his thoughts, plus a percentage of the action down the line. He doesn't take the yacht because yachts aren't his thing, but there's a place he's got in the deep countryside where he likes to put his thinking-cap on, and twenty-four hours later, not the three days Bob was on about, he's back in the penthouse suite with his *proposal*. Or in point of fact, David, three proposals. And all of them sure-fire winners, all guaranteed to yield very big returns, though not necessarily all at the same rate.

First, Bob, he tells Maxwell, there's your oil, which is obvious. If Gorby could slip you just one of the state concessions shortly to be on offer in the Caucasus, then you could auction it off to the big oil boys, or lease out the wells for a royalty. Either way, you'd be making a very large killing indeed, Bob—

And the downside? Maxwell interrupts. What's the fucking downside?

Your downside, Bob, is *time*, which as you tell me is your big problem. An oil deal that size can't happen overnight, not even with your pal in the Kremlin pulling the levers, so you won't have anything to auction for, well—

Not fucking interested. Next?

My next one, Bob, is your scrap metal. And I'm not talking pushing a barrow down Cable Street and yelling up at windows for any old iron. I'm talking the very best top-quality metal ever made, mountains of it, churned out regardless of cost by a command economy gone loco: parks full of rusty tanks, weaponry, clapped-out factories, dud power stations and all the rest of the junk left over from five-year plans, seven-year plans and no-plans-at-all. But in your world market, Bob, priceless raw metal just waiting for somebody like you to come along. And nobody needs to own it but you.

You'll be doing Russia a favour, cleaning the stuff up. A nice letter from our pal at the Kremlin thanking you for your trouble, and a couple of phone calls to people in metals I know, you're home and dry.

Except *what*?

Your downside, Bob? Is your cost of collection. Is your high personal visibility at this juncture in your life with the eyes of the world upon you, I'll put it that way. Because sooner or later somebody over there is going to ask why it's Bob Maxwell doing the cleaning up, and not someone nice and Russian.

So Maxwell asks impatiently what Barry's third proposal is. And Barry says: your blood, Bob.

*

'Your blood, Bob,' Barry tells Robert Maxwell, 'is a very valuable *commodity* in any market place. But your *Russian* blood, properly extracted and marketed, is a very serious goldmine indeed. Your Russian citizen is patriotic. When he hears on his radio or television, or reads in his Russian newspaper, that there's been a national tragedy, be it a little war somewhere, or a train smash, or a plane crash, or an earthquake, or a gas pipe blowing up, or a terrorist blowing up a market place, your Russian doesn't just sit there, he goes straight down to his nearest hospital and he gives blood. *Gives* it, Bob. For free. As the good citizen he is. Millions of gallons of it. They queue up, they stand there quietly in line, which they're used to, and they give free blood. It's what they do out of the goodness of their Russian hearts. Free.'

Barry pauses over his steak in case I have a question, but none comes to me, perhaps because I have the shivery feeling it's no longer Robert Maxwell he's pitching to, it's me.

'So given your unlimited supply of Russian blood, free at source,' Barry resumes, putting on his logistical hat, 'what else do you need? It's Russia, so organization is bound to be your first worry. The transfusion service is there, so it's already collection of a sort, but you'll have to sharpen it up. Then there's your distribution. There's cold storage in every Russian city, so all you've got to do is raise the quantity level. Bigger and better storage, more of it. Who funds your operation? The Soviet state does, what's left of it. The Soviet state, out of the goodness of its heart, improves and modernizes the service nationally, which is overdue, and Gorby gives himself a pat on the back for it. The Soviet exchequer funds the operation *centrally*, each Republic sends an agreed percentage of its take to a *central* blood bank – in Moscow, near one of your airports – as a quid pro quo for the funding. What does your central blood bank in Moscow officially use the blood for? Unspecified mega-emergencies nationwide. And what are *you* using it for? You've got a brace of refrigerated 747s working the shuttle between Sheremetyevo and Kennedy airports. You don't have to buy them. Lease them through me. Ship the blood to New York, have chemists check it for HIV en route, and I know just the boys. Have you got any idea at all what they're paying out there in the world market for a gallon of Aids-tested, Caucasian blood? I'll tell you . . .'

And the downside, Barry? This time it's me who's asking, not Maxwell, and Barry is already shaking his head.

'David, there was *not* a downside. That blood would have gone like clockwork. I'd be very surprised if it isn't going like clockwork for somebody at this very minute.'

So why not for Bob?

It's the date, David, isn't it? Barry is back to that all-important date he warned me about at the beginning of his story.

'Summer 1991, remember? Gorby is hanging on to power by his fingernails. The Party's falling apart at the seams and Yeltsin is after his balls. Come autumn, the Republics are clamouring for their independence, and nobody's thinking of sending blood to Moscow. More likely they're thinking Moscow could send a bit of something to the Republics for a change.'

And your friend Bob? I ask.

'Bob Maxwell wasn't blind and he wasn't stupid, David. Once he knew Gorby was done for, he knew blood was off the table and his last chance was gone. If he'd held on for a month, he'd have seen the Soviet Union sunk for ever, and Gorby go down with the ship. Bob knew the game was up, so he didn't hang about, did he?'

In the novel that I eventually wrote, I used Barry's idea about marketing Russian blood, but it didn't play as strongly as I meant it to, perhaps because nobody killed himself on account of it.

*

But here's a tailpiece to that twenty-five-minute lunch date with Rupert Murdoch at the Savoy Grill. One of Murdoch's ex-aides, writing of his former employer's performance before the British parliamentary committee delving into the phone-hacking conducted by one of his newspapers, described how Murdoch's advisers had urged him to remove the array of gold rings from his left hand before he informed his audience, with a clot in his voice, that this was the humblest day of his life.

20

The biggest bears in the garden

I have met two former heads of the KGB in my life and I liked them both. The last to hold the job before the KGB changed its name, though not its spots, was Vadim Bakatin. Intelligence services, somebody clever said, are like the wiring in a house: the new owner moves in, he drops the switch, and it's the same old lights that come on again.

It is 1993. Vadim Bakatin, the retired head of the extinct KGB, is drawing broken arrows on his doodle-pad. They have nicely tailored feathers and slim shafts. But halfway along they make a right-angle turn and become boomerang arrows, each tip pointing in a different direction and always out of the page. He draws them while he sits strictly to attention at the long table in my Russian publisher's conference room, his centurion's back arched and his head drawn stiffly into his shoulders as if for ceremonial inspection. *Reforma Fund* says the English side of his badly printed card. *International Fund for Social & Economic Reforms*.

He is a heavy, gingery, Nordic-looking man, with a sad smile and mottled, capable hands. Born and bred in Novosibirsk, he is by training an engineer, a former director of state construction, former member of the Communist Party's Central Committee, former Minister of Internal Affairs. Then in 1991, to his surprise and not altogether his pleasure, Mikhail Gorbachev handed him the poisoned chalice: take over the KGB for me and clean it up. Sitting listening to him now, I could well imagine what might have prompted Gorbachev to offer him the job: Bakatin's patent decency, which is of the deep-running, stubborn sort, made of awkward silences while he carefully weighs a question before delivering the carefully weighed answer.

'My recommendations were not popular with the KGB,' he observes, and draws another arrow. And as an afterthought: 'This was not an easy assignment.'

He means: not an easy assignment to breeze into KGB Headquarters in Dzerzhinsky Square one summer's morning, purge it at one blow of its autocratic tendencies and deliver a new, sanitized, socially aware spy service fit for purpose in the reconstructed democratic Russia that Gorbachev dreamed of. Bakatin knew from the beginning that the going would be tough. But how *much* he knew is anyone's guess. Was he aware that the KGB was a streamlined kleptocracy that had already pocketed a large chunk of the nation's stock of hard currency and gold reserves and stashed it abroad? That its chieftains were hand in glove with the country's organized-crime syndicates? That many were old-guard Stalinists who saw Gorbachev as the Great Destroyer?

Whatever Bakatin did or didn't know, he performed an act of such *glasnost* that it remains unique in the annals of intelligence services across the globe. Within weeks of taking office, he handed to Robert Strauss, the United States Ambassador to Russia, a chart, together with a users' handbook, of the listening devices that had been installed by the KGB's audio team in the fabric of the new building designated to replace the existing US Embassy. According to Strauss, he performed this gesture 'unconditionally, out of a sense of cooperation and goodwill'. According to Moscow's many wits, when the American sweepers had taken out the KGB's devices, the building was on the point of collapse.

'With those technical people, you could never be sure,' Bakatin earnestly confides to me. 'I told Strauss it was the best I could get out of them.'

As a reward for this courageous act of openness, he earned himself the full fury of the organization he commanded. Cries of treason went up, his post was abolished and for a short time, under the leadership of Boris Yeltsin, the KGB was parcelled out to other departments, only to have itself promptly resurrected with increased powers and a new name under the personal command of Vladimir Putin, himself a child of the old KGB.

Back to his broken arrows, Vadim Bakatin is musing about spying. Those who do it for a living are obsessives, out of touch with normal life, he says. He himself entered and left the spy business as a novice.

'You know far more about it than I do,' he adds suddenly, looking up.

'But that's not true,' I protest. 'I'm a novice too. I did the work when I was young and got out thirty years ago. I've been living off my wits ever since.'

He draws an arrow.

'So it's a game,' he says.

Does he mean *I'm* a game? Or the spying industry is? He shakes his head, as if to say it doesn't matter either way. Suddenly his questions become the mystified outcry of a man deprived of his convictions. Where is the world going? Where is Russia going? Where is the middle way, the humanitarian one, between capitalist and socialist excess? He's a socialist, he says. He grew up a socialist:

'I was brought up from childhood to believe that communism was the only true path for humanity. Okay, things went wrong. Power got into the wrong hands, the Party took some wrong turnings. But I still believe that we were the moral force for good in the world. What are we now? Where is the moral force?'

*

It would be hard to find a greater contrast between two men: the introspective Bakatin, engineer and Party stalwart from Novosibirsk, and the Georgian-bred Yevgeny Primakov, half-Jewish son of a woman doctor and a politically persecuted father, scholar, Arabist, statesman, academician and – in the course of half a century's service to a system not famed for its tenderness towards those who fall foul of it – master survivor.

Unlike Bakatin, Yevgeny Primakov was eminently qualified to take over the KGB or any other heavyweight intelligence service. As a young Soviet field agent, codenamed MAKSIM, he had spied in the Middle East and in the United States, now as correspondent for Moscow Radio, now as a print journalist for *Pravda*. But even while he was in the field, his ascent through the scientific and political ranks of Soviet power continued. And when Soviet power ended, Primakov continued to prevail, so it surprised nobody when, after five years as head of the Russian Foreign Intelligence Service, he was promoted to Russian Foreign Minister, in which capacity he came one day to London to discuss NATO matters with the British Foreign Secretary, Malcolm Rifkind.

And it was on the evening of that same day that my wife and I were summoned at no notice to dine with Primakov and his wife at the Russian Embassy in Kensington Palace Gardens. In the morning, my literary agent had taken a breathless call from Rifkind's Private Office: the Foreign Secretary requires a signed book of mine to present to his Russian opposite number, Yevgeny Primakov.

A particular book, or just any book? my agent asks.

Smiley's People. And he needs it fast.

I don't keep stacks of my books around me, but I managed to dig out a hardback copy of *Smiley's People* in reasonable condition. No doubt for reasons of national economy, Rifkind's office had said nothing of providing a courier, so we rang for one, wrapped up the book, addressed the parcel to Rifkind care of the Foreign Office, SW1, and dispatched it.

A couple of hours later, the Private Office rang again. No book, for God's sake, what's happened? Frantic calls by my wife to the courier service. Package under advisement was delivered to Foreign Office at such-and-such an hour and signed for by recipient. We relay this information to the Private Office. Oh Christ, then it must be stuck in bloody Security, we'll check. They check. The book, having presumably been sniffed at and shaken and X-rayed, is wrested from the clutches of bloody Security, and perhaps Rifkind adds his name to mine, along with a collegial line or two, one foreign minister to the other. We shall never know because neither my agent nor I had another peep out of Rifkind or his Private Office.

*

Time to dress up and call a black cab. My wife has invested in white orchids in a pot for our hostess, the Russian Ambassador's wife. I have put together a carrier bag of books and videos for Primakov. Our cab pulls up outside the Russian Embassy. No lights burn. I am obsessive about punctuality, so we're a quarter of an hour early. But it's a balmy evening and there's a red diplomatic police car parked a few yards down the kerb.

Good evening, officers.

Good evening to you, sir and madam.

We have a small problem, officers. We're dining at the Russian Embassy, but we're early, and we've brought these gifts for our hosts. May we leave them in your care while we take a stroll round Kensington Palace Gardens?

Of course you may, sir, but not in the car, I'm afraid. Put them down on the pavement there and we'll keep an eye on them for you.

We put our parcels down on the pavement, stroll, return, collect our parcels, which in the meantime have not exploded. We mount the Embassy steps. A sudden blaze of light, the front door opens. Very big men in suits glower at our parcels. One of them reaches for the orchids, another pokes inside my carrier bag. We are nodded through to the splendid drawing room. It's empty. I am assailed by inappropriate memories. At the age of twenty-odd, as an aspiring young spy in the British interest, I had attended a string of awful Anglo-Soviet Friendship meetings in this very room, before being spirited upstairs by over-friendly KGB talent-spotters, there to watch

Eisenstein's *Battleship Potemkin* for the umpteenth time and submit to yet another courteous inquisition about my life, origins, girl-friends, political leanings and aspirations, all in the vain hope that I shall become the target of a Soviet intelligence pass and thus acquire in the eyes of my British masters the coveted status of double agent. It never happened, which – given the scale of Soviet penetration of our intelligence services in those days – should not surprise anyone. Or perhaps I just didn't smell right, which wouldn't surprise me either.

Back then, there was also a tiny bar in a corner of this beautiful room. It dispensed warm white wine to any comrade hardy enough to fight his way through the crush. It is still there, and tonight it is manned by a *babushka* in her seventies.

'You want drink?'

'Very much.'

'What you want drink?'

'Scotch, please. Two.'

'Whisky?'

'Yes, whisky.'

'You want two? For her also?'

'Please. With soda, no ice.'

'Water?'

'Water's fine.'

But we have barely taken a first sip when the double doors fly open and enter Primakov, escorted by his wife and the Russian Ambassador's wife, then the Ambassador himself and a troupe of suntanned power-men in lightweight suits. Coming to a halt before us, Primakov pulls a comic smile and points an accusing finger at my glass.

'What are you drinking?'

'Scotch.'

'You are in Russia now. Drink vodka.'

We return our un-drunk Scotches to the *babushka*, join the troupe and at light-infantry speed proceed to the elegant pre-Revolutionary dining room. One long table, candlelit. I sit as directed, three feet across it from Primakov. My wife is two stops down on the same side, looking a lot calmer than I feel. Big-shouldered waiters fill our vodka glasses to the brim. Primakov, I suspect, has already refreshed himself. He is very jolly, very twinkly. His wife sits beside him. She is a blonde and beautiful Estonian doctor with a motherly glow. On his other side sits his interpreter, but Primakov prefers his own vigorous style of English with an occasional prompt.

The power-men in lightweight suits, I have meanwhile been told, are Russian ambassadors from across the Middle East, summoned to London for a conference. My wife and I are the only non-Russians at the table.

'You will call me Yevgeny, I will call you David,' Primakov informs me.

Dinner has begun. When Primakov speaks, no one else does. He speaks suddenly, after much thought, consulting his interpreter only when he's stumped for a word. Like most Russian intellectuals I have met, he has no time for small talk. His subjects for tonight, in the following order, are Saddam Hussein, President George Bush Senior, Prime Minister Margaret Thatcher and his own abortive efforts to head off the Gulf War. He is an agile and vivid communicator of great charm. His eyes do not lightly let you go. Periodically he breaks off, beams at me, raises his glass, proposes a toast. I raise my glass, beam back and respond. There must be a waiter with a vodka bottle for every guest. There is certainly one for me. When you're caught for a vodka marathon, an English friend urged me the first time I went to Russia, stick to vodka and don't for God's sake go for that lethal Crimean *Sekt* (champagne). I have never been more grateful for his advice.

'You know Desert Storm, David?' Primakov demands.

Yes, Yevgeny, I know Desert Storm.

'Saddam, he was a *friend* from me. You know what I mean by *friend*, David?'

Yes, Yevgeny, I think in this context I know what you mean by friend.

'Saddam, he *telephones* to me' – indignation mounting – '"Yevgeny. Save my face. Get me out of *Kuwait.*"'

He allows time for the significance of this request to sink in. Gradually it does. He is telling me that Saddam Hussein asked him to persuade George Bush Senior to let him pull his forces out of Kuwait with dignity – save his face – in which case there need be no war between the United States and Iraq.

'So I go to *Bush*,' he continues, striking angrily at the name. 'This man is' – tense discussion with the interpreter. If it is on the tip of Primakov's tongue to use strong language to describe George Bush Senior, he restrains himself.

'This Bush is *not cooperative*,' he asserts reluctantly, and allows himself a grimace of indignation. 'Therefore I come to *England*,' he resumes. 'To *Britain*. To your *Thatcher*. I come' – another flurried consultation with his interpreter, and this time I catch the Russian word *dacha*, which is about the only one I know.

'*Chequers*,' says the interpreter.

'So I come to *Chequers*.' A hand flies up commanding our silence, but the entire table is dead silent already. 'For *one hour* this woman *lectures* me. They *want* the war!'

*

It is after midnight when my wife and I return down the Russian Embassy's front doorsteps to England. Did Primakov ask me a single personal or political question during that whole long evening? Did we talk literature, spying, life? If we did, I have no memory of it. I remember only that he seemed to want me to share his frustration; to know that as a peacemaker and a reasonable human being, he had done his damnedest to stop a war, and that his efforts had foundered on what he regarded as the pig-headedness of two Western leaders.

There is an ironic epilogue to this tale that I only recently caught up with. It's a decade later. With the younger Bush in power and the invasion of Iraq again imminent, Primakov flies to Baghdad and urges his old friend Saddam to hand over whatever weapons of mass destruction he may or may not have to the United Nations for safe-keeping. This time it's not Bush Junior but Saddam who gives him the brush-off, on the grounds that the Americans would never dare do it to him: they had too many secrets in common.

I had not seen Primakov or spoken to him since that dinner. No letter, no email had passed between us. Now and then an invitation trickled down at third hand: tell David any time he's in Moscow, et cetera. But Putin's Russia didn't draw me, and I didn't call him. Then, come the spring of 2015, I received a message that he was ailing and would I send him some more of my books to read. Since nobody said which books, my wife and I made up a great box of them in hardback. I signed each book, added a dedication, and we dispatched the box by courier to the address we'd been given, only to have it returned by Russian customs on the grounds that it contained too many books at one time. We broke the books up into smaller lots and presumably they made it through the lines, although no word came back.

And now it never will, because Yevgeny Primakov died before he could read them. In his memoirs, I'm told, he writes kindly about me, which pleases me very much. As I write, I am trying to get my hands on the text. But this is Russia.*

How do I see that evening from this distance? I have long ago discovered that on the odd occasions when I come face to face with people of power, my critical faculties go out of the window and all I

---

*In Primakov's „Vstrechi na perekrestkach" (*Meetings at Crossroads*, (https://www .litres.ru/evgeniy-primakov/vstrechi-na-perekrestkah-2/chitat-onlayn/): Another "surprise" that was waiting for me in London during my visit to the British capital in March 1997, as Minister for Foreign Affairs, was that I had a meeting with one of the best — at least, I think so — authors of political thrillers, John le Carré. Our ambassador Adamishin invited him and his wife to dinner at my request. The meeting was completely relaxed. Me and my wife enjoyed the conversation with this interesting person. As long-time admirers of the former spy David Cornwell, who has earned worldwide fame under the name of le Carré, we were particularly pleased to receive the recently published book *Smiley's People* with an inscription from the author: "To Evgeny Maksimovich Primakov my sincere warm wishes and hope that we will live in a better world than the one described here."

want to do is be there, listen and watch. To Primakov, I was an evening's curiosity, a bit of time out, but also, as I like to think, a chance to speak from the heart to a writer whose work had rung bells with him.

Vadim Bakatin had only agreed to talk to me as a favour to a friend, but once again I like to think I provided him with an opportunity to speak as he felt. People at the epicentre, in my limited experience of the breed, have little idea of what's going on around them. The fact that they are themselves the epicentre makes it all the harder. It took an American visitor to Moscow to ask Primakov which character in my books he related to:

'Why, *George Smiley* of course!'

*

Oldřich Černý should in no way be compared with either Bakatin or Primakov, both professed communists of their day. In 1993, four years after the Berlin Wall came down, Oldřich Černý – Olda to his friends – took over the Czech foreign intelligence service and, at the behest of his old friend and fellow dissident, Václav Havel, set about turning it into a place fit for habitation by the Western spy community. Over the five years in which he ran it, he struck up a close relationship with Britain's MI6, notably with Richard Dearlove, who later became its Chief under Tony Blair. Quite soon after Černý's retirement from the post, I visited him in Prague and we spent a couple of days together, now in his tiny apartment with Helena, his companion of many years, and now out and about in one of the city's many cellar bars, drinking Scotch at scrubbed pine tables.

Before getting the job, Černý, like Vadim Bakatin, knew nothing whatever of intelligence work which, as Havel explained, was why he had chosen him. Once he took it over, he couldn't believe what he had walked into:

'The bastards didn't know the fucking Cold War was over,' he exclaimed between gusts of laughter.

Few foreigners can swear convincingly in English, but Černý was the exception. He had studied at Newcastle on a grant awarded him during the Prague Spring, so perhaps that's where he learned the art. On his return to a country once again under Russia's heel, he translated children's books by day and wrote anonymous dissident tracts by night.

'We had guys spying on *Germany*!' he went on incredulously. 'In nineteen-fucking-ninety-three! We had guys out in the street with truncheons looking for priests and anti-Party elements they could beat the shit out of! "Listen," I told them. "We don't do that stuff any more. We're a fucking *democracy*!"'

If Černý talked with the exuberance of a man released, he had every right to. He was an anti-communist by nature and by birth. His father, a wartime Czech resistance fighter, had been imprisoned in Buchenwald by the Nazis, then given twenty years for treason by the communists. One of his earliest memories was seeing his father's coffin being dumped on the family doorstep by the prison goons.

Little wonder then that Černý the writer, dramatist, translator and graduate in English Literature should have waged a lifelong battle against political tyranny; or that he was repeatedly hauled in for interrogation by the KGB and Czech intelligence who, having failed to recruit him, persecuted him instead.

And it is interesting that, for all his protestations of being hopelessly ill-equipped to take over his country's spies after its split with Slovakia, he held the job down for five years, retired with distinction, went on to direct a human rights foundation established by his friend Havel, and set up his own Security Studies think-tank that, fifteen years later and three years after his death, flourishes undiminished.

*

In London, shortly before Černý's death, I met the ageing Václav Havel at a private luncheon given by the Czech Ambassador. Tired and visibly ill, he sat alone and largely silent. Those who knew him best, knew to leave him to himself. Timidly, I approached him and mentioned Černý's name. I said I had had a good time with him in Prague. Suddenly he brightened:

'Then you were lucky,' he said, and sat smiling for a while.

21

Among the Ingush

I had heard of Issa Kostoev, but if you're under fifty you probably won't have done. He was the Russian police officer in charge of Crimes of Special Importance who in 1990 artfully coaxed a confession from the serial killer Andrei Chikatilo, a Ukrainian engineer with fifty-three victims to his name. Today, Kostoev is a tireless and outspoken member of the Russian parliament, urging greater respect and citizens' rights for the people of the North Caucasus, and particularly for his own people, the Ingush, whose fate he feels is unknown to the wider world.

He was barely born when Stalin declared all Chechen and Ingush to be criminals for collaborating with the German invader – a thing they had emphatically not done. The entire Ingush nation – his mother included – was forcibly deported to slave-labour camps in Kazakhstan. One of his earliest childhood memories is watching Russian guards on horseback whipping his mother for gleaning corn. The Ingush, he says darkly, hate all invaders equally. Even when Stalin died and they were grudgingly allowed home, they found their houses given over to the Ossetians, a tribe of Christianized usurpers from south of the mountains, and Stalin's former henchmen. But what angers him most is the racial discrimination of the average Russian towards his people.

'I'm a Russian *nigger*,' he insists, yanking furiously at his Asian nose and ears. 'I can be arrested in the Moscow streets any time, just for having *these!*' Then without apology he changes metaphors, claiming that the Ingush are Russia's Palestinians: 'First they kick us out of our towns and villages, then they hate us for surviving.'

He tells me he will get a group of men together and take me to Ingushetia, why not? It's a spontaneous invitation but, as I quickly realize, a genuine one. We will explore the glories of the landscape together, we will meet the people of Ingushetia, and I will judge for myself. And while my head is still reeling, I reply that I am honoured, and nothing would give me greater pleasure, and we shake hands on it then and there. The year is 1993.

*

All the best interrogators have a certain way with them, some personal characteristic they have learned to turn into a weapon of persuasion. Some present themselves as the soul of sweet reason, others strive to scare or unsettle; others to overwhelm you with their frankness and charm. But big, very tough, utterly inconsolable Issa Kostoev, from the moment you meet him, instils in you an urge to please. Nothing you can say or do, it seems, will dispel the air of perpetual sadness that accompanies his kind, elderly smile.

'And Chikatilo?' I ask him. 'What was your moment of breakthrough?'

A half-lowering of the heavy eyelids, a small sigh. 'The reek of his breath,' he replies, after a long pull at his cigarette. 'Chikatilo ate the private parts of his victims. Over time it affected his digestion.'

A two-way radio crackles. We are sitting head to head in the permanent dusk of the upper floor of a rickety old building in Moscow with the curtains drawn. Armed men knock, enter, exchange a word, go out again. Are they cops? Ingush patriots? Are we in an office or a safe house? And yes, he's right: I am among exiles. The stern young woman who is introduced to me only as 'the Prosecutor' could as well be one of Salah Tamari's fighters in Sidon or Beirut. The wheezing photocopier, the ancient typewriter, the half-eaten sandwiches, the overflowing ashtrays and tins of warm Coke are the mandatory furnishings of a Palestinian freedom fighter's tenuous existence. So is the enormous pistol Kostoev keeps strapped to his rump, except for the times when he slides it into his groin for greater comfort.

I was interested in the Ingush partly because, as Kostoev rightly said, nobody in the Western world seemed to have heard of them: my American literary agent even asked me whether I had invented them. But mainly I was interested because on my travels I had become drawn to the fate of subject nations after the end of the Cold War. It was the same curiosity that led me at different times to Kenya, Congo, Hong Kong and Panama. In the early nineties the future of the Muslim republics of the North Caucasus was still on the scales. Would the Cold War 'spheres of interest' endure? With Russians freed from the chains of Bolshevism, might their southern dependencies wish to be free of Russia? And if so, will their age-old wars with the Bear be resumed?

The short answer, as we now know, is yes, they would indeed be resumed, and at frightful cost. But at the time of my conversation with Kostoev, the Asian republics' cry for independence was deafening and nobody seemed to foresee – or, if they did, to care – that the price of suppression might be the radicalization of millions of moderate Muslims.

I had planned to set my new novel in Chechnya, but now I'd met Kostoev I preferred the cause of the Ingush next door, whose little country had been given away in their absence. Back home in Cornwall, I set about preparing for our promised trip. I applied for a visa and, with Kostoev's support, got one. From the sports shop in Penzance I bought a rucksack and, surprisingly, a money-belt, in anticipation of my trip. I tried to get a little fitter so that I wouldn't disgrace myself in the highest mountains in Europe. I contacted British academics who specialized in Russia's Muslim communities, and discovered, as you always seem to when you start to delve, that there was an international community of impassioned scholars who talked and breathed nothing but the North Caucasus. I became its temporary and very junior member. I cultivated expatriate Chechens and Ingush in Europe, and picked their brains.

For reasons that I didn't enquire into, but could well understand, Kostoev preferred to communicate through non-Caucasian intermediaries. He said I should be sure to provide myself with plenty of American cigarettes and a few trinkets. He recommended a cheap wristwatch, gold plated, a Zippo cigarette lighter or two, and a couple of ballpoint pens with metal cases. These were for the likelihood that our train southward was stopped by bandits. They were decent bandits, Kostoev insisted, and they didn't want to kill anyone. It was just that they felt they had a right to exact a charge from anyone passing through their territory.

He had reduced our bodyguard to six. Six would be plenty. I bought the trinkets and the Zippos and added them to my rucksack. Forty-eight hours before I was due to depart for Moscow, and thence for Nazran, our intermediary phoned to say the trip had been called off. The 'appropriate authorities' could not be responsible for my safe passage and wished me not to come until things had settled down. Which authorities I never knew, but when I turned on the evening news a couple of days later I had reason to be grateful to them. The Red Army had launched a massive land and air attack on Chechnya, and neighbouring Ingushetia looked like being dragged into the war.

*

Fifteen years on, when I came to write *A Most Wanted Man*, I chose a Chechen for my innocent young Russian Muslim caught up in the so-called war on terror. And I called him Issa, after Issa Kostoev.

22

Joseph Brodsky's prize

Autumn 1987, a sunny day. My wife and I are having lunch in a Chinese restaurant in Hampstead. Our one guest is Joseph Brodsky: Russian exile, former Soviet political prisoner, poet and to his many admirers the very soul of Russia. We have known Joseph off and on over a few years, but to be truthful we're not quite sure why we've been recruited to entertain him today.

'Whatever you do, don't on any account let him drink or smoke,' his London hostess, a lady of wide cultural connection, had warned. Despite recurrent heart problems, he was liable to do both. I said I would do my best but that, from the little I knew of Joseph, he would do whatever he wanted.

Joseph was not always an easy conversation partner, but over lunch he was unusually bonny, thanks not least to several large Black Label whiskies, consumed over my wife's gentle protests, and several cigarettes, washed down with bird-like sips of chicken noodle soup.

Literary people seldom, in my experience, have much to say to one another beyond grousing about agents, publishers and readers – or certainly not to me – and it's hard for me in retrospect to imagine what we talked about, since the gap between us could scarcely have been wider. I had read his poems, but felt I needed the handbook. I had delighted in his essays – particularly the one on Leningrad, where he was imprisoned – and was moved by his adoration of the late Akhmatova. But if I had to guess, I would say he hadn't read a word I had written, and that he felt no obligation to.

Yet somehow we were having a jolly time until Joseph's hostess, a tall, elegant woman, appeared in the doorway looking severe. My first thought was that, having run an eye over the bottles on our table and the clouds of cigarette smoke hanging over it, she was about to rebuke us for allowing Joseph to break loose. I quickly realized that she was trying to contain her excitement.

'Joseph,' she said breathlessly. 'You have won the *prize*.'

Long silence while Joseph draws on his cigarette and scowls into the smoke.

'What prize?' he growls.

'Joseph, you have won the Nobel Prize for Literature.'

Joseph's hand closes quickly over his mouth as if to suppress something shocking it's about to say. He appeals to me with his eyes as if for help: as well he might, because neither my wife nor I had the smallest notion that he was in the running for the Nobel, let alone that today was the day of the announcement.

I ask his hostess the obvious question:

'How do you know?'

'Because we have Scandinavian journalists on the doorstep *now*, Joseph, and they wish to *congratulate* you, and *interview* you. Joseph!'

Joseph's pained eyes are still appealing to me. Do something, they seem to be saying. Get me out of this. I turn again to his hostess:

'Maybe the Scandinavian journalists are interviewing everybody on the shortlist. Not just the winner. All of them.'

There is a public telephone in the corridor. His hostess knows that Joseph's American publisher, Roger Straus, has flown to London to be on hand for this moment. A woman of decision, she promptly rings his hotel and asks for him. When she rings off, she is smiling.

'You must come home now, Joseph,' she says gently, and touches his arm.

Joseph takes a last loving pull of his Scotch and with painful slowness rises to his feet. He embraces his hostess and receives her congratulations. My wife and I add ours. The four of us stand on the sunny pavement. Joseph and I are face to face. For a moment I feel I am the prisoner's friend before he is taken down to the cells of Leningrad. With Russian impetuosity, he throws his arms round me, then with his hands on my shoulders, shoves me back and lets me see the tears forming in his eyes.

'Now for a year of being glib,' he declares, then obediently allows himself to be taken off to face his interrogators.

23

The wrong horse's mouth

You would not, I imagine, if you were on the lookout for the inside story of Grand Prix racing, choose for your source a junior mechanic with a hyperactive imagination and zero experience of the race track. Yet that is a fair analogy of what it felt like to be appointed, overnight and solely on the strength of my fictions, to the status of guru on all matters of secret intelligence.

When the mantle was first thrust on me, I resisted it on the very real grounds that I was forbidden by the Official Secrets Act to admit that I had so much as scented the wind of intelligence work. The fear that my former Service, already regretting that it had passed my books for publication, might in its disgruntlement decide to make an example of me was never far from my thoughts, though Heaven knows I had little enough in the way of secret knowledge to reveal. But more important to me, I suspect, even if I didn't admit it to myself, was my writer's *amour-propre*. I wanted my stories to be read not as the disguised revelations of a literary defector but as works of imagination that owed only a nod to the reality that had spawned them.

Meanwhile, my claims never to have set foot inside the secret world rang more hollow by the day, thanks not least to my former colleagues who had no such reservations about blowing my cover. And when the truth overtook me, and I feebly protested that I was a writer who had once happened to be a spy rather than a spy who had turned to writing, the broad message I got back was, forget it: once a spy, always a spy, and if I didn't believe my own fictions, other people did, so live with it.

And live with it I did, like it or not. For years on end as it seems to me now – for my golden years, if you like – barely a week went by but a reader wrote asking how he or she could become a spy, to which I would primly answer: write to your MP or to the Foreign Office or, if you are still at school, consult your careers adviser.

But the reality was, in those days you *couldn't* apply, and you weren't meant to. You couldn't just Google MI5 or MI6 or GCHQ, Britain's once ultra-secret codebreaking agency, but you can now. There were no advertisements on the front page of the *Guardian* telling you that if you are able to talk three people in a room into doing what you want them to do, then maybe spying is for you. You had to be *spotted*. If you applied you could be enemy, whereas if you were spotted, you couldn't possibly be. And we all know how well that worked.

And to be spotted you had to be born lucky. You had to have gone to a good school, preferably a private one, and to a university, preferably Oxbridge. Ideally, there should already be spies in your family background, or at least a soldier or two. Failing that, at some point unknown to you, you had to catch the eye of a headmaster, tutor or dean who, having judged you a suitable candidate for recruitment, summoned you to his rooms, closed the door and offered you a glass of sherry and an opportunity to meet interesting friends in London.

And if you said yes, you were interested in these interesting friends, then a letter to you might arrive in an eye-catching double-scaled pale-blue envelope with an embossed official crest, inviting you to present yourself at an address Somewhere in Whitehall, and your life as a spy might or might not have begun. In my day the invitation included lunch in a cavernous Pall Mall club with an intimidating admiral who asked me whether I was an indoor man or an outdoor man. I am still wondering how to reply.

＊

If aspiring spies took up the larger part of my fan mail in those days, victims of persecution by secret forces ran a close second. The desperate appeals had a certain uniformity. My writers were being shadowed, their phones were being tapped, their cars and houses bugged, neighbours suborned. Their letters were arriving a day late, their husbands, wives and lovers were reporting on them, they couldn't park their cars without getting a ticket. The taxman was after them and there were men who didn't look at all like real work-men doing something to the drains outside the house, they'd been loitering there all week and achieved nothing. It would have served no useful purpose to tell my correspondents that just possibly they were right on every count.

But there were other times when my spurious identity as a master spy came home to roost with a vengeance, such as when, in 1982, a bunch of youthful Polish dissidents described as 'members of a Pol-ish insurgent home army' took charge of their country's Embassy in Bern, where I happened to have studied, and settled themselves in for what turned out to be a three-day siege.

It was the middle of the night when my phone rang in London. The caller was an illustrious gentleman of the Swiss political hierarchy with whom I had struck up a chance acquaintance. He needed my advice promptly in strict confidence, he said. As did his colleagues. He sounded unusually sonorous, but perhaps I was a bit slow waking up. He held no brief for communists, he said. In fact he loathed the ground they walked on. He assumed I did. Nevertheless, the Polish govern-ment, communist or not, was legitimate and its Embassy in Bern was entitled to the full protection of its host country.

Was I with him so far? I was. Good. Because a group of young Pol-ish men had just taken over Poland's Embassy in Bern at pistol point, mercifully without thus far firing a single shot. Was I still listening? I was. And these young men were *anti*-communists, and in any other circumstance to be cheered on. But this was no time to indulge one's personal preferences, was it, David?

No. It wasn't.

So the boys had to be disarmed, didn't they? They had to be got out of the Embassy and out of the country as fast and discreetly as possible. And since I knew all about these things, would I please come and get them out?

In a voice that must have sounded near-hysterical, I vowed to my caller that I had no earthly expertise in such matters, knew not a word of Polish, knew nothing of Polish resistance movements, and less than nothing about the arts of sweet-talking hostage-takers, Polish, communist, non-communist or other. Having thus pleaded my unsuitability any way I could, I think I suggested that he and his colleagues find themselves a Polish-speaking priest. If that failed, haul the British Ambassador in Bern out of bed and formally request the assistance of our Special Forces.

Whether he and his colleagues followed my advice is also something I shall never know. My illustrious friend never told me how the story had ended, though press reports indicate that Swiss police stormed the Embassy, seized the four rebels and freed the hostages. When I bumped into him half a year later on the ski slopes and taxed him about the matter, he replied airily that it had all been a harmless joke: which I took to mean that, whatever deal had been struck by the Swiss authorities, it was not to be shared with a mere foreigner.

*

And then there was the President of Italy.

When the Italian Cultural Attaché in London called to inform me that President Cossiga of Italy was a fan, and wished to invite me to lunch at the Quirinal Palace in Rome, I enjoyed a glow of pride such as few writers are privileged to feel. Did I make any move to inform myself of the President's political posture or his standing in the eyes of his people at this juncture? I have no memory of doing so. I was walking on air.

So might there possibly be a book of mine, I enquired shyly of the Cultural Attaché, that the President particularly admired? Or did his approval perhaps cover my entire oeuvre? The Attaché would enquire. A title was duly named: *Tinker Tailor Soldier Spy.*

So would His Excellency the President prefer the English version, or might he, for ease of reading, prefer a copy in Italian? The reply went straight to my heart: the President preferred to read me in my native tongue.

Next day I took a copy of the chosen work to the *dernier cri* of London's bookbinders, Messrs Sangorski & Sutcliffe, to be encased, regardless of cost, in finest calfskin – royal blue, so far as I remember, with the author's name done rather prominently in gold leaf. The effect – since the interiors of British books in those days tended to appear shabby even when brand new – was of some illustrious old manuscript rebound.

I endowed the title page with my inscription: to Francesco Cossiga, President of the Italian Republic. And then my pen name, writ large. And probably I added my homage, or my profound respects, or eternal allegiance. And I'm sure that, before I put whatever I put, I spent a lot of time thinking of an appropriate form of words, and practising them on a bit of spare paper before committing them to history.

And so, with the bound book in hand, I set off for Rome.

I believe the hotel that had been chosen for me was called the Grand, and I'm sure I slept poorly and made nothing of my breakfast and spent a lot of time in front of a mirror worrying about my hair, which in stress has a way of growing sideways. And probably I purchased a vastly overpriced silk tie from one of the hotel's little glass boutiques to which the concierge had the key.

And well before the time appointed I was hovering on the hotel's forecourt expecting at the very most a public relations person with a car and driver. Certainly nothing had prepared me for the resplendent limousine with curtained windows that drew up at the hotel entrance, or the troop of white-clad motorcycle policemen with blue lights winking and sirens wailing that attended it. All for me. I got in, and in less time than I might have wished, got out again, to a bank of flashing cameras. On the great steps, as I ascended them, serious men in medieval tights and spectacles came to attention as I passed.

It is necessary to understand that I have by now taken leave of everything we call reality. The occasion, the place, are a time warp to this day. Now I am standing in an enormous room, alone, clutching my Sangorski-bound book. Who is equal to these dimensions? The question is answered by a man in a grey suit slowly descending a magnificent stone staircase. He is the quintessential President of Italy. His extreme elegance, his caressing words of welcome, softly spoken in Italian-English as he advances on me with his hands outstretched in pleasure, exude confidence, reassurance and power.

'Mr le Carré. All my life. Every word you have written. Every syllable, in my memory' – a sigh of pleasure – 'welcome, *welcome* to the Quirinal.'

I stammer my thanks. A misty army of middle-aged men in grey suits assembles behind us, but out of respect they keep their distance.

'How about, before we go upstairs, you allow I show you certain features of the Palace?' my host enquires in the same liquid voice.

I allow. Side by side, we progress along a superb corridor with tall windows overlooking the eternal city. At a respectful distance, the grey army soundlessly keeps pace with us. My host pauses for a moment of light humour:

'Here to our right side, we see this little room. It is where we were keeping Galileo while he was waiting to change his mind.'

I chuckle. He chuckles. We walk on and stop again, this time before a great window. All Rome is at our feet.

'And here to our left side is the *Vatican*. We did not always *agree* with the Vatican.'

More wise smiles. We round a corner. For a moment we are all alone. In two swift gestures, I wipe the sweat from Sangorski's calfskin and hand it to my host.

I brought you *this*, I say.

He takes the book, smiles graciously, admires it, opens it, reads my inscription. He hands me back the book.

'Very beautiful,' he replies. 'Why don't you give it to the President?'

*

Of the lunch, I remember little. That is to say, I have no recollection of what we ate or drank, but no doubt it was exquisite. We sat at a long table, thirty-odd of us including the misty grey army, in a medieval penthouse of celestial beauty. President Francesco Cossiga, a depressed-looking man in tinted spectacles, sat with bowed shoulders at its centre. Despite the assurances of his Cultural Attaché in London, he appeared to have little English. A lady interpreter was on hand to demonstrate her skills, which became redundant when we settled on French. It was soon evident that she wasn't interpreting for the two of us alone, but for the grey army either side of us.

I don't remember handing over the calf-bound book a second time, though I must have done. Only the general topic of our conversation remains with me, since it was not about literature or art or architecture or politics, but spies, and it came in a series of sudden and unpredictable charges each time Cossiga raised his head and stared at me with unsettling intensity through his tinted spectacles.

Could societies do without spies altogether? he wished to know. What did *I* think? How was a supposed democracy to control its spies? How should *Italy* control them? – as if Italy were a separate case, not a democracy but just *Italy* in italics. What was my opinion, bluntly, in my own words please, of the Italian intelligence services *en général*? Were they worth their salt? Were they a negative force or a positive one, would I say?

To all of which I had, and still have, no answer worth a bean. I knew nothing about the workings of the Italian intelligence services. I noticed as I trotted out such wisdoms as I could muster that every time the President fired a question at me, the grey army around us

stopped eating and raised their heads as if to the command of a con-
ductor's baton, only resuming when I had ground to a halt.

Suddenly the President had gone. Perhaps he'd had enough of me.
Perhaps he had the world to run. He bounded to his feet, vouchsafed
me another piercing glance, shook my hand and left me to my fellow
guests.

Servants ushered us to an adjoining room where coffee and
liqueurs awaited. Still nobody spoke. Seated in soft chairs round a
low table, the grey-suited men exchanged only a muttered word with
one another, as if they feared to be overheard; and with me, no word
at all. Then, one by one, with a handshake and a nod, each took his
leave.

It wasn't till I returned to London that I was informed, by people
who should know, that I had lunched with the assembled chieftains
of Italy's many intelligence services. Cossiga had evidently thought
they could pick up a few hints from the horse's mouth. Mortified,
embarrassed, feeling a fool, I made enquiries about my host, only to
learn what I should have learned before I set out for Messrs Sangorski & Sutcliffe.

President Cossiga, having on his election declared himself the
father of his nation, had become its scourge. He had lashed out so
vigorously against former colleagues of left and right that he had
acquired the nickname 'pickaxe-man'. He was given to maintaining
that Italy was a country of the insane.

A radically conservative Roman Catholic who saw communism as
the anti-Christ, Cossiga went to his reward in 2010. In old age, according to his obituary in the *Guardian*, he got battier still. It is not recorded
whether he ever benefited from my advice, whatever that was.

*

Mrs Thatcher also invited me to lunch. Her office wished to recom-
mend me for a medal, and I had declined. I had not voted for her,
but that fact had nothing to do with my decision. I felt, as I feel today,

171

that I was not cut out for our honours system, that it represents much of what I most dislike about our country and that we were better apart, and finally, if there has to be a finally, that since I had no regard for our British literary commentariat, I consequently had none for its selections, even if they included me. In my letter of reply, I took care to assure the Prime Minister's office that my churlishness did not spring from any personal or political animosity, offered my thanks and compliments to the Prime Minister, and assumed I would hear no more.

I was wrong. In a second letter her office struck a more intimate note. Lest I was regretting a decision taken in heat, the writer wished me to know that the door to an honour was still open. I replied, equally courteously I hope, that as far as I was concerned the door was firmly shut, and would remain so in any similar contingency. Again, my thanks. Again, my compliments to the Prime Minister. And again I assumed the matter was closed, until a third letter arrived, inviting me to lunch.

There were six tables set in the dining room of 10 Downing Street that day, but I only remember ours, which had Mrs Thatcher at its head and the Dutch Prime Minister Ruud Lubbers on her right, and myself in a tight new grey suit on her left. The year must have been 1982. I was just back from the Middle East, Lubbers had just been appointed. Our other three guests remain a pink blob to me. I assumed, for reasons that today escape me, that they were industrialists from the north. Neither do I remember any opening exchanges between the six of us, but perhaps they had happened over cocktails before we sat down. But I do remember Mrs Thatcher turning to the Dutch Prime Minister, and acquainting him with my distinction.

'Now, Mr Lubbers,' she announced in a tone to prepare him for a nice surprise. 'This is Mr *Cornwell*, but *you* will know him better as the writer John le Carré.'

Leaning forward, Mr Lubbers took a close look at me. He had a youthful face, almost a playful one. He smiled, I smiled: really friendly smiles.

'No,' he said.

And sat back in his chair, still smiling.

But Mrs Thatcher, it is well known, did not lightly take no for an answer.

'Oh, *come*, Mr Lubbers. You've heard of *John le Carré*. He wrote *The Spy Who Came in from the Cold*, and . . .' – fumbling slightly – '. . . other wonderful books.'

Lubbers, nothing if not a politician, reconsidered his position. Again he leaned forward and took another, longer look at me, as amiable as the first, but more considered, more statesmanlike.

'No,' he repeated.

And evidently satisfied that he had made the correct finding, again sat back.

Now it was Mrs Thatcher's turn to take a long look at me, and I underwent something of what her all-male* cabinet must have experienced when they too incurred her displeasure.

'*Well*, Mr Cornwell,' she said, as to an errant schoolboy who had been brought to account. 'Since you're *here*' – implying that I had somehow talked my way in – 'have you anything you wish to say to me?'

Belatedly, it occurred to me that I had indeed something to say to her, if badly. Having recently returned from South Lebanon, I felt obliged to plead the cause of stateless Palestinians. Lubbers listened. The gentlemen from the industrial north listened. But Mrs Thatcher listened more attentively than all of them, and with no sign of the impatience of which she was frequently accused. Even when I had stumbled to the end of my aria, she went on listening before delivering herself of her response.

'Don't give me *sob stories*,' she ordered me with sudden vehemence, striking the key words for emphasis. 'Every day people appeal to my *emotions*. You can't *govern* that way. It simply isn't *fair*.'

---

* My researches tell me there was in fact one woman, Baroness Young, in her cabinet, none in her inner cabinet.

Whereupon, appealing to my emotions, she reminded me that it was the Palestinians who had trained the IRA bombers who had murdered her friend Airey Neave, the British war hero and politician, and her close adviser. After that, I don't believe we spoke to each other much. I expect that, very sensibly, she preferred to devote herself to Mr Lubbers and her industrialists.

Occasionally I do ask myself whether Mrs Thatcher nevertheless had an ulterior motive in inviting me. Was she, for instance, sizing me up for one of her quangos – those strange quasi-official public bodies that have authority but no power, or is it the other way round?

But I found it hard to imagine what possible use she could have for me – unless of course she wanted guidance from the horse's mouth on how to sort out her squabbling spies.

24

His brother's keeper

I hesitated before including Nicholas Elliott's account of his relationship with his friend and fellow spy, the British traitor Kim Philby. My first reason: as it stands, his account is a fiction that he has come to believe, rather than the objective truth; and my second, whatever Philby means to my generation, his name may not resonate so loudly in the ears of the present one. But in the end I couldn't resist offering it, shorn of its expository passages, as a window on the British espionage establishment in the post-war years, on its class assumptions and its mind-set.

The scale of Philby's betrayal is barely imaginable to anyone who has not been in the business. In Eastern Europe alone, dozens and perhaps hundreds of British agents were imprisoned, tortured and shot. Those who had not been betrayed by Philby were betrayed by George Blake, another MI6 double agent.

I had always had a bee in my bonnet about Philby, and as I have reported elsewhere it had led me into a public dispute with his friend Graham Greene, which I regretted, and with such luminaries as Hugh Trevor-Roper, which I didn't regret at all. For them, Philby was just another brilliant child of the thirties, a decade that belonged to them and not to us. Forced to choose between capitalism on the one hand – to leftists of the day synonymous with fascism – and the New Dawn of communism on the other, he had opted for communism, whereas Greene had opted for Catholicism and Trevor-Roper for neither. And all right, Philby's decision happened to be hostile to Western interests, but it was his to take, and he was entitled to it. End of argument.

To me, on the other hand, Philby's motive for betraying his

country smacked a great deal more of an addiction to deceit. What may have begun as an ideological commitment became a psychological dependency, then a craving. One side wasn't enough for him. He needed to play the world's game. It therefore came as no surprise to me to read, in Ben Macintyre's excellent portrayal of the Philby–Elliott friendship,* that when Philby was in limbo in Beirut, living out the inglorious end of his career as an MI6 and KGB agent and fearing that his Soviet controllers had given up on him, what he missed most, apart from watching cricket, was the prickle of the double life that had for so long sustained him.

Has my animosity towards Philby mellowed over the years? Not that I'm aware of. There is a type of entitled Briton who, while deploring the sins of imperialism, attaches himself to the next great imperial power in the delusion that he can steer its destiny. Philby, I believe, was such a man. In conversation with his biographer, Phil Knightley, he apparently wondered aloud why I nursed a grudge against him. I can only reply that, like Philby, I knew a thing or two about the conflicting storms aroused by a maverick father, but there are better ways of punishing society.

Enter now Nicholas Elliott, Philby's most loyal friend, confidant and devoted brother-in-arms in war and peace, child of Eton, son of its former headmaster, adventurer, alpinist and dupe – and surely the most entertaining spy I ever met. In retrospect, he also remains the most enigmatic. To describe his appearance is, these days, to invite ridicule. He was a sparkling bon vivant of the old school. I never once saw him in anything but an immaculately cut, dark three-piece suit. He was thin as a wand, and seemed always to hover slightly above the ground at a jaunty angle, a quiet smile on his face and one elbow cocked for the martini glass or cigarette. His waistcoats curved inwards, never outwards. He looked like a P. G. Wodehouse man-about-town, and spoke like one, with the difference that his conversation was startlingly forthright, knowledgeable and recklessly disrespectful of

* *A Spy Among Friends*, published by Bloomsbury, 2014.

authority. I never got the wrong side of him to my knowledge, but not for nothing did Tiny Rowland, one of the City of London's tougher nuts, describe him as 'the Harry Lime of Cheapside'.

Among the many extraordinary things that Elliott had done in his life, however, the most extraordinary and undoubtedly the most painful was to sit face to face in Beirut with his close friend, colleague and mentor Kim Philby, and hear him admit that he had been a Soviet spy for all the years that they had known each other.

*

During my own years in MI6, Elliott and I had been on nodding terms at most. When I was first interviewed for the Service, he was on the selection board. When I became a new entrant, he was a fifth-floor grandee whose espionage coups were held up to trainees as examples of what a resourceful field officer could achieve. Flitting elegantly in and out of Head Office from the Middle East, he would deliver a lecture, attend an operational conference and be gone.

I resigned from the Service in 1964 at the age of thirty-three, having made a negligible contribution. Elliott resigned in 1969, aged fifty-three, having been central to every major operation that the Service had undertaken since the outbreak of the Second World War. Intermittently, we kept in touch. He was frustrated by our former Service's refusal to let him reveal secrets that in his opinion had long ago passed their keep-by date. He believed he had a right, indeed a duty, to give his story to posterity. Perhaps that's where he thought I might come in – as some sort of go-between or cut-out who would help him get his unique exploits out into the open where they belonged.

So it happened that one evening in May 1986 in my house in Hampstead, twenty-three years after he had received Philby's partial confession, he poured out his heart to me in what turned out to be the first in a succession of such meetings. While he talked I scribbled in a notebook. Looking over my notes some three decades later – handwritten, fading notepaper, a rusty staple at one corner – I am comforted that there is hardly a crossing out. At some point in our discussions I tried to enlist his collaboration in a two-handed play starring Kim and Nicholas, but the real Elliott would have none of it.

'May we not ever again think about *the play*,' he wrote to me in 1991. And today, thanks to Ben Macintyre, I'm thoroughly glad we didn't, because what Elliott was telling me was not the story, but the cover story of his life. No amount of the caustic levity that was his stock-in-trade was going to take away the pain of knowing that the man to whom he had unreservedly entrusted his most intimate personal and professional secrets had, from the very first day of their long friendship, betrayed him to the Soviet enemy.

*

Elliott on Philby:

'Terrific charmer, with an impulse to shock. I knew him terribly well, especially the family. I really cared for them. I never knew a fellow like him for getting pissed. I'd interrogate him, he'd drink Scotch the whole time, I'd literally have to load him into a cab to send him home. Give the driver five quid to cart him upstairs. Took him to a dinner party once. Charmed everyone, then suddenly he started talking about his hostess's tits. Said she had the best breasts in the Service. Totally off-colour. I mean you don't, at a dinner party, start talking about your hostess's tits. But that's how he was. Liked to shock. I knew the father too. I had him to dinner in Beirut the night he died. Fascinating chap. Talked endlessly about his relationship with Ibn Saud.* Eleanor, Philby's third wife, adored him. The old boy managed to make a pass at someone's wife, then left. A few hours later he'd died. Last words were "God I'm bored."'

*

* Founder and first monarch of Saudi Arabia.

'My interrogation of Philby lasted a long time. The one in Beirut was the end of a series. We had two sources. One was a pretty good defector. The other was this mother figure. The Office shrink had told me about her. He rang me up, the shrink. He'd been treating Aileen, Philby's second wife, and he said, "She's released me from my Hippocratic Oath. I've got to talk to you." So I went and saw him and he told me Philby was homosexual. Never mind all his philandering, never mind that Aileen, whom I knew pretty well, said Philby liked his sex and was pretty good at it. He was homosexual, all part of a syndrome, and the psychiatrist, on no evidence he knew of, was also convinced he was bad. Working for the Russians. Or something. He couldn't be precise but he was sure of it. He advised me to look for a mother figure. Somewhere there'll be a mother figure, he said. It was this woman Solomon.* Jewish woman. She was working in Marks & Spencer's, a buyer or something. They'd been communists together. She was angry with Philby over the Jewish thing. Philby had been working for Colonel Teague, who was Head of Station in Jerusalem, and Teague was anti-Jewish, and she was angry. So she told us some things about him. The old communist connection. Five [MI5] were running the case by then, and I passed it all on to Five – get the mother figure, Solomon. Wouldn't listen of course, they're too bureaucratic.'

*

'People were so *naughty* about Philby. Sinclair and Menzies [former Chiefs of MI6] – well, they just wouldn't listen to anything against him.'

*

'So this cable came, saying they had the proof, and I cabled back to White [Sir Dick White, former Director General of MI5 now Chief

---

* Flora Solomon, who introduced Philby to Aileen in 1939.

179

of MI6] saying I must go and confront him. It had been an ongoing thing for so long, and I owed it to the family to get it out of him. Feel? Well, I don't think I'm an emotional sort of chap, much, but I was fond of his women and children, and I always had the feeling that Philby himself would like to get the whole thing off his chest and settle down and follow cricket, which was what he loved. He knew cricket averages backwards and forwards. He could recite cricket till the cows came home. So Dick White said okay. Go. So I flew to Beirut and I saw him and I said to him, if you're as intelligent as I think you are, and for the sake of your family, you'll come clean, because the game is up. Anyway we could never have nailed him in court, he'd have denied it. Between you and me the deal was perfectly simple. He had to make a clean breast of it, which I thought he wanted to do anyway, which was where he fooled me, and he had to give us everything, but *everything* on damage. That was paramount. The damage limitation. After all, I mean one of the things the KGB would have been asking him was, who can we approach independently of you, who's in the Service, who might work for us? He might have suggested people. We had to know all that. Then whatever else he'd given them. We were completely firm on that.'

My notes resort to straight dialogue:

Self: 'So what were your sanctions if he didn't cooperate?'

Elliott: 'What's that, old boy?'

'Your sanctions, Nick, what you could threaten him with in the extreme case. Could you have him sandbagged, for instance, and flown to London?'

'Nobody wanted him in London, old boy.'

'Well, what about the ultimate sanction then – forgive me – could you have him killed, liquidated?'

'My dear chap. One of us.'

'So what *could* you do?'

'I told him, the alternative was a *total* cut-off. There wouldn't be an embassy, a consulate, a legation, in the whole of the Middle East that would have the first bloody thing to do with him. The business community wouldn't touch him, his journalistic career would be dead in the water. He'd have been a leper. His whole life would have been over. It never even crossed my mind he'd go to Moscow. He'd done this one thing in the past, he wanted it out of the way, so he'd got to come clean. After that we'd forget it. What about his family and Eleanor?'

I mention the fate of one of Britain's less socially favoured traitors who gave away far less than Philby but spent years in prison for it.

'Ah well, *Vassall** – well, he wasn't top league, was he?'

*

Elliott resumes:

'That was the first session and we agreed to meet again at four o'clock and at four o'clock he turned up with a confession, sheets of it, eight or nine closely typed pages of stuff, on the damage, on every-thing, masses of it. Then he says, you could do me a favour actually. Eleanor knows you're in town. She doesn't know anything about me. But if you don't come round for a drink she'll smell a rat. So I say all right, for Eleanor's sake I'll come round and have a drink with you. But first of all I've got to encode this stuff and cable it to Dick White, which I did. When I got to his place for a drink, he'd passed out. Pissed. Lying on the floor. Eleanor and I had to put him to bed. She took his head, I took his feet. He never said anything when he was pissed. Never spoke a loose word in his life, far as I know. So I told her. I said to her, "You know what this is about, don't you?" She said, "No," so I said, "He's a bloody Russian spy." He'd told me she hadn't rumbled him, and he was right. So I went home to London and left him to Peter Lunn† to carry on the interrogation. Dick White had

---

* John William Vassall, homosexual son of an Anglican parson and clerk to the Naval Attaché at the British Embassy in Moscow, was sentenced to eighteen years for spying for the KGB.
† Peter Lunn, head of MI6 station, Beirut, and the first of my two heads of station in Bonn.

handled the case jolly well, but he hadn't said a word to the Americans. So I had to dash over to Washington and tell them. Poor old Jim Angleton.* He'd made such a fuss of Philby when he was head of the Service's station in Washington, and when Angleton found out – when I told him, that is – he sort of went all the other way. I had dinner with him just a few days ago.'

*

'My theory is, you see, that one day the KGB will publish the rest of Philby's autobiography. The first book sort of cut itself dead at 1947. My guess is, they've got another book in their locker. One of the things Philby *has* told them is to polish up their goons. Make 'em dress properly, smell less. Sophisticated. They're a totally different-looking crowd these days. Smart as hell, smooth, first-class chaps. Philby's work, that was, you bet your boots. No, we never thought of killing him. He fooled me though. I thought he wanted to stay where he was.'

*

'You know, looking back though – don't you agree? – at all the things we got up to – all right we had some belly-laughs – my God we had some belly-laughs – we were terribly amateurish, in a way. I mean those lines through the Caucasus, agents going in and out, it was so *amateurish*. Well, he betrayed Volkov, of course, and they killed him.† So when Philby wrote to me and invited me to go and meet

---

* James Jesus Angleton, delusional alcoholic head of the CIA's counter-intelligence arm, who convinced himself that the red web of the KGB had spread itself to every corner of the Western world. While stationed in Washington, Philby had counselled him, over liquid games of chess, on the art of running double agents.
† In 1945 Konstantin Volkov, a career intelligence officer in the Soviet Consulate in Istanbul, claimed knowledge of three Soviet spies inside the British Foreign Office, one of them in counter-intelligence. Philby took charge of the case and a

him in Berlin or Helsinki, and not tell my wife Elizabeth or Dick White, I wrote back and told him to put some flowers on Volkov's grave for me. I thought that was rather good.

'I mean, who the *hell* did he think I was, not telling them? The first person I'd tell was Elizabeth, and *immediately* after that, I'd tell Dick White. I'd been out to dinner with Gehlen – did you know Gehlen?* – came back late at night, and there was this plain envelope on the doormat with "Nick" written on it. Dropped in by hand. "If you can come, send me a postcard with Nelson's Column on it for Helsinki, Horse Guards for Berlin," some damned thing. Who the hell did he think I was? The Albanian operation?† Well yes, he probably blew that too. I mean we had some fucking good assets in Russia too in the old days. Don't know what happened to them either. Then he wants to meet me because he's lonely. Well of course he's lonely. He shouldn't have gone. He fooled me. I've written about him. The Sherwood Press. The big publishers all wanted me to write about the interrogation, but I wouldn't. It's more for one's climbing friends, a memoir.‡ You can't write about the Office. Interrogation's an art. You understand that. It went on over a long time. Where was I?'

*

Sometimes Elliott drifted off into reminiscences of other cases that he had been involved in. The most significant was that of Oleg Penkovsky, a GRU colonel who provided the West with vital Soviet

heavily bandaged Volkov was hustled on to a Soviet transport plane bound for Moscow. I used a version of this episode in *Tinker Tailor Soldier Spy*.
* Reinhard Gehlen, at that time Director of the BND, West Germany's secret service. See Chapter 8 of this volume.
† A doomed attempt by MI6 and the CIA in 1949 to subvert the Albanian government, resulting in the deaths of at least 300 agents, and uncounted arrests and executions among the populace. Kim Philby was one of the planners.
‡ Elliott, like his father, was a keen alpinist.

defence secrets in the run-up to the Cuba missile crisis. Elliott was infuriated by a book concocted by the CIA as a piece of Cold War propaganda and published under the title *The Penkovsky Papers*.

'Frightful book. Made out the fellow was some kind of saint or hero. He was nothing of the sort, he'd been passed over and he was pissed off. The Americans turned him down but Shergy* knew he was all right. Shergy had the nose. We couldn't have been less similar but we got on marvellously. *Les extrêmes se touchent.* I was in charge of Ops, Shergy was my number two. Marvellous field man, very sensitive, almost never wrong. He'd been right about Philby too, from very early. Shergold looked Penkovsky over and thought yes, so we took him on. Very brave thing, in spying, to put your faith in someone. Any fool can go back to his desk and say, "I don't altogether trust this chap. On the one hand, on the other hand." It takes a lot of guts to take a flyer and say, "I believe in him." That's what Shergy did, and we went along with him. Women. Penkovsky had these whores in Paris, we laid them on, and he complained he couldn't do anything with them: once a night and that was it. We had to send the Office doctor out to Paris to give him a shot in the bum so that he could get it up. You do get some belly-laughs, they were what one lived for sometimes. These marvellous belly-laughs. I mean how could you crack up Penkovsky to be a hero? Mind you, betrayal takes courage. You have to hand it to Philby too. He had courage. Shergy resigned once. He was frightfully temperamental. I came in, found his resignation on my desk. "In view of the fact that Dick White" – he put CSS [Chief of the Secret Service] of course – "has passed information to the Americans without my consent, and has therefore endangered my very sensitive source, I wish to resign as an example to other members of the Service" – something like that. White apologized and Shergy took back his resignation. I had to talk him round

* Harold (Shergy) Shergold, Controller of MI6's Soviet Bloc operations.

though. Wasn't easy. Very temperamental chap. But a marvellous field man. And he got Penkovsky dead right. Artist.'

*

Elliott on Sir Claude Dansey, also known as Colonel Z, Deputy Chief of MI6 during the Second World War:

'Utter shit. Stupid too. But tough and rude. Wrote these awful short minutes to people. Carried on feuds. I mean a real shit. I took over his networks when I became Head of Station in Bern after the war. Well he did have these high-level business sources. *They* were good. He had a knack of getting these businessmen to do things for him. He was good at that.'

On Sir George Young, Vice Chief to Sir Dick White during the Cold War:

'Flawed. Brilliant, coarse, always had to be out on his own. He went to Hambro's [Bank] after the Service. I asked them later: how did you make out with George? Were you up or down? They said they reckoned about even. He got them some of the Shah's money, but he made perfectly awful balls-ups that cost them about as much as he got for them.'

On Professor Hugh Trevor-Roper, historian and wartime member of SIS:

'Brilliant scholar, all that, but wet and useless. Something perverse inside him. Laughed my head off when he took a dive on those Hitler diaries. The whole Service knew they were fake. But Hugh walked straight in. How *could* Hitler have written them? I wouldn't have the chap near me in the war. When I was head man in Cyprus I told my sentry at the door that if a Captain Trevor-Roper showed up, he should shove his bayonet up his arse. He showed up, the sentry told him what I'd said. Hugh was puzzled. Belly-laughs. That's what I liked about the Service. Marvellous belly-laughs.'

On providing a prostitute for a potential SIS asset from the Middle East:

'St Ermin's Hotel. She wouldn't go. Too near the House of Commons. "My husband's an MP." She had to have Fourth of June off so that she could take her boy out from Eton. "Well, perhaps you'd rather we got someone else?" I said. Didn't hesitate. "All I want to know is, how much?"'

On Graham Greene:

'I met him in Sierra Leone in the war. Greene was waiting for me at the harbour. "Have you brought any French letters?" he yelled at me as I came within earshot. He had this fixation about eunuchs. He'd been reading the station codebook and found that the Service actually had a code group for eunuch. Must have been from the days when we were running eunuchs in the harems as agents. He was dying to make a signal with eunuch in it. Then one day he found a way. Head Office wanted him to attend a conference somewhere. Cape Town I think. He had some operation fixed or something. Not an operation, knowing him, he never mounted one. Anyway he signalled back "Like the eunuch I can't come."'

A wartime reminiscence of life in Turkey under diplomatic cover:

'Dinner at the Ambassador's. Middle of the war. Ambassadress lets out a yell because I've cut off the nose. "Nose of what?" "The cheese." "The valet *handed* me the bloody cheese," I tell her. "And you cut the nose off it," she says. Hell did they get it from? Middle of the bloody war. Cheddar. And the chap who'd handed it to me was Cicero,* the fellow who sold all our secrets to the Abwehr. The D-Day landings. The lot. And the Huns didn't believe him. Typical. No faith.'

I am describing to Elliott how, while I was in MI5, Graham Greene's *Our Man in Havana* was published and the Service's legal adviser wanted to prosecute him under the Official Secrets Act for

---

* Cicero was a German secret agent named Elyesa Bazna, who worked as a valet to Sir Hughe Knatchbull-Hugessen, the British Ambassador in Ankara. He is now believed to have been a British agent all along, tasked with planting fake intelligence on the Germans. Perhaps Elliott was doing the same to me.

revealing the relationship between a head of station and his head agent.

'Yes, and he jolly nearly got done for it. Would have served him bloody right.'

*

And most memorable of all, perhaps, Elliott recalling a passage from his early soundings of Philby concerning his Cambridge days:

'"They seem to think you're a bit *tarnished* somehow," I say.

'"By?"

'"Oh, you know, early passions, membership –"

'"Of?"

'"Jolly interesting group, actually, by the sounds of it. Exactly what university is for. Lefties all getting together. The Apostles,* wasn't it?"'

*

In 1987, two years before the Berlin Wall came down, I was visiting Moscow. At a reception given by the Union of Soviet Writers, a part-time journalist with KGB connections named Genrikh Borovik invited me to his house to meet an old friend and admirer of my work. His name, when I enquired, was Kim Philby. I now have it on pretty good authority that Philby knew he was dying and was hoping I would collaborate with him on his second volume of memoirs, the very book that Elliott was convinced he had up his sleeve. In the event, I declined to meet him. Elliott was pleased with me. At least I

---

* The Cambridge Apostles, known also as the Conversazione Society, was founded in 1820 as a secret intellectual discussion group of the University's chosen. They practised according to themselves 'homoeroticism' and 'platonic love'. In the thirties the society was exploited by Soviet talent-spotters to recruit promising young students to the communist cause. But Kim Philby is nowhere listed as an alumnus.

think he was. But perhaps he had secretly hoped, all the same, that I might bring him news of his old pal.

He had fed me a sanitized version of his last encounter with Kim Philby, and of his supposed suspicions about him in the years leading up to it. The truth, for which we must thank Ben Macintyre, is that ever since Philby had come under suspicion, Elliott had fought tooth and nail to protect his closest friend and colleague. Only when the case against Philby could no longer be denied did Elliott exert himself to obtain a confession – and a partial one at best – from his old pal. Whether by then he was under orders to give Philby the space to make good his escape to Moscow, we'll probably never know for sure. Whether he was or not, he fooled me, just as he was fooling himself.

25

Quel Panama!

In 1885, France's gargantuan efforts to build a sea-level canal across the Darien ended in disaster. Small and large investors of every stamp were ruined. In consequence there arose across the country the pained cry of 'Quel Panama!' Whether the expression has endured in the French language is doubtful, but it speaks well for my own association with that beautiful country, which began in 1947 when my father Ronnie dispatched me to Paris to collect five hundred pounds from the Panamanian Ambassador to France, one Count Mario da Bernaschina, who occupied a sweet house in one of those elegant side roads off the Elysées that smell permanently of women's scent.

It was evening when I arrived by appointment on the ambassadorial doorstep wearing my grey school suit, my hair brushed and parted. I was sixteen years old. The Ambassador, my father had advised me, was a first-class fellow and would be happy to settle a longstanding debt of honour. I wanted very much to believe him. Earlier in the day I had undertaken a similar errand to the George V Hotel, and it had not met with success. The hotel concierge, one Anatole, another first-class fellow, was looking after Ronnie's golf clubs. I should slip Anatole ten pounds for himself – a massive sum in those days and virtually all the money that Ronnie had given me for the trip – and in return Anatole would hand me the clubs.

But Anatole, having pocketed the ten pounds and enquired tenderly after Ronnie's health, regretted that, dearly as he would wish to release the clubs, he was under instructions from the management to withhold them until Ronnie paid his bill. A reverse-charge phone call to London had failed to resolve the matter.

God in Heaven, son, why didn't you send for the manager? Do they think your old man wants to diddle them, or what?

Of course not, Father.

The front door to the elegant house was opened by the most desirable woman I had ever seen. I must have been standing one step beneath her, because in my memory she is smiling down on me like my angel redeemer. She was bare-shouldered, black-haired and wore a flimsy dress in layer after layer of chiffon that failed to disguise her shape. When you are sixteen, desirable women come in all ages. From today's vantage point I would put her at a blossoming thirty-something.

'You are Ronnie's *son?*' she asked incredulously.

She stood back to let me brush past her. Laying a hand on each of my shoulders, she scrutinized me playfully from head to toe under the hall light and seemed to find everything to her satisfaction.

'And you have come to see *Mario,*' she said.

If that's all right, I said.

Her hands remained on my shoulders while her eyes of many colours continued to study me.

'And you are still a *boy,*' she remarked, as a kind of memo to herself.

The Count stood in his drawing room with his back to the fireplace, like every ambassador in every movie of the time: corpulent, in a velvet jacket, hands behind him and that perfect head of greying hair they all had – *marcelled* we used to call it – and the curved handshake, man to man, although I'm still a boy.

The Countess – for so I have cast her – doesn't ask me whether I drink alcohol, let alone whether I like daiquiri. My answer to both questions would anyway have been a truthless 'yes'. She hands me a frosted glass with a speared cherry in it, and we all sit down in soft chairs and do a bit of ambassadorial small talk. *Am I enjoying the city? Do I have many friends in Paris? A girlfriend perhaps?*

Mischievous wink. To which I no doubt give compelling and mendacious answers that make no mention of golf clubs or concierges, until a pause in the conversation tells me it's time for me to broach the purpose of my visit which, as experience has already taught me, is best done from the side rather than head on.

'And my father mentioned that you and he had a small matter of *business* to complete, sir,' I suggest, hearing myself from a distance on account of the daiquiri.

I should here explain the nature of that small matter of business which, unlike so many of Ronnie's deals, was simplicity itself. As a diplomat and a top ambassador, son – I am echoing the enthusiasm with which Ronnie had briefed me for my mission – the Count was immune from such tedious irritations as taxation and import duty. The Count could *import* what he wished, he could *export* what he wished. If someone, for instance, chose to send the Count a cask of unmatured, unbranded Scotch whisky at a couple of pence a pint under diplomatic immunity, and the Count were to bottle that whisky and ship it to Panama or wherever else he chose to ship it under diplomatic immunity, that was nobody's business but his.

Equally, if the Count chose to export the said unmatured, unbranded whisky in bottles of a certain design – akin, let us imagine, to Dimple Haig, a popular brand of the day – that too was his good right, as was the choice of label and the description of the bottle's contents. All that need concern me was that the Count should pay up – cash, son, no monkey business. Thus provided, I should treat myself to a nice mixed grill at Ronnie's expense, keep the receipt, catch the first ferry next morning and come straight to his grand offices in the West End of London with the balance.

'A matter of *business*, David?' the Count repeated in the tone of my school housemaster. 'What business can *that* be?'

'The five hundred pounds you owe him, sir.'

I remember his puzzled smile, so forbearing. I remember the richly draped sofas and silky cushions, old mirrors and gold glint, and my Countess with her long legs crossed inside the layers of chiffon. The Count continued to survey me with a mixture of puzzlement and concern. So did my Countess. Then they surveyed each other as if to compare notes about what they'd surveyed.

'Well, that's a pity, David. Because when I heard you were coming to see me I rather hoped you might be bringing *me* a portion of the large sum of money I have invested in your dear father's enterprises.'

I still don't know how I responded to this startling reply, or whether I was as startled as I should have been. I remember briefly losing my sense of time and place, and I suppose this was partly induced by the daiquiri, and partly by the recognition that I had nothing to say and no right to be sitting in their drawing room, and that the best thing I could do was make my excuses and get out. Then I realized that I was alone in the room. After a while, my host and hostess returned. The Count's smile was genial and relaxed. The Countess looked particularly pleased.

'So, David,' said the Count, as if all were forgiven. 'Why don't we go and have dinner and talk about something more pleasant?'

They had a favourite Russian restaurant fifty yards from the house. In my memory it is a tiny place and we are the only three people in it, save for a man in a baggy white shirt who plucked at a balalaika. Over dinner, while the Count talked about something more pleasant, the Countess kicked off a shoe and caressed my leg with her stockinged toe. On the tiny dance floor she sang 'Dark Eyes' to me, holding the length of me against her and nibbling my earlobe while she flirted with the balalaika man and the Count looked indulgently on. On our return to the table the Count decided that we were ready for bed. The Countess, by a squeeze of my hand, seconded the motion.

My memory has spared me the excuses I made, but somehow I made them. Somehow I found myself a bench in a park, and somehow I contrived to remain the boy she had declared me to be. Decades later, finding myself alone in Paris, I tried to seek out the very street, the house, the restaurant. But by then, no reality would have done them justice.

*

Now I am not pretending that it was the magnetic force of the Count and Countess that half a century later drew me to Panama for the space of two novels and one movie; merely that the recollection of that sensuous, unfulfilled night remained lodged in my memory, if only as one of the near-misses of interminable adolescence. Within days of my arrival in Panama City I was enquiring after the name. *Bernaschina?* Nobody had heard of the fellow. A *Count?* From *Panama?* It seemed most improbable. Maybe I had dreamed the whole thing? I hadn't.

I had come to Panama to research a novel. Unusually, it already had a title: *The Night Manager.* I was looking for the sort of crooks, smooth talkers and dirty deals that would brighten the life of an amoral English arms seller named Richard Onslow Roper. Roper would be a high-flyer where my father Ronnie had been a low one who frequently crashed. Ronnie had tried selling arms in Indonesia and gone to jail for it. Roper was too big to fail, until he met his destiny in the shape of a former Special Forces soldier turned hotel night manager named Jonathan Pine.

With Pine as my secret sharer, I had found a hideaway for Pine and his mistress amid the splendours of Luxor; explored the luxury hotels of Cairo and Zurich, and the forests and goldmines of northern Quebec province; thence to Miami to seek the advice of the US Drug Enforcement Administration, who assured me that there was no finer place for Roper to go about a drugs-for-arms deal than Panama's free zone of Colón at the western gateway to the Canal. In Colón, they said, Roper could be assured of all the official inattention his project demanded.

And if Roper wished to stage an ostentatious demonstration of his wares without arousing needless interest? I asked. Panama again, they said. Go for the central mountains. Nobody asks questions up there.

*

In a dripping Panamanian hill forest near the Costa Rican border, an American military adviser – now retired, he insists – gives me the tour of a grisly encampment where CIA instructors once trained the Special Forces of half-a-dozen Central American countries in the days when the United States was supporting every narco-tyrant in the region in its fight against whatever passed for communism. At the tug of a wire, bullet-spattered targets, garishly painted, lurch out of the undergrowth: a Spanish colonial lady with bared breasts, toting a Kalashnikov; a bloodied pirate with tricorn and raised cutlass; a little red-haired girl, her mouth open in a scream that is supposed to say 'Don't shoot me, I'm a child.' And at the forest's edge, wooden cages for the camp's trapped wild animals: mountain tigers, jungle cats, bucks, snakes, monkeys, all starved to death and rotting in their cells. And in a filthy aviary, the remains of parakeets, eagles, cranes, kites and vultures.

To teach the boys to be fierce, my guide explains. To teach them to be heartless.

*

In Panama City, a courtly Panamanian named Luis escorts me to the Palace of the Herons to meet the reigning President Endara. On our way to the Palace he regales me with the scandals of the day.

The traditional herons that I would see strutting the Palace forecourt are not the descendants of many generations of heron, as popularly supposed. They are impostors, says Luis with pretended indignation, smuggled into the Palace at dead of night. When President Jimmy Carter came to visit his Panamanian colleague, his Secret Service men had sprayed the Palace with disinfectant. By nightfall the entire flock of presidential herons lay dead in the forecourt. Substitute birds of no known provenance, netted in Colón, were flown in by passenger plane minutes before Carter's arrival.

Endara, recently widowed, married his mistress within months of his first wife's demise, Luis rattles on. The President is fifty-four, his bride, a student at Panama University, twenty-two. Panama's press are making sport of the event, dubbing Endara 'El Gordo Feliz', or 'Happy Fatty'.

We cross the Palace forecourt, admire the counterfeit herons, ascend the superb Spanish colonial staircase. Early photographs depict Endara as the street brawler he once was, but the Endara who receives me looks so like my Count that if it weren't for the tail suit and red sash across the vast white waistcoat, I might in my dreams have asked him for five hundred pounds. A young woman is crouched on all fours at his feet, her shapely rump pressed into designer jeans as she wrestles with a Lego palace she is building with the President's children.

'Darling,' Endara cries down to her, in English for my benefit. 'See who is here! You have heard of . . .' et cetera.

Still kneeling, the First Lady looks me cursorily up and down and resumes her building.

'But darling, of *course* you have heard of him!' the President implores her. 'You have read his wonderful books! We both have!'

Belatedly, the former diplomat in me stirs.

'Madame President. There is no reason on earth why you should have heard of me. But you have surely heard of Sean Connery, the actor, who was in my recent film?'

Long silence.

'You are *friend* of Mr Connery?'

'Indeed I am,' I reply, though I scarcely know him.

'You are very welcome in Panama,' she says.

*

In the Club Union, where Panama's rich and famous have their presence here on earth, I enquire yet again after the Count Mario da Bernaschina, Ambassador to France, putative husband to the Countess, purveyor of unbranded Scotch. Nobody remembers him, or if they do, they prefer not to. It takes an indefatigable Panamanian friend called Roberto to report, after prolonged enquiry, that the Count had not only existed, but played an insignificant role in the volatile history of his country.

The title of Count 'came from Spain via Switzerland', whatever that meant. He had been a friend of Arnulfo Arias, President of Panama. When Arias was toppled by Torrijos, Bernaschina had fled to the American Canal Zone, claiming to be Arias' ex-Foreign Minister. He was nothing of the kind. Nevertheless, he lived large for several years until an evening when, dining at an American club, I like to think lavishly, he was kidnapped by Torrijos' secret police. Incarcerated in the notorious La Modelo prison, he was charged with conspiracy against the state, treason and sedition. Three months later he was mysteriously released. Though in age he boasted of his twenty-five years as a Panamanian diplomat, he had never so much as belonged to the Panamanian foreign service. Least of all had he been Panama's Ambassador to France. Of the Countess, if such she was, mercifully nothing: my boyhood fantasies could remain intact.

As to that cask of unbranded whisky and the unsolved matter of who, if anyone, was owed five hundred pounds, of one thing only we may be certain: when conman meets conman, both sides will end up crying foul.

*

Countries are characters too. After a walk-on part in *The Night Manager*, Panama is insisting on star billing in a new novel I am planning, although it is five years later. My hero-to-be is that much neglected denizen of the spy world, the intelligence fabricator or, as the trade jargon has it, pedlar. True, Graham Greene celebrated the fabricator's calling in *Our Man in Havana*. But no sudden war resulted from poor Wormold's fabrications. I wanted the farce to turn to tragedy. The United States had already achieved the remarkable feat of invading Panama while it still occupied the country. Then let it invade a second time, on the strength of my pedlar's cooked-up intelligence.

But who would play the part of my pedlar? He must be socially trivial, benign, innocent, lovable, a non-player in the world's game, but a striver for all that. He must be loyal to whatever he loves most: his wife, his children, his profession. He must be a fantasist. Intelligence services are famously susceptible to fantasists. Many of its most famous children – Allen Dulles for one – have been fantasists in their own right. He must be engaged in a service industry where he rubs shoulders with the great, the good, the influential and the credulous. A fashionable hairdresser then, a *Figaro*? An antique dealer? A gallery owner?

Or a tailor?

There are only two or three books of mine of which I can truthfully say, 'This is where it began.' *The Spy Who Came in from the Cold* began in London airport, when a stocky man in his forties flopped on to a bar stool beside me, delved in his raincoat pocket and poured a handful of loose change in half-a-dozen currencies on to the bar. With a fighter's thick hands, he raked through the coins till he had enough of one currency.

'Large Scotch,' he ordered. 'No bloody ice.'

It was all I ever heard him say, or so I now believe, but I fancied I caught a whiff of Irish in his voice. When his glass came, he ducked his lips to it in the practised movement of an habitual drinker and emptied it in two gulps. Then he shuffled off, looking at nobody. For all I'll ever know he was a commercial traveller down on his luck. Whoever he was, he became my spy, Alec Leamas, in *The Spy Who Came in from the Cold*.

*

Then there was Doug.

An American friend visiting London suggests we drop in on his tailor, Doug Hayward, who has his premises in Mount Street in the West End. We are in the mid-nineties. My friend is from Hollywood. Doug Hayward dresses a lot of film stars and actors, he says. Somehow you don't expect tailors to be sitting down, but Doug when we find him is enthroned in a winged armchair, talking on the telephone. One reason he sat a lot, he later told me, was that he was tall and didn't want to tower over his customers.

He is talking to a woman, or I guess she's a woman because there are a lot of dears and darlings and references to her old man. His voice is theatrical and authoritative, with the Cockney traces ironed out of it, but the cadences still there. When Doug was young, he had spent a lot of time practising his elocution so that he could talk posh in front of shop. Then the sixties came along, posh was out, regional came back in, and thanks not least to the actor Michael Caine, a client of Doug's, Cockney was the flavour of the decade. But Doug wasn't about to have learned his posh for nothing. So he stuck to it, while the posh blokes went off round the corner and learned how to talk common.

'Now listen, darling,' Doug is saying into the telephone. 'I'm sorry to hear your old man's playing around, because I like you both. But look at it this way. When you two got together, you were his bit on the side and he had a regular missus. Then he gets rid of his missus and he marries his bit on the side.' Pause for effect, because by now he knows we're listening. 'So there's a vacancy, isn't there, darling?'

'Tailoring is theatre,' Doug tells us over lunch. 'Nobody comes to me because they *need* a suit. They come for the buzz. They come to get their youth back, or have a natter. Do they know what they want? Of course they don't. Anyone can dress a Michael Caine, but can you dress Charles Laughton? Somebody has to be in *charge* of a suit. I had a bloke the other day asking me why I don't make suits like Armani. "Listen," I told him. "Armani makes better Armani suits than I do. If you want an Armani, go down to Bond Street, save your-self six hundred quid and buy one.'"

I named my tailor Pendel, not Hayward, and called the book *The Tailor of Panama*, with tacit acknowledgement to Beatrix Potter's *The Tailor of Gloucester*. I gave him a half-Jewish background because, like the earliest American moviemakers, most of our tailoring families in those days were East End immigrants from middle Europe. And Pendel after the German word for pendulum, because I liked to think of him swinging back and forth between truth and fiction. All I needed now was a decadent, well-born British rascal who could recruit my Pendel and use him to line his own pocket. But for anyone who has taught at Eton, as I had, there were candidates galore.

26

Under deep cover

It's only a few years since we said our goodbyes to him, but I may not tell you when or where. I may not tell you whether we burned or buried him, whether we did it in the town or in the country, or whether his name was Tom, Dick or Harry, or the funeral was Christian or of another sort.

I will call him Harry.

Harry's wife was at the funeral, standing very straight, the same wife he had had for fifty years. She had been spat on in the fish queue for him, jeered at by neighbours for him and had her house burgled by the police who thought they were doing their duty by shaking out the local Communist Party firebrand. There was a child there too, now grown, who had suffered similar humiliations at school and later. But I may not tell you whether this was a boy or a girl child, or whether he or she has found a safe corner in the world Harry believed he was protecting. The wife, now widow, stood as steady as she had always done under pressure, but the grown-up child was crumpled with grief, to the mother's evident contempt. A life of hardship had taught her to value bearing, and she expected it of her offspring.

*

I went to the funeral because long ago I had had the management of Harry, which was a sacred trust as well as a delicate one since all his energies from late childhood onward had been directed at frustrating his country's perceived enemies by becoming one of them. Harry had absorbed the Party's dogma until it was second nature to him. He had bent his mind until he scarcely knew its old shape any more. With our help he had schooled himself to think and react from the hip as one of its faithful. Yet he always managed to come up smiling for his weekly debriefings with his case officer:

All right then, Harry? I would ask.

'Hunky-dory, thanks. How's your good self and the missus?'

Harry had taken on all the Party's dirty jobs, in the evenings and on weekends, that other comrades were only too glad to be relieved of. He had sold or failed to sell the *Daily Worker* at street corners, ditched his unsold copies and turned in the cash we gave him to cover them. He had acted as runner and talent-spotter for visiting Soviet cultural attachés and third secretaries of the KGB, and accepted their dreary assignments to collect tittle-tattle about technical industries in the area where he lived. And if no tittle-tattle came his way, we provided him with that too, having first made sure it was harmless.

Gradually, through diligence and devotion to the cause, Harry rose to become a valued comrade, entrusted with semi-conspiratorial errands that, though he played them for all they were worth, and so did we, seldom amounted to anything of substance in the intelligence market place. But this lack of success didn't matter, we assured Harry, because he was the right man in the right place, the essential listening post. If you didn't hear anything, Harry, we told him, that's fine too because it means we can sleep a little easier at night. And Harry would remark cheerfully that, well, John – or whatever I called myself – somebody has to clean out the drains, don't they? And we'd say, somebody has to, Harry, and thank you for being the one.

From time to time, perhaps to bolster his morale, we'd enter the virtual world of staybehind: if those Reds ever do come, Harry, and you happen to wake up to find yourself the Party's grand poobah for your district – that's when you'll become the link man for the resistance movement that's going to have to drive those bastards back into the sea. In earnest of which fantasy, we would dig his radio transmitter out of its hiding place in his attic, blow the dust off it and watch him send dummy messages to an imaginary underground headquarters, and receive dummy orders in return, all by way of practice for the imminent Soviet occupation of Britain. We felt a little awkward doing this, and so did Harry, but it was part of the job, so we got on with it.

Ever since I left the secret world, I pondered the motives of Harry and his wife, and of other Harrys and their wives. Shrinks would have had a field day with Harry, but Harry would have had one with the shrinks, too. 'So what am I supposed to do, then?' he'd have asked them. 'Let the Party steal the bloody country from underneath my nose?'

Harry took no delight in his duplicity. He bore it as a necessary burden of his calling. We paid him a pittance, and if we'd paid him more, he'd have been embarrassed. Besides, he could never have enjoyed his money. So we gave him a tiny private income and a tiny pension and called it his alimony, and we threw in all the respect and friendship that security allowed. With time, furtively, Harry and his wife, who posed as the good comrade's wife, became mildly religious. The minister of the religion they espoused seems never to have asked why two such avid communists came to him to pray.

When the funeral was over, and the friends and family and Party comrades had dispersed, a pleasant-faced man in a raincoat and black tie walked over to my car and shook my hand. 'I'm from the Office,' he murmured shyly. 'Harry's my third this month. They all seem to be dying off at the same time.'

Harry was one of the poor bloody infantry of honourable men and women who believed that the communists were set on destroying the country they loved, and felt they'd better do something about it. He thought the Reds were a nice enough bunch in their way, idealistic but a bit warped. So he put his life where his convictions were and died an unknown soldier of the Cold War. The practice of infiltrating spies into supposedly subversive organizations is as ancient as the hills. As J. Edgar Hoover reportedly said with unusual wit when told the news that Kim Philby was a Soviet double agent:

'Tell 'em, Jesus Christ only had twelve, and one of them was a double.'

Today, when we read of undercover policemen worming their way into peace and animal-rights organizations, taking lovers and fathering children under false identities, we are repelled because we know at once that the targets never justified the deception or the human cost. Harry, thank God, did not operate that way, and he believed absolutely that his work was morally justified. He saw international communism as his country's enemy, and its British manifestation as the enemy inside the home camp. No British communist I ever met would have subscribed to that view. The British establishment emphatically did, and that was good enough for Harry.

27

Hunting for warlords

The novel had everything, even a title: *The Mission Song*. It was set in London and the Eastern Congo, and had a central character called Salvo, short for Salvador, the son of an erring Irish missionary and a Congolese headman's daughter. Salvo had been brainwashed by zealous Christian missionaries from infancy, and punished as an outcast for his father's supposed sins, so it wasn't hard for me to cry in my beer and identify with him.

I had three Congolese warlords, each a standard-bearer of the tribe or social group that had spawned him. I had separately wined and dined a small platoon of British and South African mercenaries, and devised a plot flexible enough to respond to the needs and whims of its characters as the story developed on the page.

I had a beautiful, young female Congolese nurse, a daughter of Kivu, working in an East London hospital and longing only to return to her own people. I had walked her hospital's corridors, sat in its waiting rooms, and watched the doctors and nurses come and go. I had staked out the changing of the shifts, and from a respectful distance followed groups of weary female nurses as they trekked back to their sleeping quarters and hostels. In London and Ostend I had spent long hours head to head with huddles of Congo's secret exiles, listening to tales of mass rape and persecution.

But there was one small snag. I didn't know anything at first hand about the country I was describing, and knew next to nothing about its indigenous people. The three Congolese warlords that Maxie, my head mercenary, had embroiled in an operation to seize the reins of power in

Kivu, were not real characters at all: just identikit men, cobbled together from hearsay and my uninformed imagination. As to the great province of Kivu itself and its capital city Bukavu, they were fantasy places to me, conjured out of old guidebooks and the internet. The whole construct had been dreamed up at a moment in my life when, for family reasons, I had been unable to travel. Only now was I free to do what in better circumstances I would have done a year ago: go there.

The lure was irresistible. Bukavu, built in the early twentieth century by Belgian colonialists at the southern end of Lake Kivu, the highest and coolest of Africa's great lakes, read like a lost paradise. I had visions of a misted Shangri-La of wide, bougainvillea-laden streets, and villas with lush gardens sloping to the lake's shore. The volcanic soil of the surrounding hillsides is so fertile, the same guidebooks told me, and the climate so benign, that there is scarcely a fruit, flower or vegetable that doesn't thrive there.

The Eastern Congo was also a death trap. I had read about that too. Its riches had for centuries lured every species of human predator, from roaming Rwandan militias to corporate carpetbaggers with shiny offices in London, Houston, Petersburg or Beijing. Since the Rwandan genocide, Bukavu had been in the front line of the refugee crisis. Hutu insurgents, fleeing across the border from Rwanda, had used the town as a base to get their own back on the government that had driven them out. In what became known as the First Congo War, the town had been laid waste.

So what did it all look like now? And what did it *feel* like? Bukavu was the town of my hero Salvo's birth. Somewhere close by in the bush lurked the Roman Catholic seminary that had housed Salvo's father, the big-hearted, fallible Irish priest who had yielded to the charms of a tribal woman. It would be nice to find the seminary too.

*

I had read *In the Footsteps of Mr Kurtz* by Michela Wrong, and greatly admired it. Wrong had lived in the Congolese capital,

Kinshasa, and spent altogether twelve years on the African continent. She had covered Rwanda for Reuters and the BBC in the aftermath of the genocide. I invited her to lunch. Might she help? She might. Might she even accompany me to Bukavu? She might, but on terms. Jason Stearns would have to come too.

At twenty-nine, Jason Stearns, polyglot and African scholar, was a senior analyst with the International Crisis Group. Almost unbelievably, from my point of view, he had actually served three years in the city of Bukavu as political adviser to the United Nations. He spoke immaculate French, Swahili and an unknown number of other African languages. He was one of the West's leading authorities on the Congo.

Amazingly also, it turned out that both Jason and Michela had their own professional purposes in East Congo. They agreed to coincide their visits with mine. They ploughed through an embarrassing early draft of my novel and pinpointed its many transgressions. Nevertheless, it gave them an idea of the people I was keen to meet and the places I needed to see. At the top of my list came the three warlords; after them, the Catholic missionaries, seminaries and schools of Salvo's childhood.

Foreign Office advice was for once clear: don't travel to the Eastern Congo. But Jason had taken soundings of his own and reported that Bukavu was pretty quiet, given that the Democratic Republic of Congo was about to hold its first multi-party election in forty-one years, and there was a certain nervousness in the air. For my two companions this made it the perfect time to go, as it was for myself and my characters, since the novel was set in the run-up to the same elections. The year was 2006, so twelve years since the Rwandan genocide.

Looking back, I'm a bit ashamed that I prevailed on them to take me with them at all. If something had gone wrong, which in Kivu was practically mandatory, they'd have been saddled with a not very agile, white-haired septuagenarian.

*

Long before our Jeep had left the Rwandan capital, Kigali, and reached the Congolese border my imagined world had receded and the real one taken over. The Hôtel des Mille Collines in Kigali, alias the Hotel Rwanda in that movie, had an air of oppressive normality. I looked in vain for a commemorative photograph of the actor Don Cheadle, or his alter ego Paul Rusesabagina, the real-life hotel manager who in 1994 had turned the Mille Collines into a secret refuge for Tutsis in terror of the panga and the gun.

But that story, in the minds of those now in power, was no longer operative. Ten minutes into Rwanda with your eyes open, you knew that the Tutsi-led government ran a very tight ship indeed. From the windows of our car as we wove over the hills towards Bukavu, we glimpsed Rwandan justice at work. In tailored meadows that would not have been out of place in a Swiss valley, villagers crouched in rings like summer schoolchildren. At their centre, in place of teachers, men in prison pink gesticulated or hung their heads. To break the backlog of suspected *génocidaires* awaiting trial, Kigali had reinstated traditional village courts. Anyone might accuse, anyone might defend. But the judges were appointed by the new government.

An hour short of the Congolese border we turned off the road and climbed a hill in order to take a look at a few of the *génocidaires'* victims. A former secondary school looked down on lovingly tended valleys. The curator, himself an improbable survivor, led us from one classroom to another. The dead – hundreds of them, whole families, tricked into assembling for their own protection and every one of them hand-killed – had been laid out in fours and sixes on wooden pallets and coated with what looked like congealed flour and water. A lady with a facemask and bucket was giving them an extra coat. For how long would she go on painting them? How long would they last? Many were children. In a country where farmers do their own slaughtering, the technique had come naturally: first cut the tendons, then take your time. Hands, arms and feet were stored separately in baskets. Torn clothing, brown with blood and mostly children's sizes, hung from the eaves of a cavernous assembly hall.

'When will you bury them?'

'When they have done their work.'

Their work as the proof that it had really happened.

The victims have no one to name them, or mourn them, or bury them, our guide explains. The mourners are dead too. We leave the bodies on show to silence our doubters and deniers.

*

Rwandan troops in green US-style uniforms have appeared along the roadside. The Congolese frontier post is a dilapidated shed the other side of an iron bridge across an outlet of the Ruzizi River. A cluster of female officials frown over our passports and vaccination certificates, shake their heads and confer. The more chaotic a country, the more intractable its bureaucracy.

But we have Jason.

An interior door bangs open, joyous cries are exchanged. Jason disappears. To peals of congratulatory laughter, our documents are returned to us. We bid farewell to the perfect tarmac of Rwanda and for five minutes lurch over giant pot-holes of red Kivu mud to our hotel. Jason, like my Salvo, is a master of African dialects. When passions flare, he first joins in the excitement, then gently talks the protagonists down. It's not a tactical thing, it comes instinctively to him. I can imagine my Salvo – child of conflict, natural appeaser – doing exactly the same.

*

In every trouble spot I have cautiously visited, there has always been one watering hole where, as if by secret rite, hacks, spies, aid workers and carpetbaggers converge. In Saigon, it was the Continental; in Phnom Penh, the Phnom; in Vientiane, the Constellation; in Beirut, the Commodore. And here in Bukavu it's the Orchid, a gated, low-built, lakeside colonial villa surrounded by discreet cabins. The owner is a worldly-wise Belgian *colon* who would have bled to death in one of Kivu's wars had not his late brother smuggled him to safety. In a corner of the dining room sits a German lady of age who talks wistfully to strangers of the days when Bukavu was all white, and she could drive her Alfa at sixty down the boulevard. Next morning we retrace her route, but not at her speed.

The boulevard is wide and straight but, like every street in Bukavu, pitted by red rainwater gushing off the surrounding mountains. The houses are fallen gems of art nouveau, with rounded corners, long windows and porches like old cinema organs. The town is built on five peninsulas, 'a green hand dipped in the lake', as the more lyrical guidebooks have it. The largest and once the most fashionable peninsula is La Botte, where Mobutu, mad King-Emperor of Zaire, kept one of his many residences. According to the soldiers who bar our entry, the villa is being refurbished for the new Congolese President, Joseph Kabila, Kivu-born son of a Marxist-Maoist revolutionary. In 1997 Kabila's father had ousted Mobutu from power, only to be murdered by his own bodyguard four years later.

A steamy haze hangs over the lake. The border with Rwanda splits it longways. The toe of La Botte tips eastward. The fish are very small. The lake's monster is called *mamba mutu* and is half-woman, half-crocodile. What she likes best is eating human brains. Listening to my guide I scribble notes of all this, knowing I shall never make use of them. Cameras don't work for me. When I write a note my memory stores the thought. When I take a photograph, the camera steals my job.

We enter a Roman Catholic seminary. Salvo's father was one of the Brothers here. Its windowless brick walls are unlike anything around them in the street. Behind them lies a world of gardens, satellite dishes, guest rooms, conference rooms, computers, libraries and mute servants. In the canteen, an old white priest in jeans shuffles to the coffee urn, vouchsafes us a long, unearthly stare and goes his way. If Salvo's father were still alive, I am thinking, this is how he might look today.

A Congolese priest in brown habit is lamenting how his fellow African Brothers are at risk from penitents who confess their ethnic hatreds too eloquently. Inflamed by passionate rhetoric they are supposed to assuage, he says, they are capable of becoming the worst extremists of them all. Thus it was in Rwanda that otherwise good priests were known to summon all Tutsis in their parish to the church, which was then torched or bulldozed with the priests' blessing.

While he talks, I write in my notebook: not as he might suppose, his golden words, but rather how he speaks them: the slow, guttural elegance of his educated African-French, and the sadness with which he recounts the sins of his Brothers.

*

Thomas is so far removed from my version of him that again I abandon all preconceptions. He is tall and suave and wears a well-cut blue suit. He receives us with consummate diplomatic ease. His house, guarded by sentries with semi-automatic rifles, is spacious and representational. A massive television screen plays silent football while we talk. No warlord of my uninformed imaginings was ever like this.

Thomas is a Banyamulenge. His people have been fighting wars in the Congo ceaselessly for the last twenty years. They are pasturalists who came originally from Rwanda and over the last couple of hundred years settled the high plateaux of the Mulenge mountains of South Kivu. Famed for their battle skills and reclusiveness, hated for their supposed affinity with Rwanda, they are the first to be picked on in times of discontent.

I ask him whether the upcoming multi-party election makes things better for them. His reply is not encouraging. The losers will say the vote was rigged, and they'll be right. The winner will take all, and the Banyamulenge will be blamed for all of it as usual. Not for nothing are they called the Jews of West Africa: if anything is amiss, it must be the Banyamulenge's fault. He was similarly unimpressed by Kinshasa's efforts to forge Congo's militias into a single national army:

'A lot of our boys joined, then defected to the mountains. In the army they kill us and insult us, despite the fact that we have fought and won many battles for them.'

There is one chink of hope, Thomas concedes. The Mai Mai, who see it as their job to keep Congo free of all 'foreigners' – and specifically the Banyamulenge – are learning the high cost of becoming a soldier of Kinshasa. He does not elaborate.

'Maybe as the Mai Mai learn to mistrust Kinshasa, they will draw closer to us.'

We are about to find out. Jason has arranged for us to meet a colonel of the Mai Mai, the largest and most notorious of Congo's many armed militias, and the second of my warlords.

*

Like Thomas, the Colonel is immaculately turned out, not in a well-cut blue suit, but in the dress uniform of Congo's maligned national army. His Kinshasa-issue khaki drills are ironed and pressed, his badges of rank glisten in the midday sun. He wears gold rings on all the fingers of his right hand. Two cellphones lie on the table before him. We are sitting in an open-air café. From a sandbagged emplacement across the road, blue-helmeted Pakistani troops of the United Nations watch us over their gun barrels. Fighting has been my life, the Colonel says. In his day he commanded fighters as young as eight. Now they're all adults.

'There are ethnic groups in my country that do not deserve to be here. We fight them because we fear they will claim our sacred Congolese land. No government in Kinshasa can be trusted to do this, therefore we do it ourselves. When Mobutu's power failed, we stood in the breach with our pangas, bows and arrows. The Mai Mai is a force created by our ancestors. Our *dawa* is our shield.'

By *dawa* he is referring to the Mai Mai's magic powers that enable them to divert flying bullets or turn them into water: *Mai*.

'When you are face to face with an AK47 that is firing straight at you and nothing happens, you know our *dawa* is authentic.'

In that case, I ask, as delicately as I may, how does the Mai Mai explain its dead and wounded?

'If one of our warriors is struck down, it is because he is a thief or rapist or has disobeyed our rituals or was harbouring bad thoughts about a comrade when he went into battle. Our dead are our sinners. We let our witch doctors bury them without ceremony.'

And the Banyamulenge? How does the Colonel regard them in the present political climate?

'If they start another war, we shall kill them.'

Venting his hatred of Kinshasa, however, he comes closer than he knows to sharing the views of his sworn enemy Thomas of the night before:

'The *salauds* in Kinshasa have marginalized the Mai Mai. They forget that we fought for them and saved their fat arses. They don't pay us and don't listen to us. For as long as we're soldiers, they don't let us vote. Better we go back to the bush. How much does a computer cost?'

*

It was time to drive out to Bukavu airport for the action scene at the end of my novel. During the week we had a couple of riots in the town and sporadic shooting. The curfew was still running. The road to the airfield belonged to the Mai Mai, but Jason said it was safe to travel, so I assumed he had secured our passage with the Colonel. We were about to set off when we learned that, curfew or not, the centre of town had been blocked by demonstrators and burning tyres. It transpired that a man had mortgaged his house for four hundred dollars in order to buy his wife a medical operation, but when Kinshasa's unpaid soldiers got to hear about it they raided his house,

212

killed him and stole the money. Angry neighbours had seized the
soldiers and locked them up, but the soldiers' comrades sent rein-
forcements to get them back. A fifteen-year-old girl had been shot
dead and the crowd was rioting.

After a giddying drive at high speed through uneven back streets,
we reached the Goma road and drove northwards along Lake Kivu's
western shore. The airfield had recently seen serious fighting. A
Rwandan militia had taken it over, and stayed several months before
being thrown out. Now the airfield was under the joint UN protection of Indian and Uruguayan troops. The Uruguayans gave us a
lavish lunch and urged us to come back for a real party soon.

'What would you do,' I enquired of our Uruguayan host, 'if the
Rwandans came back?'

'*Vamos*,' he replied without hesitation: get the hell out.

In reality, I wanted to find out what he and his comrades would do
if a bunch of heavily armed white mercenaries landed unannounced,
which was what they do in my novel. I am shy of putting my hypoth-
eses so directly, but I had no doubt that, if he had known the true
purpose behind my question, his answer would have been the same.

We toured the airfield, and headed back to town. The red clay
road was struck by a torrential tropical downpour. We descended a
hill to be met with a rapidly filling lake that hours earlier had been a
car park. A man in a black suit was standing on the roof of his drowning car, waving his arms for help, to the entertainment of a
fast-growing crowd. The arrival of our Jeep with its two white men
and one white woman aboard added to the fun. In no time, a group
of kids had set to work rocking us from side to side. In their enthusiasm they could have rocked us into the lake if Jason hadn't hopped
out and, speaking their language, pacified them with their own
laughter.

For Michela, the moment was so run-of-the-mill that she has no
memory of it. But I have.

*

The discotheque is my last and most affecting memory of Bukavu. In my novel, it is owned by the French-educated heir to an East Congolese trading fortune, who later becomes Salvo's saviour. He too is a warlord of a sort, but his real power base is Bukavu's young intellectuals and businessmen: and here they are.

There is a curfew and the town is deadly quiet. Rain is falling. I recall no winking signs or bulky men checking us at the entrance to the nightclub: just a row of miniature Essoldo cinemas disappearing into the dark, and a rope banister descending a dimly lit stone staircase. We grope our way down. Music and strobe lights engulf us. Yells of 'Jason!' as he vanishes under a sea of welcoming black arms.

The Congolese, I have been told, know better than anybody how to have fun, and here at last they are having it. Away from the dance floor a game of pool is running, so I join the lookers-on. Round the table, tense silence attends every shot. The last ball goes down. To hoots of joy, the victor is swept off his feet and carted in triumph round the room. At the bar, beautiful girls chatter and laugh. At our table, I listen to somebody's views on Voltaire – or was it Proust? Michela is politely discouraging a drunk. Jason has joined the men on the dance floor. I will leave him with the last word:

'For all Congo's troubles, you meet fewer depressed guys on the streets of Bukavu than you do in New York.'

*

I hope I got that line into the novel, but it's a long time since I read it. The East Congo was my last excursion into the killing fields. Does the novel do justice to the experience? Of course it doesn't. But the education I received was unputdownable.

28

Richard Burton needs me

Whenever I allow myself to remember my first encounter with Martin Ritt, the veteran American director of *The Spy Who Came in from the Cold*, I blush to think of the idiotic clothes I was wearing.

It was 1963. My novel had not yet been published. Ritt had bought the film rights to it on the strength of a rogue typescript slipped to him by my literary agent or publisher, or maybe some bright soul in a duplicating office who had a pal in the studio, which was Paramount. Ritt would later boast that he stole the rights. I would later agree with him. At the time I saw him as a man of unlimited generosity who had taken the trouble to fly all the way from Los Angeles with some like-minded friends in order to give me lunch at that altar to Edwardian luxury, the Connaught Hotel, and talk flatteringly about my book.

And I had flown all the way from Bonn, capital of West Germany, at the expense of Her Majesty the Queen. I was a serving diplomat of thirty-two and had never met movie people before. In childhood, like all boys of my time, I had fallen in love with Deanna Durbin, and rolled in the aisles over the Three Stooges. In wartime cinemas, I had shot down German aeroplanes piloted by Eric Portman, and triumphed over the Gestapo with Leslie Howard. (My father was so persuaded that Portman was a Nazi that he said he should be interned.) But, what with early marriage, small children and very little money, not a lot of films since. I had a charming London-based literary agent whose life's ambition, had he allowed himself to pursue it, was to play the drums in a jazz band. His knowledge of the film world must have been greater than mine, but not, I suspect, by much. Nevertheless, it was he who had arranged the film deal, and I who, after a convivial lunch with him, had signed it.

As I have reported elsewhere, part of my job as a Second Secretary at the British Embassy in Bonn was to escort invited German dignitaries on their rounds of the British government and its parliamentary opposition, which was what had brought me to London. This explains why, when I stole away from my official duties to have lunch with Martin Ritt at the Connaught, I was wearing a tight black jacket, black waistcoat, silver tie and striped grey-and-black trousers, an outfit that the Germans call *Stresemann* after a Prussian statesman who had the brief misfortune to preside over the Weimar Republic. It also explains why Ritt enquired of me, with raucous cordiality as we shook hands, what the hell had possessed me to dress like a maître d'.

And what was Ritt himself wearing, that he felt free to ask me this challenging question? In the Connaught's dining room, a strict dress code ruled. But in the Grill they had learned by 1963, somewhat grudgingly, to stretch a point. Hunched in a corner of the grill room and flanked by four hoary cohorts from the film industry, Martin Ritt, seventeen years and several centuries my senior, wore a revolutionist's black shirt buttoned to the neck and a pair of baggy pants held up by elastic and nipped at the ankles. And of all extraordinary things, to my eye, an artisan's flat cap with the peak turned up where it should have been turned down. But *worn indoors*, you understand, which in my diplomatic England of those days was about as acceptable as eating peas off a knife. And all this on the bearish frame of an old footballer run to fat, with a broad, bronzed, mid-European face etched with the pain of ages, and thick, swept-back greying hair, and shadowed, watchful eyes framed by black-rimmed spectacles.

'Didn't I tell you he was going to be young?' he demanded proudly of his cohorts while I struggled to explain why the hell I was dressed like a maître d'.

You did, Marty, you did, they agreed, because film directors, as I now know, are always right.

*

And Marty Ritt was more right than most of them. He was an accomplished film director of great heart and daunting life experience. He had served in the US forces in the Second World War. He had been, if not a member of the Communist Party, one of its more devoted fellow-travellers. His unabashed admiration for Karl Marx had got him blacklisted by the television industry in which he had acted and directed with distinction. He had directed any amount of theatre, much of it leftist, including a show for Russian War Relief in Madison Square Garden. He had directed ten feature films back to back, notably *Hud* with Paul Newman a year previously. And he made no secret of the fact, from the moment we sat down, that he saw in my novel some kind of crossing-point from his earlier convictions to his present state of impotent disgust at McCarthyism, the cowardice of too many of his peers and comrades in the witness box, the failure of communism and the sickening sterility of the Cold War.

And Ritt, as he was quick to tell you, was Jewish to the core. If his family hadn't suffered directly in the Holocaust – though I believe it had – he personally had suffered, and continued to suffer, for his entire race. Ardently and articulately, his Jewish identity was a constant theme with him. And this became all the more relevant once we started talking about the movie he intended to make of my novel. In *The Spy Who Came in from the Cold,* two idealistic communists, one an innocent woman librarian from London, the other a member of East German Intelligence, are callously sacrificed for the greater good of the Western (capitalist) cause. Both are Jews.

For Marty Ritt, this movie was going to be personal.

And I? What qualifications from the great university of life had I to offer in return? My *Stresemann*? A British public school education, albeit truncated? A novel I had dreamed up from scraps of vicarious experience? Or the unnerving fact, which thank God I could not reveal to him, that I had spent a large chunk of my recent life toiling in the sheltered vineyards of British Intelligence, fighting the very cause to which he, by his own frank admission, had enthusiastically subscribed?

But that's something else I've picked up along the way. Never mind that I too was beginning to question the easy loyalties of my youth. Movie-making is the enforced bonding of irreconcilable opposites. And this was never more evident than when Richard Burton stepped into the leading role of Alec Leamas.

*

I forget at what point I learned that Burton had got the part. Over our lunch in the Connaught Grill, Marty Ritt had asked me who I thought should play Leamas and I had suggested Trevor Howard; or Peter Finch, but only with the proviso that Finch was willing to play English rather than Australian, because I felt strongly that this was a very British story about very British secret manners. Ritt, a good listener, said he took my point, liked both actors but feared neither was big enough to carry the budget. A few weeks later, when I again flew to London, this time on Paramount's tab to take part in a tour of locations, he told me that he had offered the role to Burt Lancaster.

To play an *Englishman*, Marty?

Canadian. Burt's a great actor. Burt will play it Canadian, David.

To which there was no useful reply. Lancaster was indeed a great actor, but my Leamas was not a great Canadian. But by then the Big Unexplained Silence had kicked in.

In the making of every film of my work – or in the non-making – there has been the First Flush, followed by the Big Unexplained Silence. This can last anything from a few months to several years, or for ever. Is the project dead in the water, or is it steaming forward and nobody's told me? Safe from the gaze of the unwashed, huge sums of money are being bandied about, scripts commissioned, written and rejected, agents joust and lie. In sealed rooms, beardless boys in ties strive to outshine each other with gems of youthful creativity. But outside the walls of Camp Hollywood hard intelligence is impossible to come by: for the good reason that, in the immortal words of William Goldman, nobody knows anything.

Richard Burton *emerged*, that's all I can say from here. No thousand violins announced his arrival, just an awe-struck: 'David, I have news for you. Richard Burton has signed to play Leamas.' And that wasn't Marty Ritt speaking to me on the phone, but my American publisher Jack Geoghegan in a ferment of religious ecstasy. 'And what's more, David, you're about to meet him!' Geoghegan was a veteran of gritty bookselling. He had started out as a shoe-leather sales rep and risen to be Head of Sales at Doubleday. Close to retirement, he had acquired his own small publishing house, Coward McCann. The improbable success of my novel and the addition of Richard Burton were a dream come true for him.

We must be looking at late 1964 by now because I had left government service and set up, first in Greece and later in Vienna, as a full-time writer. I was shaping to visit the United States for the first time, and Burton as it happened was playing Hamlet on Broadway with Gielgud co-directing and speaking the part of the Ghost. The production was described as a dress rehearsal, to be screened in movie theatres. Geoghegan would take me to see it, and afterwards he would introduce me to Burton in his dressing room. If we were about to have an audience with the Pope, he could not have been more excited.

And Burton's performance was epic. And we had the best seats. And in his dressing room he was very charming and said my book was the best thing since I don't know what. And I said his Hamlet was better than Olivier's – better even than Gielgud's, I went on recklessly, though for all I know he was in the room – better than anyone else's I could think of. But what I was secretly wondering amid this torrent of mutual compliments was: how on earth will this beautiful, thunderous, baritone Welsh voice and this overpowering Triple Alpha Male talent fit inside the character of a washed-up, middle-aged British spy not noted for his charisma, his classic articulation or the looks of a pockmarked Greek god?

And though I didn't know it at the time, the same question must have been nagging at Ritt, because one of the first of their many battles in the war that was to follow was about how to get Burton's voice back into its box, something Burton wasn't keen to do.

*

By now we are in 1965 and I have heard by chance – I still had no film agent so I must have had a spy somewhere – that in the latest film script of my novel, Alec Leamas, the part that Burton was slated to play, instead of punching a grocer and going to jail for it, was to be confined in a psychiatric hospital and escape by way of a first-floor bedroom window. The Leamas of my novel wouldn't have gone near a psychiatric hospital to save his life, so what was he doing in one? The answer seemed to be that in Hollywood's eyes psychiatry was sexier than jail.

A few weeks later, news trickled through the lines that the script's writer, who like Ritt had been blacklisted in his time, had been taken ill and the mantle had passed to Paul Dehn. I was sad for the writer, but relieved. Dehn was a fellow Brit. He had written his own film called *Orders to Kill*, which I admired. Also, he was family. During the war, he had trained Allied agents in silent killing and taken part in covert missions to France and Norway.

In London, Dehn and I met. He had no patience with psychiatric hospitals and no compunction about punching grocers. He was happy to put Leamas back in jail for as long as it took. And it was Dehn's script that a couple of months later arrived on my doorstep with a nice note from Ritt asking for my comments.

I had moved to Vienna by then, and in the best tradition of writers who have been showered with unexpected success, I was wrestling with a novel I didn't like, money I'd never dreamed of and marital mayhem entirely of my own making. I read the script, liked it, told Ritt I liked it, and went back to my novel and my mayhem. A few nights later my phone rang. It was Ritt, calling from Ardmore Studios in Ireland, where shooting was supposed to have started. His voice had the strangled throb of a man who has been taken hostage and this is his last message.

Richard needs you, David. Richard needs you so bad he won't speak his lines till you've rewritten them.

But what's wrong with Richard's lines, Marty, they seemed fine to me?

That's not the point, David. Richard needs you and he's holding up the production till he gets you. We'll pay your fare first class and give you your own suite. What more can you ask?

The answer – if it was really true that Burton was holding up the production for me – was that I could ask the moon and get it. But to my knowledge I never asked anything. It's half a century ago, and Paramount's records may tell a different tale, but I doubt it. Perhaps I was so eager to have my movie made that I didn't care or didn't dare. Perhaps I wanted to escape the mess I had created around myself in Vienna.

Or perhaps I was still so green I just didn't know that this was the kind of once-in-a-lifetime opportunity a film agent would sell his mother to exploit: a green-lit film, an entire Paramount Pictures unit in place, sixty electricians alone hanging around the lot with nothing to do but eat free hamburgers, and one of the hottest film stars of the day refusing to perform until that most despised creature in the entire film menagerie – *the writer of origin, for Christ's sake!* – is parachuted in to hold his hand.

All I know for sure is, I put down the phone and flew next morning to Dublin because Richard Needed Me.

*

Did Richard really?

Or did Marty need me more?

In theory I was in Dublin to rewrite Burton's lines, which meant reworking scenes to make them play his way. But Burton's way wasn't always Ritt's, with the result that I became, for this brief period, their go-between. I remember sitting down with Ritt and fixing a scene, then sitting down with Burton and fixing it again, then scurrying back to Ritt. But I don't remember ever sitting down with both of them together. And that process only lasted a few days, by which time Ritt had declared himself satisfied with the revisions and Burton had ceased to offer fight: or none to me. But when I told Ritt I was flying back to Vienna, he became reproachful as only he could.

Somebody has to look after Richard, David. Richard's drinking too much. Richard needs a friend.

Richard needs a *friend*? Hadn't he just married Elizabeth Taylor? Wasn't *she* a friend? Wasn't she here with him, holding up the shoot every time she arrived on set in a white Rolls-Royce, surrounded by *other* friends, such as Yul Brynner and Franco Zeffirelli; such as visiting agents and lawyers; such as the reputedly seventeen-strong Burton household that occupied the whole of one floor of Dublin's grandest hotel comprising, as I understood it, their various children by different marriages, tutors for said children, hairdressers, secretaries and, in the words of one disrespectful member of the unit, the fellow who clipped their parrot's claws? All these, and Richard still needed *me*?

Of course he did. He was being Alec Leamas.

And as Alec Leamas he was a prowling solitary going to seed, his career had hit the buffers and the only people he could talk to were strangers like me. Though I scarcely realized it at the time, I was undergoing my initiation in the process of an actor plundering the darker regions of his life for the elements of the part he's about to play. And the first element you must plunder, if you are Alec Leamas going to seed, is solitude. Which in a word meant that for as long as Burton was being Leamas, the entire Burton court was his avowed enemy. If Leamas walked alone, so must Burton. If Leamas kept a half-bottle of Johnnie Walker whisky in his raincoat pocket, so did Burton. And took healthy swigs of it whenever the solitude became too much for him, even if – as quickly became apparent – the one thing Leamas had got that Burton absolutely hadn't was a head for booze.

How this affected his domestic life, I have no idea, beyond the occasional bit of boys' talk over our nips of Scotch: he was in the dog-house, Elizabeth was not best pleased. But I didn't place much faith in these confidences. Burton, like many actors, couldn't rest till he'd made an instant pal of whoever you might be, as I knew from watching him work his charm on anyone from the gaffer to the tea-girl, to the visible irritation of our director.

On the other hand, Taylor may have had her own reasons not to be best pleased. Burton had urged Ritt to cast her in the female lead, but Ritt had given the part to Claire Bloom, with whom, according to the rumour mill, Burton had once had a dalliance. And though Bloom confined herself determinedly to her caravan off screen, the scorned Elizabeth can scarcely have enjoyed the spectacle of the two of them flirting on set.

*

Imagine now a floodlit square in Dublin, and the Berlin Wall in all its hideous likeness – built in grey breeze-block and barbed wire – cutting straight across it. The pubs are closing and all Dublin has turned out to watch the spectacle, and who wouldn't? For once it's not raining, so a team of Dublin fire engines is on standby. Oswald Morris, our director of photography, likes his night streets wet. Along the wall, set designers and technicians are having a last fidget. There is a point where iron bolts form a crude, barely visible ladder. Oswald Morris and Ritt are busy studying it.

Any minute now, Leamas will climb this ladder, push aside the barbed wire and, sprawled across the top of the wall, stare down in horror at the dead body of the poor woman he has been tricked into betraying, lying on the other side. In the novel this woman is called Liz but in the film, for obvious reasons, she is rechristened Nan.

Any minute now, an assistant director or other functionary will descend the steps outside the window of the drab semi-basement room where Burton and I have been cloistered these last couple of hours. From it, Alec Leamas in a shabby raincoat will then emerge, take up his position at the wall and on Ritt's command begin his fateful ascent.

Except he won't. The half-bottle of Johnnie Walker whisky is long gone. And though I have managed to drink the lion's share of it, Leamas may still be in climbing shape, but Burton definitely isn't.

Meanwhile, to the delighted cheers of the crowd, the white Rolls-Royce has appeared, driven by the chauffeur, who is French, and Burton, waking belatedly to the clamour outside, gives out a throaty roar of 'Oh Christ! Elizabeth, you *fool*!' and charges up the steps into the square. Deploying at full volume the baritone voice that Ritt is determined to suppress, he rages at the chauffeur – in imperfect French, though the chauffeur speaks good English – for delivering Elizabeth into the hands of the Dublin mob: not a great threat, one might think, given that the entire Dublin police force has turned out to watch the fun.

But Burton's operatic rage is not to be withstood. With Elizabeth glowering her displeasure through the lowered window, the chauffeur throws the Rolls into reverse and hightails it back to base, leaving Marty Ritt standing beside the wall in his artisan's cap, looking like the loneliest, angriest man on the planet.

*

Both at the time and in any odd hour since, when I have been watching actors and directors working together on other films, I have wondered just what was the cause of the ever more open hostility between Burton and Ritt, and I have come to the conclusion that it was preordained. Yes, there was the irritation that Ritt had rejected Taylor for the part of Nan and given it to Bloom. But to me, the cause goes much further back: to the days when Ritt was a black-listed radical, wounded and enraged. Social awareness wasn't just an attitude, it was in his milk.

In one of the few conversations of substance that I had with Burton during our short spree together, he almost boasted of how much he despised the showman in himself; how he wished he had 'done a Paul Scofield', by which he meant eschew the big-screen heroics and the big-screen money and accept only acting parts of real artistic substance. And Ritt would have agreed with him wholeheartedly.

But that didn't let Burton off the hook. To the eye of the puritan-ical, committed, connubial leftist and activist, Burton came close to everything Ritt instinctively condemned. Look up his quotes and you find one that says it all: 'I don't have a lot of respect for talent. Talent is genetic. It's what you do with it that counts.' It was bad enough to put profit before art, or sex before family, or flaunt your wealth and your woman, or ostentatiously soak yourself in liquor, or strut the world like a god while the masses cry out for justice. But to waste your talent was a sin against gods and men. And the greater the talent – and Burton's talents were legion and extraordinary – the greater in Ritt's view the sin.

In 1952, the year Ritt was blacklisted, Burton, the twenty-six-year-old Welsh prodigy with the golden tongue, was launching himself on his Hollywood career. It is no coincidence that several members of the cast of *The Spy Who Came in from the Cold* – Claire Bloom and Sam Wanamaker for two – had also been blacklisted. Mention any-one's name from that period and Ritt's immediate question was: 'Where was *he* when we needed him?' He meant: did he or she speak up for us, betray us, or keep the coward's silence? And it would not surprise me if, always in the back of Ritt's mind, or the front of it, the same persistent question hung over his relationship with Burton.

*

We are in a windswept beach house in Scheveningen, on the Dutch coast. It's the last day of shooting *The Spy Who Came in from the Cold*. It's a tight indoor set. Leamas is negotiating his own destruction by agreeing to cross into East Germany and betray precious secrets to his country's enemies. I am hovering somewhere behind Oswald Morris and Martin Ritt, doing my best not to get in the way. The tension between Burton and Ritt is palpable. Ritt's commands are terse and monosyllabic. Burton barely responds. As always in close scenes like these, film actors speak so quietly and casually that they seem to the uninitiated to be rehearsing rather than acting. So it comes as a surprise to me when Ritt says 'wrap' and the scene is over.

But it isn't over. An expectant silence settles, as if everyone but me knows what's about to happen. Then Ritt, who after all is a substantial actor in his own right and knows a thing or two about timing, delivers the speech I believe he has been saving up for this moment:

'Richard, I've had the last good lay in an old whore, and it had to be in front of the mirror.'

True? Fair?

Not true, not by a long way, and not at all fair. Richard Burton was a literate, serious artist, a self-educated polymath with appetites and flaws that in one way or another we all share. If he was the prisoner of his own weaknesses, the dash of rectifying Welsh puritanism in him was not a hundred miles from Ritt's. He was irreverent, mischievous, generous-hearted but necessarily manipulative. For the very celebrated, being manipulative goes with the territory. I never knew him in his quieter hours, but wish I had. He was a superb Alec Leamas, and in a different year his performance might have earned him the Oscar that eluded him all his life. The film was grim and black-and-white. That wasn't what we were wearing in 1965.

If either the director or his actor had been less, then perhaps the film also would have been less. I suppose at the time, I felt more protective of the podgy, stalwart and embittered Ritt than of the flamboyant and unpredictable Burton. A director carries the whole burden of the film on his back, and that has to include the idiosyncrasies of his star. Sometimes I had the feeling that Burton was going out of his way to belittle Ritt, but in the end I guess they were pretty evenly matched. And Ritt surely had the last word. He was a brilliant and impassioned director whose righteous anger could never be stilled.

29

Alec Guinness

Alec Guinness died with his customary discretion. He had written to me a week before his death expressing concern about his wife Merula's illness. Typically he had scarcely mentioned his own.

You could never tell Alec how great he was, of course. If you were fool enough to try, you got the hairy eyeball. But in 1994, to celebrate his eightieth, a successful clandestine operation mounted by the publisher Christopher Sinclair-Stevenson produced a handsome bound volume called 'Alec', which was given to him for his birthday. It contained memoirs, poems, simple expressions of affection and thanks, mostly from old friends. I wasn't there to see the presentation, but I'm sure Alec was suitably grumpy about receiving it. But perhaps he was also a little pleased, if only because he cherished friendship as deeply as he loathed praise, and here at least was a bunch of his friends under one cover.

By comparison with most of the contributors to the presentation volume, I was a latecomer to Alec's life, but we had worked closely together on and off for five years or so, and we had remained agreeably in touch ever since. I was always proud of our relationship, but my proudest moment came when he selected the piece I had written for his eightieth birthday as a preface to his last volume of reminiscences.

Alec was adamant that he wished no memorial service, no posthumous gathering of friends, no emotional outpourings. But I have the excuse of knowing that this little portrait was one that this immensely private man was content to offer the world.

*

What follows is taken in part from my preface to his autobiographical memoir, with a few afterthoughts:

He is not a comfortable companion. Why should he be? The watching child inside this eighty-year-old man has still found no safe harbours or easy answers. The deprivals and humiliations of three-quarters of a century ago are unresolved. It is as though he were still striving to appease the adult world about him; to winkle love from it, to beg its smile, to deflect or harness its monstrosity.

But he loathes its flattery, and mistrusts its praise. He is as wary as children learn to be. He gives his trust slowly, and with the greatest care. And he is ready any time to take it back. If you are incurably fond of him, as I am, you do best to keep that fact to yourself.

Form is desperately important to him. As someone all too familiar with chaos, he treasures good manners and good order. He inclines gratefully to the good-looking, but also loves clowns, apes and quirkish figures in the street, gazing on them as if they were his natural allies.

Day and night he studies and stores away the mannerisms of the adult enemy, moulds his own face, voice and body into countless versions of us, while he simultaneously explores the possibilities of his own nature – do you like me better so? – or so? – or so? – ad infinitum. When he is composing character, he steals shamelessly from those around him.

Watching him putting on an identity is like watching a man set out on a mission into enemy territory. Is the disguise right for *him*? (*Him* being himself in his new persona.) Are his spectacles right? – No, let's try those. His shoes, are they too good, too new, will they give him away? And this walk, this thing he does with his knee, this glance, this posture – not too much, you think? And if he looks like a native, will he speak like one – does he master the vernacular?

And when the show is over, or the day's shoot, and he is once more Alec – the fluid face shiny from the makeup, the small cigar trembling slightly in the thick hand – you can't help feeling what a dull world he has come back to after all the adventures he has had out there.

He may be a solitary, but the former naval officer also loves to be part of a team. He wishes nothing better than to be well led, able to respect the meaning of his orders and the quality of his comrades. Acting with them, he knows their lines as well as he knows his own. Beyond all self-consideration, it is the collective illusion that he treasures most, called otherwise The Show: that precious other world where life has meaning, form and resolution, and events proceed according to written rules.

Working on scripts with him is what Americans call *a learning experience*. One scene may go through a dozen versions before he is persuaded by it. Another, for no reason, is nodded through without debate. It's only later, when you see what he has decided to do with it, that you discover why.

The disciplines he imposes on himself are rigorous, and he expects no less of others. I was present once when an actor who has since become teetotal turned up drunk for filming – not least because he was terrified of acting opposite Guinness. The offence, in Alec's eyes, was absolute: the poor man might as well have gone to sleep on sentry duty. But ten minutes later Alec's anger had given way to an almost desperate kindliness. The next day's shoot went like a dream.

Ask Alec to dinner, he will be on your doorstep brushed and polished while the clock is still chiming the appointed time, never mind the blizzard that has brought London to a standstill. If you are his guest – a more likely eventuality, since he is a compulsively generous host – then a postcard, in neat and beautiful handwriting sinking gracefully to the south-east, will confirm the arrangement you made on the telephone the day before.

And you will do well to repay him the courtesy of his punctuality. Your gestures matter very much to him. They are a mandatory part of life's script, they are what distinguishes us from the indignity and disorder of his wretched early years.

But God forbid that I should paint him as a stern man.

Alec's bubbling laughter and good fellowship, when they come, are all the more miraculous for the uncertain weather that preceded them. The sudden beam of pleasure, the marvellously paced anecdotes, the flashes of physical and vocal mimicry, the mischievous dolphin smile that spreads and flits away, are all before me as I write. Watch him in the company of fellow actors of every age and provenance, and you see him settle to them like a man who has found a favourite fireside. The new never shocks him. He loves to discover young talent and give it a helping hand along the hard road he has trodden.

And he reads.

Some actors, offered work, first count their lines to calculate the importance of the part. Alec is as far removed from them as it is possible to be. No film director, producer or screenwriter of my acquaintance has a better eye for structure and dialogue, or for that *extra something* that he is perennially on the scent of: the McGuffin, the bit of magic that lifts a piece out of the common ruck.

Alec's career is studded with brilliant and unlikely roles. The talent that chose them was as inspired as the talent that performed them. I have heard too – is it one of Alec's well-kept secrets? – that his wife Merula has much influence on his selections. I would not be in the least surprised. She is a wise and quiet woman, and a most gentle artist, and she sees a long way.

What joins us, then, those of us who have been lucky enough to share a mile or two of Alec's long life? I suspect, a constant bewilderment about who to be for him. You want to show him your love, but you want also to give him the space he clearly needs. His talent is so near the surface that your immediate instinct is to protect it from the buffetings of daily life. But then he can manage quite nicely by himself, thank you.

So we become like the rest of his great audience: frustrated givers, never able to express our gratitude, reconciled to being the beneficiaries of the genius he so resolutely refuses to acknowledge.

*

It is lunchtime on the top floor of the BBC, one summer's day in 1979. The cast, crew, producers, director and writer of *Tinker Tailor Soldier Spy* are gathered in their best suits, sipping at their warm white wine, one glass each, before proceeding to the dining room where a celebratory feast of cold chicken awaits them.

But there is a small delay. The gong has sounded, the BBC's barons are on parade. The writer, producers and director have long been present and correct. The barons are sticklers for time. The cast too has arrived early and Alec, as ever, earlier still. But where, oh where, is Bernard Hepton, our leading supporting actor, our Toby Esterhase?

As our glasses of wine get warmer, all eyes gravitate towards the double doors. Is Bernard ill? Has he forgotten? Is he sulking? It is rumoured there was friction on set between Alec and Bernard.

The doors part. With studious unconcern, Bernard makes his entrance, dressed not in the dreary greys and navy blues of the rest of us, but in a three-piece suit of shrill green check, set off by orange patent shoes.

As he advances smiling into the room, the melting voice of George Smiley rings out in welcome:

'Oh, Bernard. You came as a frog.'

30

Lost masterpieces

One day, I trust, it will be recognized that the best films of my work were the ones that were never made.

In 1965, the year in which the movie of *The Spy Who Came in from the Cold* was released, I was persuaded by my British publisher to attend the Frankfurt Book Fair, which I dreaded, to publicize a novel of which I had low expectations, and generally make myself agreeable and interesting to the media. Sick of the sound of my own voice – and of being passed around foreign journalists like a bag of goods – I retreated to my suite in the Frankfurter Hof to sulk.

And that was what I was doing one late afternoon when my house phone rang and a woman's voice, speaking a husky, accented English, advised me that Fritz Lang was in the lobby and wished to see me, and would I please come down?

The summons did not impress me. Langs in Germany are two-a-penny, Fritzes also. Was this the same odious literary gossip writer I had fended off earlier in the day? I suspected it was, and using a woman as his lure. I asked her the nature of Mr Lang's business.

'Fritz Lang, the *film director*,' she corrected me reprovingly, 'he wishes to discuss a proposition with you.'

If she had told me Goethe was waiting in the lobby, my reaction would not have been much different. When I was studying German in Bern in the late forties, we students had passed whole nights debating the genius of Fritz Lang, the great film director of the Weimar years.

We knew his life too, to a point: an Austrian-born Jew brought up as a Catholic, three times wounded fighting for Austria in the First World War, and thereafter in quick order actor, writer and expressionist director in the glory days of Ufa, the fabled Berlin film production company of the twenties. As students, we had earnestly discussed such expressionist classics as *Metropolis*, had sat through five hours of *Die Nibelungen* and four hours of *Dr Mabuse the Gambler*. Probably because it suited me to think of crooks as heroes, I had a particular affinity for *M*, in which Peter Lorre plays a child murderer who is hunted down by the criminal underworld.

But *after* 1933? Lang? Thirty years on? I had read that he had gone on to make movies in Hollywood, but I didn't remember seeing any. For me he was Weimar Man, and that was it. To be truthful, I didn't know he was still alive. And I still thought that the phone call might be a hoax.

'So you're telling me that *Dr Mabuse* is downstairs?' I ask the beguiling female voice, with what I hope is haughty scepticism.

'It is Mr Fritz Lang the film director and he wishes a positive discussion with you,' she repeats, not giving an inch.

If it's the real Lang, he'll be wearing the eye-patch, I tell myself as I pull on a clean shirt and select a tie.

*

He was wearing the eye-patch. He was also wearing spectacles, which confused me: why two lenses for one eye? He was a heavy, daunting man with a face made in muscular curves. A fighter's jutting jaw, a not-very-nice smile. A tall grey hat, with a brim that left his good eye in shadow from the overhead light. Seated like an old pirate, bolt upright on his hotel chair. Head tilted back, listening to something he's not sure he likes. Powerful hands clenched over the handle of a walking stick wedged between his knees. This was the man, as legend had it, who, when he was directing *M*, threw Peter Lorre down a flight of stairs in a fit of creative passion.

The husky-voiced woman I had spoken to sat beside him and I shall never know whether she was his mistress, his new young wife or his business manager. She was closer to my age than his, and clearly determined that our conversation should be a success. She ordered English tea and asked me whether I was enjoying the book fair. I lied and said very much. Lang went on smiling grimly into the distance. When we stopped talking our banalities, he left us to our silence for a while, until:

'I want to make a movie of your little book A *Murder of Quality*,' he announced in a declamatory German-American, laying a heavy hand on my forearm and keeping it there. 'You come to California. We make a script together, we make a movie. You wanna do that?'

'Little book' about summed it up, I reflected as I came to my senses. I had written it in a few weeks soon after I arrived at the British Embassy in Bonn. The story tells of a public school master on the point of retirement who murders his own pupil in order to cover up a previous crime. George Smiley, summoned to the rescue, unmasks him. And now I came to think about it, I could imagine that, for all its shortcomings, it might indeed attract the director of *M*. The only problem was George Smiley. Under the terms of a film deal I should not have signed, he was under contract to a major film studio. Lang was undeterred.

'Listen, I *know* those people. They're my *friends*. Maybe we let them finance the movie. That's a good deal for a studio. They own your character, so they get to make a movie about him. That's good business for them. You like California?'

I like California very much.

'You come to California. We work together, we make a script, we make a movie. Black-and-white, like your *Spy Who Came in*. You got a problem with black-and-white?'

No problem at all.

'You got a movie agent?'

I name my movie agent.

'Listen, I made that guy's career for him. I talk to your agent, we make a deal, after Christmas we settle down in California, write a script. After Christmas good for you?' – still smiling ahead of him, still with his hand anchored on my forearm.

After Christmas suits me fine.

By now I've noticed how the woman at his side lightly guides his free hand whenever he reaches forward for his cup. He takes a sip of tea. With her guidance he sets the cup down. He returns the hand to the crook of the walking stick. He reaches for his cup, and she guides his hand back to it.

I never again heard from Fritz Lang. My film agent said I never would. He made no mention of Lang's incipient blindness, but the death sentence he uttered was absolute all the same: Fritz Lang wasn't bankable any more.

*

In 1968, my novel A *Small Town in Germany* briefly inspired Sydney Pollack. Our collaboration, complicated by Sydney's discovery of the Swiss slopes, had not fulfilled its promise and the company that had bought the original rights had gone out of business, leaving them lost in a legal maze. If I had learned anything at all about the film business, it was never again to allow myself to be swept along by Sydney's glorious but short-lived bursts of enthusiasm.

So it was only natural that when twenty years on he called me in the middle of the night and told me at the top of his melodious voice that my new novel *The Night Manager* would be the inspirational film of his career, I dropped everything and caught the first available flight to New York. This time round, Sydney and I agreed, we were going to be older and wiser. No Swiss villages for us, no tempting snow falls, no Martin Epps, no north face of the Eiger. This time round, Robert Towne himself, in those days the biggest star in the screenwriters' universe, and surely its most expensive, would write the script for us. Paramount agreed to buy the rights.

In a safe house in Santa Monica where we were sure not to be disturbed, Sydney, Bob Towne and myself took it in turns to pace the floor and shine to one another, until an almighty explosion put an abrupt end to our deliberations. Towne, convinced that terrorists had struck, hurled himself to the floor. Sydney, intrepid man of action, called the Los Angeles Police Department on a hotline which I like to think was only available to A-list directors. I, with my usual presence of mind, seem to have done nothing except gawp.

The Police Department's response is soothing: just a minor earth tremor, Sydney, nothing to be scared of at all, and listen, what kind of movie are you boys dreaming up down there? We shone on, but not so brightly, and broke up early. Towne would do a first pass, we agreed. Sydney would then work on it with him. I would be a passive resource.

'If you ever want to try out ideas, Bob, feel free to call me,' I said magnanimously, and gave him my phone number in Cornwall.

*

Towne and I never spoke again. As my plane lifted out of Los Angeles airport, a full-scale earthquake alert was being announced over the speaking system. Sydney had said he would join me in Cornwall just as soon as we had Towne's first pass. In those days I owned a guest cottage just up the lane from our house. We made it all ready for him. He currently was editing a John Grisham thriller he had just shot, starring Tom Cruise, he said. Our project would be next. Bob really has his head down. He's crazy about your work, David. He loves the challenge. Bob is fired up and ready to go. Towne has a couple of scripts to finish off first. Then the drip-feed of bulletins, with the space between them getting a little longer every time. Towne is having trouble with the final act, and Jesus, Cornwell, why do you have to write such complicated books?

And finally – in the middle of the Cornish night, as usual – the call I have been patiently waiting for: meet me in Venice on Friday. The Cruise movie looks like breaking all records, he adds. Test showings have been rapturous. The studio's over the moon. Great, I say, fantastic, how's Bob doing? See you Friday. I'll have my people fix you a suite at the hotel. I drop everything and fly to Venice. Sydney likes his food, but he's a rapid eater, particularly when he's distracted. Bob's coming on just fine, he says vaguely, as if reporting on a distant friend's health. Got a bit hung up over the middle act. He'll get back to it soon. Middle, Sydney? I thought it was the final act he was having problems with. They're connected, Sydney says. All this while he receives a string of breathless message bearers: great reviews, Sydney – see this, five stars and two thumbs-up! – we're making entertainment history for Chrissakes! Sydney has an idea. How's about I fly with him to Deauville tomorrow? They're showing the movie there too. We can talk on the plane. No interruptions.

Next morning we fly to Deauville in Sydney's Lear. We're four: Sydney and his co-pilot, both in earphones, sitting at the controls, a spare pilot, and me in the back. Both Sydney's friend John Calley, then head of Sony Columbia, and Stanley Kubrick, another air-safety buff, have warned me never to fly with Sydney. Think of the actu- arial risk of a dude jet pilot with like zero miles in the saddle, David. Don't go there. After an improbably short journey we touch down in Deauville and Sydney is at once engulfed by a swarm of studio executives, actors' agents and publicity people. He disappears into one limousine; I am shepherded to another. At our grand hotel, another enormous suite awaits me with flowers, champagne from the management, and a note of welcome addressed to Monsieur David Carr. I call the concierge and get a list of ferry times. After several shots, I succeed in being put through to Sydney's suite. Sydney, this is all great, but you're very tied up just now and I don't think our project is foremost on your mind. Why don't I slide off home and we talk again when Bob turns in his script?

All concern now, Sydney wants to know how I propose to get from Deauville to England. A fucking *ferry*, Cornwell? Am I *crazy*? Take the fucking Lear, for Chrissakes! Sydney, honestly, the ferry's fine, thanks. There are lots of them. I love boats. I take the fucking Lear.

This time we're three: Sydney's two pilots in the front, me alone in the back. Newquay airport, which is huge but partly Royal Air Force, won't have us. We settle for Exeter. Suddenly I am standing alone on an empty runway at Exeter airport with a suitcase in my hand, and the Lear is halfway back to Deauville. I peer round for an immigration or customs shed, can't find one. A lone workman in an orange high-vis waistcoat is doing something with a pickaxe to the side of the runway. Excuse, me, I've just arrived by private plane, can you tell me where I find customs and immigration? Arrived from where then? he demands officiously, resting on his pickaxe. France? That's the fucking Common Market! He shakes his head at my obtuseness and resumes his labours. I climb a flimsy fence to the car park where my wife waits to drive me home.

It wasn't till Towne showed up at the Edinburgh Film Festival a year later and, according to my spies, spoke sagely about the insoluble problems of adapting my work for the big screen that I knew the game was up. Jesus, Cornwell, Bob just couldn't crack that last act.

*

When Francis Ford Coppola called up and invited me to stay at his winery in the Napa Valley and work with him on a film adaptation of my novel *Our Game*, I knew that this time round it was going to be the real thing. I flew to San Francisco. Coppola sent a car. Predictably, he was a dream to work with: rapid, incisive, creative, supportive. In five days, working like this, we'll have a first draft cold, he assured me. And we did. We were brilliant together. I had a cabin to myself on the estate, got up with the dawn and wrote brilliantly till midday. Elegiac family lunch at the long table, cooked by Coppola. A walk beside the lake, a swim maybe, then back to being brilliant together for the rest of the afternoon.

After five days, we were home and dry. Harrison is really going to love this, Coppola said. He means Harrison Ford. In Hollywood, surnames are for outsiders only. There was a prickly moment when

Coppola passed our script to his in-house editor and it came back scored with wavy lines and pencilled marginal comments such as 'CRAP! DON'T SAY IT, *SHOW* IT!', but Coppola laughed off such light-hearted comments. His editor was always like that, he said. Not for nothing did they call him the killer cutter. The script would go to Harrison on Monday. And I was free to return to England and await developments.

I return to England and I wait. Weeks pass. I call Coppola but get his assistant. Francis is very tied up right now, David, can I help at all? No, David, Harrison has not as yet responded. And to this day, so far as I shall ever know, Harrison still hasn't. Nobody does silence better than Hollywood.

*

My first intimation of Stanley Kubrick's interest in adapting my novel *A Perfect Spy* for the big screen came when he called me up, wanting to know why I had turned down his offer for the movie rights. *I had turned down Stanley Kubrick?* I was amazed and horrified. We knew each other, for Heaven's sake! Not well, but enough. Why hadn't he called me to tell me he was interested? And most extraordinary of all: what did my film agent think he was up to, not telling me he had an offer from Kubrick, then signing up the book with BBC television? Stanley, I said, I'm going to check this out at once and I'm going to get right back to you. D'you happen to know *when* you made this offer? As soon as I'd read the book, of course, David: why would I hang around?

My agent was as mystified as I was. There'd only been one film offer for *A Perfect Spy* apart from the BBC; but it was so trifling he hadn't thought to bother me with it. A Dr Feldman, I think his name was, of Geneva wished to acquire an option on the movie rights to my novel as a teaching tool for a course on book-into-film. It was a competition thing. The student who came up with the best screenplay would have the pleasure of seeing a minute or two of his work realized on the big screen. For the two-year option on the movie rights of A *Perfect Spy*, Dr Feldman and his colleagues were prepared to offer a five-thousand-dollar honorarium.

I was on the brink of calling Kubrick to assure him that his own offer had never reached me, but something held me back, so I called instead a big wheel in the studio Kubrick sometimes worked with: my friend John Calley. Calley gave a happy chuckle. Well, that sure as hell sounds like our Stanley all right. Always afraid his name is going to bump up the asking price.

I called Kubrick and told him with a straight face that if I'd known Dr Feldman was acting for him, I would have thought twice before optioning the rights to the BBC. Nothing daunted, Kubrick replied that he would be happy to direct the BBC series. I called Jonathan Powell, the producer at the BBC. Powell had masterminded the television versions of *Tinker Tailor Soldier Spy* and *Smiley's People*. He was in the throes of putting together A *Perfect Spy*. How about having Stanley Kubrick to direct it for you? I asked him.

Silence while Powell, not a man given to emotional outbreaks, took a moment to collect himself.

'And have the budget overrun by a few million pounds, you mean?' he enquired. 'And the series delivered a couple of years late? I think we'll stay the way we are, thank you.'

*

Kubrick's next suggestion, following hot upon the last, was that I should write him a Second World War spy movie set in France and based on the rivalry between MI6 and SOE. I said I'd think about it, thought about it, didn't like it and declined. Okay, so how about adapting an erotic *novelle* by the Austrian writer Arthur Schnitzler?* He said he owned the rights, and I didn't ask whether Dr Feldman

* Later filmed by Kubrick as *Eyes Wide Shut*, with Tom Cruise and Nicole Kidman.

of Geneva had bought them for educational purposes. I said I knew Schnitzler's work, and was interested in the idea of adapting it. I had barely put down the phone before a red Mercedes pulled up outside my house and out sprang Kubrick's Italian driver, armed with a cyclostyled English translation of Schnitzler's *Rhapsody* that I didn't need, and an armful of literary commentaries.

A couple of days later the same Mercedes conveyed me to Kubrick's vast country house near St Albans. I had been there a couple of times, but nothing had prepared me for the sight of two huge metal cages in the hallway, one occupied by cats, the other by dogs. Trap doors and metal walkways led from one cage to the other. Any cat or dog who felt moved to socialize with the opposite species could do so. Some socialized, some preferred not to, Kubrick said. It would take time. Cats and dogs had a lot of history to deal with.

Pursued by dogs but no cats, Kubrick and I stroll the grounds while at his request I pontificate on how Schnitzler's *novelle* might be adapted to the big screen. Its eroticism, I suggest, is greatly intensified by inhibition and class snobbery. Vienna of the twenties may have been a hive of sexual licence, but it was also a hive of social and religious bigotry, chronic anti-Semitism and prejudice. Anyone moving in Viennese society – for example, our young hero, the sex-obsessed medical doctor – flouted its conventions at his peril. Our hero's erotic journey, beginning with his incapacity to make love to his beautiful young wife and culminating in his frustrated attempt to take part in an orgy at the house of an Austrian nobleman, was fraught with social as well as physical danger.

Somehow, I told Kubrick, warming to my theme as we patrolled the grounds with the pack of dogs at our heels, our film must recreate this repressive atmosphere, and contrast it with our hero's search for sexual identity.

'How do we do that?' Kubrick asked, just when I was beginning to think the dogs had stolen his attention.

Well, Stanley, I've thought about this, and I believe our best bet is: go for a medieval walled city or country town that is visually confining.

No reaction.

Like Avignon, for instance – or Wells in Somerset. High walls – battlements – narrow streets – dark doorways.

No reaction.

An ecclesiastical city, Stanley, maybe Catholic like Schnitzler's Vienna, why not? With a bishop's palace, a monastery and a theological college. Handsome young men in religious gear sweeping past young nuns with their eyes not quite averted. Church bells resounding. We can practically *smell* the incense, Stanley.

Is he listening to me? Is he mesmerized, or bored stiff?

And the grand ladies of the town, Stanley – pious as hell on the surface, and so skilled at dissembling that when you're invited to dinner at the bishop's palace you don't know whether you were screwing the lady on your right at last night's orgy, or she was at home saying prayers with her children.

My aria complete, and I not a little pleased with myself, we walk for a stretch in silence. Even the dogs, it seems to me, are quietly relishing my eloquence. At length, Stanley speaks.

'I think we'll set it in New York,' he says, and we all set course for the house.

31

Bernard Pivot's necktie

Few interviews are pleasurable. All are stressful, most are boring, and some are downright awful, particularly if your interviewer is a fellow countryman: the seasoned hack with a chip on his shoulder who hasn't done his homework, hasn't read the book, thinks he's doing you a favour by making the journey and needs a drink; the aspiring novelist who thinks you're second rate but wants you to read his unfinished typescript; the feminist who believes you've only made it big because you're a plausible middle-class white male bastard, and you suspect she may be right.

Foreign journalists in my simple lexicon are by contrast sober, diligent, have read your book inside out and know your backlist better than you do – with the exception of the odd maverick such as the young Frenchman from *L'Evénement du jeudi* who, undeterred by my refusal to grant him an interview, ostentatiously staked out my Cornish house on foot, overflew it in a small low-flying aeroplane and reconnoitred it again from an inshore fishing boat before writing an article about his escapade that did full justice to his powers of invention.

Or there was the photographer – also French and young, but dispatched by some other magazine – who insisted that I inspect samples of his work before he took my portrait. Opening a greasy pocket album, he showed me photographs of such luminaries as Saul Bellow, Margaret Atwood and Philip Roth, and when I had dutifully admired each, fulsomely as is my way, he turned to his next exhibit which consisted of the rear view of an escaping cat with its tail raised.

'You like cat's arsehole?' he demanded, keenly observing my reaction.

'It's a nice shot. Well lit. Fine,' I replied, mustering whatever sang-froid I possessed.

His eyes narrowed and a smile of great cunning spread across his absurdly young face.

'The cat's arsehole is my *test*,' he explained proudly. 'If my subject is shocked, I know he is not sophisticated.'

'And I am?' I asked.

For his portrait he wanted a door. An outside door. Not of any particular character or colour, but a recessed door, with shadow. I should add that he was a very small man in stature, almost elfin, so much so that I was half inclined to offer to carry his large camera bag for him.

'I don't want to pose for a spy shot,' I said with uncharacteristic firmness.

He dismissed my concerns. The door wasn't about spies, it was about *profundity*. After some while we found one that met his strict criteria. I stood before it and looked straight into the lens as instructed. It was like no other I had ever seen: a half-globe, ten inches in diameter. He had dropped to one knee, with one eye glued to the eyepiece, when two very large men of Arab appearance drew to a halt behind him and addressed me over his back.

'Excuse me, please,' said one. 'Can you tell us the way, please, to Hampstead Underground station?'

I was on the point of directing him up Flask Walk when my photographer, furious at having his concentration disturbed, swung round and, still on one knee, screamed a piercing 'fuck off' at them. Amazingly, they did.

*

Setting such incidents aside, my French interviewers over the years have, to repeat, displayed a sensitivity that their British counterparts would have done well to emulate: which is why, or how, on the island of Capri in 1987, I signed away my life to Bernard Pivot, the shining star of French cultural television, founder, creator and anchor-man of *Apostrophes*, a weekly literary talk show that for the last thirteen years had held *la France entière* in thrall at prime time every Friday evening.

I had come to Capri in order to collect a prize. So had Pivot. Mine was for writing, his for journalism. Now imagine Capri on a perfect autumn evening. Two hundred dinner guests, all beautiful, are gathered under a starlit sky. The food is divine, the wine nectar. At a high table for the honorands, Pivot and I exchange a few merry words. He is a man in his prime – early fifties, vivid, energetic, unspoiled. Noticing that he alone of all the men is wearing a tie, he makes a joke against himself, rolls it up and jams it in his pocket. The tie is significant.

As the evening progresses, he chides me for refusing his overtures to take part in his programme. I feign embarrassment, tell him I must have been going through one of my rejection periods – I was – and somehow manage to leave the matter unresolved.

At midday the next day we present ourselves at Capri's town hall for the formal award ceremony. The lapsed diplomat in me cautions a suit and tie. Pivot dresses informally and discovers that, whereas last night he wore a tie and didn't need to, today he wears no tie when all about him are wearing theirs. In his speech of acceptance he laments this lack of social graces, and points to me as the man who gets everything right but refuses to appear on his literary programme.

Carried away by this perfectly judged charm offensive, I spring to my feet, tear off my tie, hand it to him and, before a packed crowd of enthusiastic witnesses – for the sake of the drama if no other – tell him that it's his, and that from now on he has only to show it to me and I will appear on his show. On the flight back to London next morning, I wonder whether promises made in Capri are legally binding. Within days I know they are.

I have committed myself to a live interview, in French, of

246

seventy-five minutes' duration, to be conducted by Bernard Pivot and three top-tier French journalists. There will be no prior discussion, no questions will be telegraphed in advance. But be prepared – thus my French publisher – for a wide-ranging debate covering all topics including politics, culture, literature, sex and whatever else comes into Bernard Pivot's febrile mind.

And I have barely spoken a word of French since I last taught it at O-level thirty years earlier.

*

The Alliance Française occupies a pretty corner house in Dorset Square. I drew a breath and entered. At the reception desk sat a young woman with short hair and large brown eyes.

'Hullo,' I said. 'I wondered whether I could arrange to brush up my French?'

She stared at me in stern bewilderment.

'*Quoi?*' she said, and we took it from there.

First, in whatever French remained to me, I spoke to Rita, then I spoke to Roland, and finally to Jacqueline, I think in that order. At the mention of *Apostrophes* they sprang into action. Rita and Jacqueline would take turns with me. It would be an immersion course. Rita – or was it Jacqueline? – would concentrate on my spoken French, help shape my responses to predicted questions. Jacqueline, in collaboration with Roland, would plan our military campaign. On the principle of 'know your enemy', they would make a study of Pivot's psychology, document his tradecraft and preferred areas of discussion, and keep a tight hold on the influx of daily news. The producers of *Apostrophes* set store by the programme's topicality.

To this end, Roland assembled an archive of old *Apostrophes* episodes. The rapidity and wit of the participants' exchanges terrified me. Without telling my tutors, I furtively enquired whether I might after all insist on an interpreter. Pivot's reply was instantaneous: on the strength of our conversations in Capri, he was convinced we could manage. My three other interrogators were to be Edward Behr, polyglot journalist and celebrated foreign correspondent, Philippe Labro, well-known author, journalist and film director, and Catherine David, respected literary journalist.

My distaste for interviews of any kind is not an affectation, even if now and then I give in to the temptation or bow to the pressure of my publishers. The celebrity game has nothing whatever to do with writing, and is played out in a quite different arena. I was always aware of that. A theatrical performance, yes. An exercise in self-projection, certainly. And from the publishers' point of view, the best promotional free ticket in town. But it can destroy talent as fast as it promotes it. I've met one writer at least who, after a full year of promoting his work worldwide, feels permanently drained of creativity, and I fear he may be right.

In my own case, there were two elephants in my room from the day I started writing: my father's lurid career which, if anyone had cared to make the connection, was a matter of public record; and my intelligence connections, which I was forbidden to discuss, both by law and by personal inclination. The feeling that interviews were as much about what to conceal as what to say was therefore rooted in me well before I embarked on a literary career.

*

All this in parentheses as I take my place on the platform of a packed studio in Paris and enter the land of serene unreality that lies just the other side of the fence from stage fright. Pivot produces my tie, and with gusto tells the story of how he came by it. The crowd loves it. We discuss the Berlin Wall and the Cold War. A clip from the movie of *The Spy Who Came in from the Cold* provides respite. So also do the lengthy contributions of my three interrogators, which tend to be more like mission statements than questions. We discuss Kim Philby, Oleg Penkovsky, the *perestroika, glasnost*. Did my team of advisers at Alliance Française cover these subjects during our operational briefings? Evidently it did, because by the look of me I'm reciting from memory. We admire Joseph Conrad, Maugham, Greene and Balzac. We ponder Margaret Thatcher. Was it Jacqueline who tutored me in the rhythm of the French rhetorical paragraph – state the thesis, turn it on itself, enlarge with your own summation? Whether it was Jacqueline, Rita or Roland, I protest my thanks to all three and the crowd again erupts.

Watching Pivot perform in real time before a live audience that is free-falling under his spell, it's not hard to understand how he has achieved something no other television character on earth has come within shouting distance of imitating. This isn't just charisma. This isn't just energy, charm, deftness, erudition. Pivot has the most elusive quality of them all, the one that film producers and casting directors across the globe would give their eye-teeth for: a natural generosity of spirit, better known as *heart*. In a country famous for making an art form out of ridicule, Pivot lets his subject know from the moment he or she sits down that they're going to be all right. And his audience feels that too. They're his family. No other interviewer, no other journalist of the few I now recall, has left such a deep mark on me.

The show is over. I may leave the studio. Pivot must remain on stage while he reads out church notices for next week. Robert Laffont, my publisher, guides me quickly into the street, which is empty. Not one car, not one passer-by, not one policeman. On a perfect summer's night, all Paris is wrapped in slumber.

'Where is everybody?' I ask Robert.

'Still watching Pivot, of course,' he replies contentedly.

Why do I tell this story? Maybe because I like to remind myself that, amid all the ballyhoo, this was a night of my life to remember. Of all the interviews I gave, and the many I regret, this is one I'll never take back.

32

Lunching with prisoners

There were six of us gathered round the lunch table that summer's day in Paris in the early days of the new millennium. Our host was a French publisher, and we were assembled to celebrate the success of my friend François Bizot, who had recently published a prize-winning memoir.*

Bizot, a Buddhist scholar and a fluent Khmer-speaker, remains the only Westerner to have been taken prisoner by Pol Pot's Khmer Rouge and survive. In October 1971, while working at the Angkor Conservation Centre, he was captured by the Khmer Rouge, kept in barbarous circumstances and subjected to three months of intense interrogation by the notorious Douch, who wished him to confess to being a CIA spy.

Somehow interrogator and prisoner developed a mysterious affinity, derived partly from Bizot's deep knowledge of ancient Buddhist culture, and partly, I suspect, from his sheer power of personality. Then, in what was surely a similarly extraordinary act of courage, Douch wrote a report to the Khmer Rouge high command exonerating Bizot from the charge of espionage. Extraordinarily also, Bizot was released, and Douch went on to manage one of Pol Pot's largest torture and execution centres. In my novel *The Secret Pilgrim*, there is a story about 'Jungle Hansen', where at several removes I attempt – unsuccessfully I fear – to do justice to Bizot's experience.

As we sat at table, it was a full thirty years since Bizot's ordeal, yet the fate of Douch still hung in the balance, his trial repeatedly

---

* *The Gate (Le Portail)*, published by Harvill Press.

dclaycd by political apathy and intrigue. And Bizot, we were now learning, had meanwhile rallied to his cause. His argument, vigorously expressed as ever, was that many of Douch's accusers in the present Khmer government were themselves steeped in blood, and wished only to make Douch responsible for all their sins.

Bizot was therefore conducting a one-man campaign, not in defence of Douch, but to demonstrate that he was neither more nor less guilty than those who were presuming to judge him.

While Bizot set out his case we all listened attentively, save for one guest who remained curiously unmoved. He was sitting directly across the table from me, a small, intense man with a wide brow and a dark, alert gaze that kept returning to mine. He had been introduced to me as the writer Jean-Paul Kauffmann, and I had read his recent book *The Dark Room at Longwood* with great pleasure. Longwood was the house in St Helena where Napoleon had spent his last humiliating years of exile. Kauffmann had made the long sea journey to St Helena, and described with impressive empathy the solitude, claustrophobia and systematic degradation of the world's most famous, admired and reviled prisoner.

Not having been told in advance that I was about to meet the author, I was able to express my spontaneous pleasure. So why on earth was he now eyeing me with such disfavour? Had I misspoken in some way? Did he know something disgraceful about me, always possible? Or had we met before and I'd clean forgotten, which even in those days was a racing possibility?

Either I must have asked him something to this effect, or my body language asked it for me. In a sudden reversal of roles, it was my turn to do the staring.

*

In May 1985, Jean-Paul Kauffmann, French foreign correspondent, had been taken hostage in Beirut by Hezbollah, whose secret prisoner he remained for three years. When his captors needed to move him from one safe house to another, they gagged him, bound him from head to foot and rolled him up in an oriental blanket in which he nearly died of asphyxia. He had been staring at me across the lunch table because in one of the hideouts where he was confined he had come upon a crumpled paperback novel of mine and devoured it over and over again, investing in it, I am sure, greater profundities than it had ever contained. He explained this to me in the matter-of-fact tone that I was familiar with in other victims of torture, for whom the unbanished experience has become part of the daily grind of life.

And I, speechless in response. For what, after all, was there to say? 'Thank you for reading me'? 'Sorry if my profundities were a bit on the shallow side'?

So probably I just tried to sound as humble as I felt, and probably after we parted I went back to *The Dark Room at Longwood* and made the connection I ought to have made when I'd read it: that this was one haunted prisoner writing about another – perhaps the greatest prisoner of all time.

The lunch took place at the beginning of the century, but the memory remains fresh although I have not met Kauffmann since, or corresponded with him. So while writing this book I looked him up on the internet, established that he was alive, and after some asking around, got his email address, with the warning that he might not respond.

I had by then also noted, I confess in some surprise, that the book that by a miracle of chance had saved him from despair and madness had been Leo Tolstoy's *War and Peace* which, like my own novel apparently, he had also devoured; and surely he had drawn from it a great deal more spiritual and intellectual nourishment than anything mine had to offer. Were there then two lucky finds? Or was one of our memories playing tricks with us?

Cautiously, I wrote to him, and after a few weeks this is what he generously wrote in reply:

During my captivity I missed books enormously. Occasionally our jailers would bring them. The arrival of a book brought a sense of

252

indescribable happiness. I would read it not just once, twice, forty times, but also reread it by starting at the end or in the middle. I hoped that this game might occupy me for at least two months. During my three years of misery, I experienced intense moments of joy. *The Spy Who Came in from the Cold* was one of those moments. I saw it as a nod from fate; our jailers brought us any old thing: cheap novels, the second volume of Tolstoy's *War and Peace*, incomprehensible treatises. But this time, here was a writer I admired . . . I had read all of your books including *The Spy* but in my new circumstances it was not the same book. It didn't even seem to have anything to do with my memory of it. Everything had changed. Each line was fraught with meaning. In a situation like mine, reading became a serious and even dangerous business because the slightest fact felt connected to this game of double or quits, which is the very existence of a hostage. The opening of a cell door, announcing the arrival of a Hezbollah official, could mean freedom or death. Every sign, every allusion became an omen, symbol or parable. There are many in *The Spy*.

With this book, I felt that climate of concealment and manipulation (the Shiite *taqiyya*) in my innermost being. Our captors were far from having the professionalism of the men of the KGB or the CIA but, like them, they were conceited fools, brutal cynics who used religion and the credulity of young militants to satisfy their appetite for power.

Like your characters, my captors were experts in paranoia: pathological mistrust, manic rage, false judgement, delusions, systematic aggression, a neurotic appetite for lies. Leamas' arid and absurd world, where human lives are nothing but pawns, was our world. How often have I felt like an abandoned man, forsaken. And above all, exhausted. This duplicitous world also taught me to reflect on my profession as a journalist. In the end, we are double agents. Or triple. We must empathize with others to understand and be accepted, then we betray.

Your vision of mankind is pessimistic. We are pitiful creatures; individually we don't count for much. Happily, this doesn't apply to everyone (see the character of Liz).

In this book I found reasons to hope. The most important is a voice, a presence. Yours. The jubilation of a writer who describes a cruel and colourless world and delights in rendering it so grey and hopeless. You feel it almost physically. Someone is talking to you, you are no longer alone. In my jail, I was no longer abandoned. A man came into my cell with his words and his vision of the world. Someone shared their power with me. I would make it through . . .*

*

And there you are; that's human memory for you, Kauffmann's, mine, both. I could have sworn the book he was talking about over lunch was *Smiley's People*, not *The Spy Who Came in from the Cold*, and that seems to be my wife's memory too.

33

Son of the author's father

It took me a long while to get on writing terms with Ronnie, con-man, fantasist, occasional jailbird, and my father.

From the day I made my first faltering attempts at a novel, he was the one I wanted to get to grips with, but I was light years away from being up to the job. My earliest drafts of what eventually became *A Perfect Spy* dripped with self-pity: cast your eye, gentle reader, upon this emotionally crippled boy, crushed underfoot by his tyrannical father. It was only when he was safely dead and I took up the novel again that I did what I should have done at the beginning, and made the sins of the son a whole lot more reprehensible than the sins of the father.

With that settled, I was able to honour the legacy of his tempestuous life: a cast of characters to make the most blasé writer's mouth water, from eminent legal brains of the day and stars of sport and screen to the finest of London's criminal underworld and the beautiful creatures who trailed in their wake. Wherever Ronnie went, the unpredictable went with him. Are we up or down? Can we fill up the car on tick at the local garage? Has he fled the country or will he be proudly parking the Bentley in the drive tonight? Or hiding it in the back garden, turning out the house lights, checking doors and windows, and murmuring into the telephone if it hasn't been cut off? Or is he enjoying the safety and comfort of one of his alternative wives?

Of Ronnie's dealings with organized crime, if any, I know lamentably little. Yes, he rubbed shoulders with the notorious Kray twins, but that may just have been celebrity-hunting. And yes, he did business of a sort with London's worst-ever landlord Peter Rachman, and my best guess would be that when Rachman's thugs had got rid of Ronnie's tenants for him, he sold off the houses and gave Rachman a piece.

But a full-on criminal partnership? Not the Ronnie I knew. Con-men are aesthetes. They wear nice suits, have clean fingernails and are well spoken at all times. Policemen in Ronnie's book were first-rate fellows who were open to negotiation. The same could not be said of 'the boys' as he called them, and you messed with the boys at your peril.

Tension? Ronnie's entire life was spent walking on the thinnest, slipperiest layer of ice you can imagine. He saw no paradox between being on the Wanted list for fraud and sporting a grey topper in the Owners' enclosure at Ascot. A reception at Claridge's to celebrate his second marriage was interrupted while he persuaded two Scotland Yard detectives to put off arresting him until the party was over – and meanwhile, come in and join the fun, which they duly did.

But I don't think Ronnie could have lived any other way. I don't think he wanted to. He was a crisis addict, a performance addict, a shameless pulpit orator and a scene-grabber. He was a delusional enchanter and a persuader who saw himself as God's golden boy, and he wrecked a lot of people's lives.

Graham Greene tells us that childhood is the credit balance of the writer. By that measure at least, I was born a millionaire.

*

For the last third of Ronnie's life – he died suddenly at the age of sixty-nine – we were estranged or at loggerheads. Almost by mutual consent, there were terrible obligatory scenes, and when we buried the hatchet we always remembered where we'd put it. Do I feel more kindly towards him today than I did then? Sometimes I walk round him, sometimes he's the mountain I still have to climb. Either way, he's always there, which I can't say for my mother, because to this day I have no idea what sort of person she was. The versions of her that have been offered me by those who were close to her and loved her have not been enlightening. Perhaps I didn't want them to be. I ran her to earth when I was twenty-one, and thereafter broadly attended to her needs, not always with good grace. But from the day of our reunion until she died, the frozen child in me showed not the smallest sign of thawing out. Did she love animals? Landscape? The sea that she lived beside? Music? Painting? Me? Did she read books? Certainly she had no high opinion of mine, but what about other people's?

In the nursing home where she stayed during her last years, we spent much of our time deploring or laughing at my father's misdeeds. As my visits continued, I came to realize that she had created for herself – and for me – an idyllic mother–son relationship that had flowed uninterrupted from my birth till now.

Today, I don't remember feeling any affection in childhood except for my elder brother, who for a time was my only parent. I remember a constant tension in myself that even in great age has not relaxed. I remember little of being very young. I remember the dissembling as we grew up, and the need to cobble together an identity for myself, and how in order to do this I filched from the manners and lifestyle of my peers and betters, even to the extent of pretending I had a settled home life with real parents and ponies. Listening to myself today, watching myself when I have to, I can still detect traces of the lost originals, chief among them obviously my father.

All this no doubt made me an ideal recruit to the secret flag. But nothing lasted: not the Eton schoolmaster, not the MI5 man, not the MI6 man. Only the writer in me stuck the course. If I look over my life from here, I see it as a succession of engagements and escapes, and I thank goodness that the writing kept me relatively straight and largely sane. My father's refusal to accept the simplest truth about himself set me on a path of enquiry from which I never returned. In the absence of a mother or sisters I learned women late, if ever, and we all paid a price for that.

In my childhood, everyone around me tried to sell me the Christian God in one form or another. I got the low church from my aunts, uncles and grandparents, and the high church from my schools. When I was brought to the bishop to be confirmed, I tried my hardest to feel pious, and felt nothing. For another ten years I went on trying to acquire some sort of religious conviction, then gave it up as a bad job. Today, I have no god but landscape, and no expectation of death but extinction. I rejoice constantly in my family and the people who love me, and whom I love in return. Walking the Cornish cliffs, I am overtaken with surges of gratitude for my life.

*

Yes, I have seen the house where I was born. Cheerful aunts pointed it out to me a hundred times as we skimmed by. But the house of my birth that I prefer is a different one, built in my imagination. It's red brick and clattery and due for demolition, with broken windows, a 'For Sale' sign, and an old bath in the garden. It stands in a plot of weeds and builders' junk, with a bit of stained glass in the smashed front door – a place for kids to hide in, rather than be born. But born there I was, or so my imagination insists, and what's more I was born in the attic, among a stack of brown boxes that my father always carted round with him when he was on the run.

When I made my first clandestine inspection of those boxes, some time around the outbreak of the Second World War – for by the age of eight I was already a well-trained spy – they contained only personal stuff: his Masonic regalia, the barrister's wig and gown with which he proposed to astonish a waiting world as soon as he had got round to studying law, and such top-secret items as his plans for selling fleets of airships to the Aga Khan. But once war finally broke out, the brown boxes offered more substantial fare: black-market Mars bars, Benzedrine inhalers for shooting stimulant up your nose and, after D-Day, nylon stockings and ballpoint pens.

Ronnie had a penchant for weird commodities provided they were rationed or not available. Two decades later, when Germany was still divided and I was a British diplomat living on the banks of the River Rhine in Bonn, he appeared unannounced in my gateway, his ample frame squeezed inside a steel coracle with wheels attached. It was an amphibious motorcar, he explained. A prototype. He had acquired the British patent from its manufacturers in Berlin, and it was about to make our fortunes. He had driven it down the interzonal corridor under the gaze of East German frontier guards, and now he proposed to launch it, with my help, into the Rhine, which happened to be swollen at the time, and very fast flowing.

I dissuaded him despite my children's enthusiasm and gave him lunch instead. Refreshed, he set off in great excitement for Ostend and England. How far he got I don't know, for the car was not spoken of again. I assume that somewhere along the journey creditors caught up with him and removed it.

But that didn't stop him from popping up in Berlin two years later, announcing himself as my 'professional adviser', in which capacity he received a VIP tour of West Berlin's largest film studio, and no doubt a great deal of the studio's hospitality and a starlet or two, and a lot of sales patter about tax breaks and subsidies on offer to foreign filmmakers, and notably to the makers of the movie of my recent novel, *The Spy Who Came in from the Cold*.

It goes without saying that neither I nor Paramount Pictures, who had already made their deal with Ardmore Studios in Ireland, had the smallest idea of what he was up to.

*

There's no electricity in the house of my birth, and no heating, so the light comes from the gas lamps on Constitution Hill, which give the attic a creamy glow. My mother lies on a camp bed, pitifully doing her best, whatever her best may entail – I was not conversant with the niceties of childbirth when I first pictured this scene. Ronnie is champing in the doorway, wearing a snappy gent's double-breasted and the brown-and-white brogues he played golf in, keeping an eye to the street while in pounding cadences he urges my mother to greater efforts:

'God in Heaven, Wiggly, why can't you get a move on for once? It's a damned shame is what it is, and no two ways about it. There's poor old Humphries, sitting in the car out there, catching his death and all you do is shilly-shally.'

Though my mother's first name was Olive, my father called her Wiggly, rain or shine. Later, when technically I grew up, I too gave women silly nicknames in order to make them less formidable.

Ronnie's voice when I was young was still Dorset, with heavy 'r's and long 'a's. But the self-laundering was in progress and by the time I was an adolescent he was almost – but never quite – well spoken. Englishmen, we are told, are branded on the tongue, and in those days being well spoken could gain you a military commission, bank credit, respectful treatment from policemen and a job in the City of London. And it's one of the ironies of Ronnie's mercurial life that, by realizing his ambition of sending my brother and me to posh schools, he placed himself socially below us by the cruel standards of the time. Tony and I were whisked effortlessly through the class sound barrier, while Ronnie remained stuck the other side.

Not that he exactly paid for our education – or not always, so far as I can make out – but either way he fixed it. One school, after a taste of his ways, bravely demanded its fees up front. It received them at Ronnie's leisure in deferred black-market dried fruit – figs, bananas, prunes – and a case of unobtainable gin for the staff.

Yet he remained, which was his genius, to all outward appearances a most respectable man. Respect, not money, was what he cared for above everything. Every day he had to have his magic recognized. His judgement of other people depended entirely on how much they respected him. At the humble level of life, there's a Ronnie in every second street in London, in every county town. He's the back-slapping, two-fisted tearaway naughty boy with a touch of the blarney, who throws champagne parties for people who aren't used to being given champagne, opens his garden to the local Baptists for their fête though he never sets foot inside their church, is honorary president of the boys' football team and the men's cricket team and presents them with silver cups for their championships.

Until one day it turns out he hasn't paid the milkman for a year, or the local garage, or the newspaper shop, or the wine shop, or the shop that sold him the silver sports cups, and maybe he goes bankrupt or goes to jail, and his wife takes the children to live with her mother, and eventually she divorces him because she discovers – and her mother knew it all along – that he's been screwing every girl in the neighbourhood and has kids he hasn't mentioned. And when our naughty boy comes out or gets himself temporarily straight, he lives small for a while and does good works and takes pleasure in simple things, till the sap rises again and he's back to his old games.

*

My father was that fellow, no question, all of the above. But that was only the beginning. The difference is in scale, in his episcopal bearing, his ecumenical voice and his air of injured sanctity when anyone dares to doubt his word, and his infinite powers of self-delusion. While your run-of-the-mill naughty boy is blowing the last of the housekeeping money on the three-thirty handicap at Newmarket, Ronnie is relaxing serenely at the big table in Monte Carlo with a complimentary brandy-and-ginger in front of him, with myself aged seventeen and pretending to be older, seated on one side of him and King Farouk's equerry, aged fifty-plus, on the other. The equerry is most welcome at this table. He has bought it many times over. He is polished, grey-haired, innocuous and very tired. The white telephone at his elbow links him directly to his Egyptian king, who is surrounded by astrologers. The white phone rings, the equerry removes his hand from his chin, raises the receiver, listens with his long eyelids lowered and dutifully transfers another chunk of the wealth of Egypt to red, or black, or whatever number is considered propitious by the zodiacal wizards of Alexandria or Cairo.

For some while now Ronnie has been observing this process, a combative little smile to himself that says, 'If that's the way you want it, old son, that's the way it's got to be.' And he starts to raise his own bids around the table. Purposefully. Tens become twenties. Twenties, fifties. And as he splashes out the last of his chips and beckons imperiously for more, I realize he is not playing a hunch, or playing the house, or playing the numbers. He is playing King Farouk. If Farouk favours black, Ronnie goes for red. If Farouk backs odd, Ronnie raises him on even. We are talking hundreds by now (these days thousands). And what Ronnie is telling His Egyptian Majesty – as a term's worth, then a year's worth, of my school fees vanish into the croupier's maw – is that Ronnie's line to the Almighty is a great deal more efficacious than some tin-pot Arab potentate's.

In the soft blue twilight of Monte Carlo before dawn, father and son saunter side by side along the esplanade to a twenty-four-hour jeweller's shop to pawn his platinum cigarette case, gold fountain pen and wristwatch. Bucherer? Boucheron? I'm warm. 'Win it all back tomorrow with interest, right, old son?' he says as we retire to bed in the Hôtel de Paris, where he has mercifully prepaid our room bills. 'Ten o'clock sharp,' he adds severely, lest I am thinking of malingering.

*

So I am born. Of my mother, Olive. Obediently, with the haste Ronnie has demanded of her. In a final push to forestall creditors and prevent Mr Humphries from catching his death while he crouches outside in his Lanchester. For Mr Humphries is not just a cab driver but a valued confederate, as well as a fully paid-up member of the exotic Court with which Ronnie surrounds himself, and a distinguished amateur conjuror who does tricks with bits of rope like hangman's nooses. In high times he is replaced by Mr Nutbeam and a Bentley, but in low times Mr Humphries with his Lanchester is always ready to oblige.

I am born, and packed up with my mother's few possessions, for we have recently suffered another bailiff's visitation and are travelling light. I am loaded into the boot of Mr Humphries' taxi like one of Ronnie's contraband hams a few years hence. The brown boxes are thrown in after me and the lid of the boot is locked from the outside. I peer around in the darkness for a sign of my elder brother, Tony. He is not in evidence. Neither is Olive, alias Wiggly. Never mind, I have been born and, like a brand-new foal, am already on the run. I have been on the run ever since.

*

I have another confected childhood memory that, according to my father, who had every right to know, is equally inaccurate. It is four years later and I am in the city of Exeter, walking across a patch of wasteland. I am holding the hand of my mother, Olive, alias Wiggly. As we are both wearing gloves, there is no fleshly contact between us. And indeed, so far as I recall, there never was any. It was Ronnie who did the hugging, never Olive. She was the mother who had no smell, whereas Ronnie smelled of fine cigars, and pear-droppy hair oil from Taylor of Old Bond Street, Court Hairdressers, and when you put your nose into the fleecy cloth of one of Mr Berman's tailored suits you seemed to smell his women there as well. Yet when, at the age of twenty-one, I advanced on Olive down No. 1 platform at Ipswich railway station for our great reunion after sixteen hugless years, I couldn't work out for the life of me where to grab hold of her. She was as tall as I remembered her, but all elbow and no huggable contours. With her toppling walk and long, vulnerable face she could have been my brother Tony in Ronnie's legal wig.

I am in Exeter again, swinging on Olive's gloved hand. At the far side of the wasteland is a road from which I see a high, red brick wall with spikes and broken glass along its top, and behind the wall a

263

grim flat-fronted building with barred windows and no light inside them. And in one of these barred windows, looking exactly like a Monopoly convict when you go directly to jail, without passing go or collecting two hundred pounds, stands my father from the shoulders up. Like the Monopoly man, he is clutching the bars with both big hands. Women always told him what lovely hands he had and he was forever grooming them with clippers from his jacket pocket. His wide, white forehead is pressed against the bars. He never had much hair, and what there was of it ran fore and aft over his crown in a tight black, sweet-smelling river, stopping short of the dome that did so much for his saintly image of himself. As he grew older, the river turned grey, then dried up altogether, but the wrinkles of age and dissolution that he had so richly earned never materialized. Goethe's Eternal Feminine prevailed in him till the end.

He was as proud of his head as he was of his hands, according to Olive, and soon after their marriage mortgaged it for fifty pounds to medical science, cash in advance and the goods to be delivered on his death. I don't know when she told me this, but I know that from the day this knowledge was entrusted to me, I eyed Ronnie with something of the detachment of an executioner. His neck was very broad, hardly a kink where it joined his upper body. I wondered where I would aim the axe if I were doing the job. Killing him was an early preoccupation of mine, and it has endured off and on even after his death. Probably it is no more than my exasperation that I could absolutely never pin him down.

Still clutching Olive's gloved hand, I wave at Ronnie high up in the wall and Ronnie waves the way he always waved: leaning back and with the upper body dead still while one prophetic arm commands the skies above his head. 'Daddy, Daddy!' I yell. My voice is a giant frog's. On Olive's hand I march back to the car feeling thoroughly pleased with myself. Not every small boy, after all, has his mother to himself and keeps his father in a cage.

But, according to my father, none of this happened. The notion that I might have seen him in any of his prisons offended him very

much – 'Sheer invention from start to finish, son.' All right, he con-
ceded, he did a bit of time in Exeter, but mostly he was in Winchester
and the Scrubs. He'd done nothing criminal, nothing that couldn't
have been sorted out between reasonable people. He'd been in the position of the office boy who'd borrowed a few bob from the stamp box
and been caught before he had a chance to put them back. But that
wasn't the point, he insisted. The point, as he confided to my half-sister
Charlotte, his daughter by another marriage, when he was complaining
about my generally disrespectful behaviour towards him – i.e. I wouldn't
give him a cut of my royalties or put up a few hundred thousand to
develop a nice bit of green belt he'd gulled out of some misguided local
council   the point *was* that anyone who knows the inside of Exeter jail
knows perfectly well you can't see the road from the cells.

*

And I believe him. Still. I'm wrong and he was right. He was never
at that window and I never waved to him. But what's the truth?
What's memory? We should find another name for the way we see
past events that are still alive in us. I *saw* him in that window but I
also *see* him there now, grasping the bars, his bull's chest encased in
the convict's uniform, with arrows printed on it, as worn in all the
best school comics. There is a part of me that never afterwards saw
him wearing anything else. And I know I was four years old when I
saw him because a year later he was at large again, and a few weeks
or months after that my mother slipped away in the night, disappearing for sixteen years before I rediscovered her in Suffolk, the mother
of two other children who had grown up unaware of their
half-brothers' existence. She took with her one fine white hide suitcase by Harrods, silk-lined, which I found in her cottage when she
died. It was the only thing in the whole house that bore witness to
her first marriage, and I have it still.

I saw him crouching in his cell, too, on the edge of his bunk with
his mortgaged head in his hands, a proud young man who'd never in

his life gone hungry or washed his own socks or made his own bed, thinking of his three pious doting sisters and two adoring parents, his mother heartbroken and forever wringing her hands and asking God, 'Why, why?' in her Irish brogue, and his father a former mayor of Poole, an alderman and Freemason. Both serving Ronnie's time with him in their minds. Both turning prematurely white-haired while they waited for him.

How could Ronnie bear knowing all that while he stared at the wall? With his pride and prodigious energy and drive, how did he cope with the confinement? I'm as restless as he was. I can't sit still for an hour. I can't read a book for an hour unless it's in German, which somehow keeps me in my chair. Even at a good play, I long for the interval and a stretch. When I'm writing, I'm forever bouncing up from my desk and charging round the garden or up the street. I've only to lock myself in the loo for three seconds – the key has fallen out of its hold and I'm fumbling to get it back in – and I'm in a Force 12 sweat and screaming to be let out. Yet Ronnie at the prime of his life did serious time – three or four years. He was still serving one sentence when they slapped some more charges on him and gave him a second, this time with hard labour or, as we might call it today with our horrible misuse of the word, *enhanced* incarceration. The stretches he did in later life – Hong Kong, Singapore, Jakarta, Zurich – were, to the best of my knowledge, short. Researching *The Honourable Schoolboy* in Hong Kong, I came face to face with his ex-jailer at the Jardine Matheson tent at Happy Valley racecourse.

'Mr Cornwell, sir, your father is one of the finest men I ever met. It was a privilege to look after him. I'm retiring soon and when I get back to London he's going to fix me up in business.' Even in prison, Ronnie was fattening his jailer for the pot.

*

I am in Chicago, supporting a lacklustre campaign to sell British goods abroad. The British Consul General, with whom I am staying, hands me a telegram. It is from our Ambassador in Jakarta telling me that Ronnie is in prison and will I buy him out? I promise to pay whatever needs to be paid. To my alarm, it is only a few hundred. Ronnie must be down on his luck.

*

From the Bezirksgefängnis in Zurich, where he has been imprisoned for hotel fraud, Ronnie telephones me, reversing the charges. 'Son? It's your old man.' What can I do for you, Father? 'You can get me out of this damned jail, son. It's all a misunderstanding. These boys just won't look at the facts.' How much? No answer. Just an actor's gulp before a drowning voice delivers the punch line: 'I can't do any more prison, son.' Then the sobs that as usual go through me like slow knives.

*

I asked my two surviving aunts. They spoke the way Ronnie spoke when he was young: in light, unconscious Dorset accents that I really like. How did Ronnie take it, that first stretch? How did it affect him? Who was he before prison? Who was he after it? But the aunts are not historians, they're sisters. They love Ronnie, and prefer not to think beyond their love. The scene they remember best was Ronnie shaving on the morning of the day the verdict was to be announced at Winchester Assizes. He had defended himself from the dock the previous day and was certain he would be home free that evening. It was the first time the aunts were allowed to watch him shave. But the only answer I get from them is in their eyes and dropped words: 'It was terrible. Just terrible.' They are talking about the shame as if it were yesterday rather than seventy years ago.

Sixty-something years back I had asked my mother, Olive, the same question. Unlike the aunts, who prefer to keep their memories to themselves, Olive was a tap you couldn't turn off. From the moment of our reunion at Ipswich railway station, she talked about Ronnie non-stop. She talked about his sexuality long before I had sorted out mine, and for ease of reference gave me a tattered hardback copy of Krafft-Ebing's *Psychopathia Sexualis* as a map to guide me through her husband's appetites before and after jail.

'*Changed*, dear? In *prison*? Not a bit of it! You were totally *un*changed. You'd lost weight, of course – well, you would. Prison food isn't *meant* to be nice.' And then the image that will never leave me, not least because she seemed unaware of what she was saying: 'And you did have this silly habit of stopping in front of doors and waiting at attention with your head down till I opened them for you. They were perfectly *ordinary* doors, not locked or anything, but you obviously weren't *expecting* to be able to open them for yourself.'

Why did Olive refer to Ronnie as *you*? *You* meaning *he*, but subconsciously recruiting me to be his surrogate, which by the time of her death was what I had become. There is an audiotape that Olive made for my brother Tony, all about her life with Ronnie. I still can't bear to play it, so all I've ever heard is scraps. On the tape she describes how Ronnie used to beat her up, which, according to Olive, was what prompted her to bolt. Ronnie's violence was not news to me because he had made a habit of beating up his second wife as well: so often and so purposefully and coming home at such odd hours of the night to do it that, seized by a chivalrous impulse, I appointed myself her ridiculous protector, sleeping on a mattress in front of her bedroom door and clutching a golf iron so that Ronnie would have to reckon with me before he got at her.

Would I really have struck him on his mortgaged head? Might I indeed have killed him, and followed in his footsteps to prison? Or just given him a hug and wished him goodnight? I'll never know, but I have played the possibilities in my memory so often that all of them are true.

Certainly Ronnie beat me up, too, but only a few times and not with much conviction. It was the shaping up that was the scary part: the lowering and readying of the shoulders, the resetting of the jaw.

And when I was grown up Ronnie tried to sue me, which I suppose is violence in disguise. He had watched a television documentary of my life and decided there was an implicit slander in my failure to mention that I owed everything to him.

*

How did Olive and Ronnie first get together? I asked her this question in my Krafft-Ebing period, not long after that first remembered hug at Ipswich station. 'Through your Uncle Alec, dear,' she replied. She was referring to her estranged brother, her senior by twenty-five years. Their parents were both long dead, so Uncle Alec, a grandee of Poole, Member of Parliament and fabled local preacher, was her effective father. Like Olive, he was thin and bony and very tall, but also vain, a natty dresser with a great sense of his social importance. Appointed to present a cup to a local football team, Uncle Alec took Olive along with him, in the manner of one schooling a future princess in the exercise of her public duties.

Ronnie was the team's centre forward. Where else could he possibly play? As Uncle Alec moved along the line, shaking hands with each player, Olive trailed behind him, pinning a badge to each proud breast. But when she pinned one to Ronnie's he fell dramatically to his knees, complaining she had pierced him to the heart, which he was clutching with both hands. Uncle Alec, who on all known evidence was a pompous arse, loftily condoned the horseplay, and Ronnie with impressive meekness enquired whether he might call at the great house on Sunday afternoons to pay his respects – not to Olive, naturally, who was socially far above him – but to an Irish housemaid with whom he had struck up an acquaintance. Uncle Alec graciously gave his consent and Ronnie, under cover of wooing the maid, seduced Olive.

'I was so lonely, darling. And you were such a ball of fire.' The fire, of course, was Ronnie, not me.

Uncle Alec was my first secret source and I blew him sky high. It was to Alec that I had secretly written on my twenty-first birthday – Alec Glassey, MP, care of the House of Commons, *Private* – to enquire whether his sister, my mother, was alive and, if so, where she might be found. Glassey had long ceased to be an MP, but miraculously the Commons authorities forwarded my letter. I had asked Ronnie the same question when I was younger, but he had only frowned and shaken his head, so after a few more shots I gave up. In a two-line scrawl Uncle Alec advised me that I would find her address on the attached piece of paper. A condition of this information was that I should never tell 'the person concerned' where I had it from. Stimulated by the injunction, I blurted out the truth to Olive within moments of our meeting.

'Then we must be grateful to him, dear,' she said, and that was all.

Or it *should* have been all, except that forty years later in New Mexico, and several years after my mother's death, my brother Tony informed me that on his twenty-first birthday, two years before mine, he, too, had written to Alec, had taken the train to Olive, hugged her on the No. 1 platform and probably, thanks to his height, achieved a better grasp than I had. And he had debriefed her.

So why had Tony not told me all this? Why hadn't I told him? Why had Olive told neither of us about the other? Why had Alec tried to keep us all apart? The answer is fear of Ronnie, which for all of us was like fear of life itself. His reach, psychological and physical, and his terrible charm were inescapable. He was a walking Rolodex of connections. When one of his women was discovered to be consoling herself with a lover, Ronnie went to work like a one-man war room. Within an hour he had a line to the wretched man's employer, his bank manager, his landlord and his wife's father. Each was recruited as an agent of destruction.

And what Ronnie had done to a helpless erring husband he could do to all of us tenfold. Ronnie wrecked as he created. Every time I am moved to admire him, I remember his victims. His own mother, freshly bereaved, the sobbing executrix of his father's estate; his second wife's mother, also widowed, also in dazed possession of her late husband's fortune: Ronnie robbed them both, depriving them of their husbands' savings and the proper heirs of their inheritance. Dozens, scores of others, all trusting, all by Ronnie's noble standards deserving of his protection: conned, robbed, ripped off by their knight errant. How did he explain this to himself, if at all? The race-horses, parties, women and Bentleys that furnished his other life while he was gulling money out of people so helpless with love for him that they couldn't say no? Did Ronnie ever count the cost of being God's chosen boy?

*

I keep few letters, and most of Ronnie's to me were so awful I destroyed them almost before I read them: begging letters from America, India, Singapore and Indonesia; hortatory letters forgiving me my trespasses and urging me to love him, pray for him, make the best use of the advantages he had lavished on me, and send him money; bullying demands that I repay the cost of my education; and doom-laden prognostications of his imminent death. I don't regret having thrown them away; sometimes I wish I could throw away the memory of them, too. Occasionally, despite my best efforts, a shred of his inextinguishable past turns up to tease me: a page of one of his typed letters on flimsy airmail paper, for instance, advising me of some crazy scheme he wants me to 'bring to the Attention of your Advisors with a View to Early Investment'. Or an old business adversary of Ronnie writes to me, always tenderly, always grateful to have known him, even if the experience proved costly.

*

Some years back, dickering on the brink of an autobiography and frustrated by the poverty of collateral information, I hired a pair of detectives, one thin, one fat, both recommended by a rugged London solicitor, and both good eaters. Go out into the world, I said to them airily. Be my guests. Find the living witnesses and the written record and bring me a factual account of myself and my family and my father and I will reward you. I'm a liar, I explained. Born to lying, bred to it, trained to it by an industry that lies for a living, practised in it as a novelist. As a maker of fictions, I invent versions of myself, never the real thing, if it exists.

So what I'll do is this, I said. I'll let my imaginative memory rip on the left-hand page, and I'll put your factual record on the right-hand page, unchanged and unadorned. And in that way my readers will see for themselves to what extent an old writer's memory is the whore of his imagination. We all reinvent our pasts, I said, but writers are in a class of their own. Even when they know the truth, it's never enough for them. I directed them to Ronnie's dates and names and places and suggested they dig out the court records. I imagined them hunting down vital sources while there were still a few around, former secretaries, prison officers and policemen. I told them to do the same with my school record, my army record, and, since I had several times been the subject of official security checks, the assessments of my trustworthiness by the services we used to regard as secret. I urged them to stop at nothing in their search for me. I told them about my father's scams, domestic and foreign, everything I could remember: how he attempted to con the prime ministers of Singapore and Malaysia into a dubious football-pools operation and came within a whisker of bringing it off. But it was the same whisker that always let him down.

I told them about his little 'extra families' and mistress-mothers, keepers of the flame, who, in his own words to me, were always there to cook him a sausage if he dropped by. I gave them the names of a couple of the women I knew about, and an address or two, and the names of the children – whose is anybody's guess. I told them about Ronnie's war service, which consisted of using every trick in the book not to do any, including standing in parliamentary by-elections under such rousing banners as 'Independent Progressive', which obliged the army to release him to exercise his democratic rights.

And how, even while he was being trained, he kept a couple of courtiers and a secretary or two on hand, billeted in local hotels, so that he could pursue his legitimate business of war profiteer and trader in shortages. In the immediate post-war years, it is my conviction, Ronnie improved upon his army record by awarding himself the alias of Colonel Cornhill, by which name he was well known in the shadier corners of the West End. When my half-sister Charlotte was playing in a film about the notorious gangland family in east London called *The Krays*, she consulted the eldest brother, Charlie, in order to collect material for the part. Over a nice cup of tea, Charlie Kray dug out the family photo album, and there was Ronnie with an arm round the two younger brothers.

I told them about the night I checked into the Royal Hotel in Copenhagen and was at once invited to visit the manager. I assumed my fame had gone ahead of me. It hadn't, but Ronnie's had. He was wanted by the Danish police. And there they were, two of them, upright like schoolboys in correction chairs against one wall. Ronnie, they said, had entered Copenhagen illegally from the United States with the assistance of a couple of Scandinavian pilots whom he had fleeced at poker in a New York dive. Instead of cash, he had suggested they give him a free ride to Denmark, which they duly did, spiriting him through customs and immigration when they landed. Did I by any chance, the Danish policemen enquired, happen to know where they could find my father? I didn't. And, thank God, I really didn't. I'd last heard of Ronnie a year earlier, when he had tiptoed out of Britain in order to escape a creditor, or arrest, or the mob, or all three.

So there was another lead for my detectives, I told them: let's find out what Ronnie was running away from in Britain, and why he had to get out of America the hard way, too. I told them about Ronnie's racehorses, which he kept going even when he was an undischarged bankrupt: horses in Newmarket, in Ireland and at Maisons-Laffitte, outside Paris. I gave them the names of trainers and jockeys and told them how Lester Piggott had ridden for him while Lester was still an apprentice; and how Gordon Richards had advised him on his buy-ing. And how I had once come upon young Lester in the back of a horse trailer, lounging in the straw in Ronnie's silks, reading a boys' comic before the race. Ronnie's racehorses were named after his beloved children: Dato, God help us, for David and Tony; Tummy Tunmers, which combined the name of his house with his affection for his own stomach; Prince Rupert – the only horse that showed any form – after my half-brother, Rupert; and Rose Sang, in arch refer-ence to my half-sister Charlotte's red hair. And how in my late teens I used to go to race meetings in Ronnie's stead after he had been warned off the course for not paying his gambling debts. And how when Prince Rupert to everyone's amazement took a place in – was it the Cesarewitch? – I returned to London on the same train as the bookies Ronnie hadn't paid, lugging a briefcase stuffed with bank-notes from bets I'd placed for him around the course.

I told my detectives about Ronnie's Court, as I had always secretly called it: the motley of genteel ex-prisoners who formed the nucleus of his corporate family – ex-schoolmasters, ex-lawyers, ex-everything. And how one of them, called Reg, took me aside after Ronnie's death and tearfully gave me what he called the bottom line. Reg had done prison for Ronnie, he said. And he wasn't alone in that distinction. So had George-Percival, another courtier. So had Eric and Arthur. All four had taken the rap for Ronnie at one time or another, rather than see the Court robbed of its guiding genius. But that wasn't Reg's point. His point, David – through his tears – was that they were a bunch of bloody idiots who had let Ronnie con them every time. And they still were. And if Ronnie rose from his grave today and asked Reg to do another stretch for him, Reg would do it, the same as George-Percival and Eric and Arthur would. Because where Ron-nie was concerned – and Reg was happy to admit this – the whole lot of them were soft in the head.

'We was all bent, son,' Reg added in a last respectful epitaph to a friend. 'But your dad was very, very bent indeed.'

I told the detectives how Ronnie had stood as a Liberal

parliamentary candidate for Yarmouth in the general election of 1950, taking the Court with him, Liberals to a man. And how the Conservative candidate's agent met Ronnie by appointment in a private place and, fearful that Ronnie was going to split the vote in Labour's favour, warned him that the Tories would leak his prison record and one or two other tidbits about him if he didn't stand down, which Ronnie, after consulting a plenary session of the Court, of which I was an ex-officio member, refused to do. Was Uncle Alec the Tories' Deep Throat? Had he sent them one of his secret letters exhorting them not to reveal the source? I have always suspected so. In any event, the Tories did exactly as they had threatened. They leaked Ronnie's prison record, and Ronnie as predicted split the vote and Labour won.

Perhaps by way of friendly warning to my detectives, or as a bit of a boast, I impressed upon them the extent of Ronnie's network of connections, and the lines he had to the most unlikely people. In the late forties and early fifties, his golden years, Ronnie could throw parties at his house in Chalfont St Peter which included directors of Arsenal football club, Permanent Under-Secretaries, champion jockeys, film stars, radio stars, snooker kings, ex-lord mayors of London, the entire cast of the Crazy Gang then playing at the Victoria Palace, not to mention a handpicked selection of lovelies from wherever he got them, and the Australian or West Indian Test cricket teams if they were visiting. Don Bradman came, and so did most of the great and good players of the post-war years. To which should be added a choir of leading judges and barristers of the day and a troop of ranking Scotland Yard police officers in off-duty blazers with crests on the pocket.

Ronnie with his early education in police methods could spot a flexible copper a mile off. He knew at a glance what they ate and drank and what made them happy, how far they would bend and where they would snap. It was one of his pleasures to extend police protection to his friends, so that if someone's son, dead drunk, rolled his parents' Riley into a ditch, it was Ronnie who received the first frantic phone call from the child's mother, Ronnie again who waved his wand and caused the blood tests to be muddled in the police laboratory, to the profuse apologies of the prosecution for wasting Your Worship's valuable time: with the further happy outcome that Ronnie notched up yet another favour to his account in the great Promise Bank where he kept his only assets.

In briefing my detectives I was, of course, beating the air. No detective on earth could have found what I was looking for, and two were no better than one. Ten thousand pounds and several excellent meals later, all they had to offer was a bunch of press clippings about old bankruptcies and the Yarmouth election, and a pile of useless company records. No trial records, no retired jailers, no golden-bullet witnesses or smoking gun. Not a single mention of Ronnie's trial at Winchester Assizes, where by his own account he defended himself brilliantly against a young advocate named Norman Birkett, later Sir Norman, then Lord, who served as a British judge at the Nuremberg trials.

From prison – this much Ronnie told me himself – he had written to Birkett, and, in the sporting spirit dear to both of them, congratulated the great barrister on his performance. And Birkett was flattered to receive such a letter from a poor prisoner who was paying his debt to society, and wrote back. And thus a correspondence developed in which Ronnie pledged his lifelong determination to study for the law. And as soon as he came out of prison he enrolled himself as a student at Gray's Inn. It was on the strength of this heroic act that he bought himself the wig and gown that I still see trailing after him in their cardboard box as he criss-crosses the globe in his search for El Dorado.

*

My mother, Olive, crept out of our lives when I was five and my brother Tony was seven and both of us were fast asleep. In the creaking jargon of the secret world I later entered, her departure was a well-planned exfiltration operation, executed in accordance with the best principles of need-to-know security. The conspirators selected a night when my father, Ronnie, was billed to come home from London late or not at all. This was not hard. Fresh from the deprivations of prison, Ronnie had set himself up in business in the West End, where he was diligently making up for lost time. What kind of business we could only guess, but its rise had been mercurial.

Ronnie had barely drawn his first breath of free air before he had gathered to himself the scattered nucleus of his Court. At the same dizzy speed, we abandoned the humble brick house in St Albans to which my grandfather with much frowning and finger-wagging had conducted us upon Ronnie's release, and established ourselves in the riding-school-and-limousine suburb of Rickmansworth, less than an hour's drive from London's most expensive fleshpots. With the Court in attendance we had wintered in splendour at the Kulm Hotel in St Moritz. In Rickmansworth our bedroom cupboards were stuffed with new toys on an Arab scale. Weekends were one long adult revel while Tony and I persuaded riotous uncles to kick footballs with us, and gazed at the bookless walls of our nursery while we listened to the music from downstairs. Among the less probable visitors of those days was Learie Constantine, later Sir Learie and later still Lord Constantine, arguably the greatest West Indian cricketer of all time. It is one of the many paradoxes of Ronnie's nature that he liked to be seen in the company of people of brown or black skin, which in those days made him a rarity. Learie Constantine played 'French cricket' with us and we loved him dearly. I have a memory of a jovial domestic ceremony in which, without benefit of priest, he was formally inducted as either my godfather or my brother's, neither of us seems sure which.

'But where did the money come from?' I asked my mother at one of the many debriefings that attended our reunion. She had no idea. Business was either beneath her or over her head. The rougher it got, the further she stayed away from it. Ronnie was crooked, she said, but wasn't everyone in business crooked?

The house from which Olive made her covert exit was a mock-Tudor mansion called Hazel Cottage. In darkness, the long, descending garden and diamond-leaded windows gave it the appearance of a forest hunting-lodge. I imagine a slim new moon, or none. All through the interminable day of her escape, I see her engaged in surreptitious preparations, filling her white hide Harrods suitcase with operational necessities – a warm pullover, East Anglia will be freezing; where in heaven's name did I leave my driving licence? – casting nervous glances at her St Moritz gold watch while maintaining her composure towards her children, the cook, the cleaning woman, the gardener and the German nanny, Annaliese.

Olive no longer trusts any of us. Her sons are Ronnie's wholly owned subsidiaries. Annaliese, she suspects, has been sleeping with the enemy. Olive's close friend Mabel lives only a few miles away with her parents in a flat overlooking Moor Park Golf Club, but Mabel is no more privy to the escape plan than is Annaliese. Mabel has had two abortions in three years after becoming pregnant by a man she refuses to identify, and Olive is beginning to smell a rat. In the mock-raftered drawing room, as she tiptoes through it with her white suitcase, stands one of the earliest pre-war television sets, an upended mahogany coffin with a tiny screen that shows fast-moving spots and just occasionally the misted features of a man in a dinner jacket. It is switched off. Muzzled. She will never watch it again.

'Why didn't you take us with you?' I asked her at one debriefing.

'Because you'd have come after us, darling,' Olive replied, meaning as usual not me, but Ronnie. 'You wouldn't have rested till you got your precious boys back.'

Besides, she said, there was the all-important question of our education. Ronnie was so ambitious for his sons that somehow, more by crook than by hook but never mind, he would get us into classy schools. Olive would never have been able to manage that. Well, would she, darling?

I can't describe Olive well. As a child, I didn't know her, and as an adult I didn't understand her. Of her abilities, I know as little as I know of anything else about her. Was she kind-hearted but weak? Was she tortured by her separation from her two growing first-born children, or was she a woman of no particularly deep emotions who was simply dragged through life by other people's decisions? Did she have latent talents crying to come to the surface, but never succeeding? In any one of these identities I would willingly recognize myself, but I don't know which, if any, to choose.

The white hide suitcase sits today in my house in London and has become an object of intense speculation to me. As with all major works of art, there is tension in its immobility. Will it suddenly leap off again, leaving no forwarding address? Outwardly, it is a well-to-do bride's honeymoon suitcase with a good brand name. The two uniformed doormen who in my memory stand forever before the glass doors of the Kulm Hotel in St Moritz, brushing the snow from guests' boots with a dramatic flourish, would immediately identify its owner as a member of the tipping classes. But when I am tired and my memory is out foraging for itself, the interior of the suitcase breathes a heavy sexuality.

Partly, the tattered pink silk lining is the reason: a skimpy petticoat waiting to be ripped off. But there is also somewhere in my head a hazily remembered image of carnal flurry – of a bedroom skirmish I have intruded upon when I am very young – and pink is its colour. Was this the time I saw Ronnie and Annaliese making love? Or Ronnie and Olive? Or Olive and Annaliese? Or all three of them together? Or none of them, except in my dreams? And does this pseudo-memory portray some kind of childish erotic paradise from which I was shut out once Olive had packed her bag and left?

As an historical artefact, the suitcase is beyond price. It is the only known object that bears Olive's initials from her Ronnie period: O.M.C. for Olive Moore Cornwell, printed in black beneath the sweated leather handle. Whose sweat? Olive's? Or the sweat of her fellow conspirator and rescuer, a gingery, irascible land agent who was also the driver of her getaway car? I have an idea that, like Olive, her rescuer was married, and, like Olive, had children. If that's so, were they, too, fast asleep? As the professional intimate of landed gentry, her rescuer also had class, whereas Ronnie in Olive's judgement had none. Olive never forgave Ronnie for marrying above himself.

All through her later life she hammered this theme, until I began to understand that Ronnie's social inferiority was the fig leaf of dignity which she clutched to herself while she continued to trail helplessly after him in the years of their supposed estrangement. She let him take her out to lunches in the West End, listening to his fantasized accounts of his prodigious wealth, though little if any of it ever reached her, and after the coffee and the brandy – or so I picture it – yielded to him in some safe house before he scurried off to make another fantasy million. By keeping open the wounds that Ronnie's low breeding had inflicted on her, by deriding to herself his vulgarities of speech and lapses of social delicacy, she was able to blame him for everything and herself for nothing, except her stupid acquiescence.

Yet Olive was anything but stupid. She had a witty, barbed and lucid tongue. Her long, clear sentences were print-ready, her letters cogent, rhythmical and amusing. In my presence, she was painfully well spoken, like Mrs Thatcher halfway through her elocution course. But in other people's presence, I learned recently from one who knew her better than I did, she was a mynah bird, instantly adopting the vocal effects of whoever she was with, even if it took her all the way down the social scale. And yes, I too have an ear for voices. So perhaps that's a bit I got from her, for Ronnie had none. And I love to mimic them, and get them on to the page. But what she read, if anything at all, I've no more idea than I have of her genetic contribution to my existence. Looking back, listening to her other children, I know there was a mother there to be learned. But I never learned her, and perhaps I didn't want to.

In computer-dating terms, it has always seemed to me, Ronnie and Olive were nevertheless remarkably well matched. But while Olive was willing to be defined by whoever claimed to love her,

Ronnie was a five-star conman endowed with the unfortunate gift of awakening love in men and women equally. Olive's resentment of my father's social origins did not stop at the principal offender. Ronnie's father – my own revered grandfather, Frank, ex-Mayor of Poole, Freemason, teetotaller, preacher, icon of our family probity, no less – was, according to Olive, as bent as Ronnie. It was Frank who had put Ronnie up to his first scam, had financed it, remote-controlled it, then kept his head down when Ronnie took the fall. She even found a bad word for Ronnie's *grandfather*, whom I remember as a white-bearded D. H. Lawrence lookalike riding a tricycle at ninety. Where on earth I was supposed to stand in this wholesale condemnation of our male line remained unsaid. But then I'd had the education, hadn't I, darling? I'd had the language and manners of respectable people beaten into me.

*

There's a family anecdote about Ronnie that remains unverified, but I would like to believe it because it speaks for the good heart in Ronnie that so often, and so frustratingly, defied his detractors.

Ronnie is on the run but hasn't yet skipped England. The fraud charges are so pressing that the British police have launched a manhunt. Amid the hue and cry, an old business pal of Ronnie's has died suddenly and must be buried. In the hope that Ronnie will attend the funeral, the police stake it out. Plainclothes detectives mingle with the mourners, but Ronnie is not among them. Next day, a member of the grieving family goes to tend the new grave. Ronnie is standing alone at the graveside.

*

Now move to the eighties, and this isn't just a family tale, it happened in broad daylight in the presence of my British publisher, my literary agent and my wife.

281

I'm on a book tour in Southern Australia. Luncheon in the great marquee. I sit at a trestle table, my wife and my publisher beside me, my agent looking on. I'm signing my latest novel, A *Perfect Spy*, which contains a not very veiled portrait of Ronnie, whose life I have touched on in my after-lunch speech. A lady of age in a wheelchair rolls energetically past the queue, and tells me with some heat that I've got it completely wrong about Ronnie being in prison in Hong Kong. She was living with him all the time he was in the colony, so he couldn't possibly have gone to prison, or she'd have noticed, wouldn't she?

While I'm still measuring my response – for instance, to the effect that I had recently had a friendly chat with Ronnie's Hong Kong jailer – a second lady of similar age bowls up.

'Utter bloody nonsense!' she thunders. 'He was living with *me* in Bangkok and only *commuting* to Hong Kong!'

I assure them that they are both probably right.

*

You will not be surprised to read then that in low moments, like many sons of many fathers, I ask myself which bits of me still belong to Ronnie, and how much of me is mine. Is there really a big difference, I wonder, between the man who sits at his desk and dreams up scams on the blank page (*me*), and the man who puts on a clean shirt every morning and, with nothing in his pocket but imagination, sallies forth to con his victim (*Ronnie*)?

Ronnie the conman could spin you a story out of the air, sketch in a character who did not exist, and paint a golden opportunity when there wasn't one. He could blind you with bogus detail or helpfully clarify a non-existent knotty point if you weren't quick enough on the uptake to grasp the technicalities of his con first time round. He could withhold a great secret on grounds of confidentiality, then whisper it to your ear alone because he has decided to trust you.

And if all that isn't part and parcel of the writer's art, tell me what is.

*

It was Ronnie's misfortune to be an anachronism in his own lifetime. In the twenties when he set out in business, an unscrupulous trader could bankrupt himself in one town, and next day raise credit in another fifty miles away. But as time went by, communications began to catch up with Ronnie the way they caught up with Butch Cassidy and the Sundance Kid. I am sure he was deeply shocked when Singapore Special Branch confronted him with his British police record. And shocked again when, summarily deported to Indonesia, he was put behind bars for currency offences and gun-running. And more shocked still when a few years later the Swiss police dragged him out of his hotel bedroom in the Dolder Grand hotel in Zurich, and banged him up in the district jail. Reading recently how the gentlemen of FIFA were whisked from their beds in the Baur au Lac in Zurich and distributed to selected prison cells around the town, I see Ronnie forty-odd years ago suffering the same humiliation at the same hour at the hands of the same Swiss police.

Grand hotels are the conman's catnip. Until that dawn in Zurich, Ronnie had stayed in any number of them and his system had never failed: take the best suite the best hotel has to offer, entertain lavishly, endear yourself to the doormen, headwaiters and above all the concierges, i.e. tip them handsomely and often. Make phone calls all over the world and when the hotel presents its first bill, say you have passed it to your people for settlement. Or, if you are playing the long game, delay the first bill then settle it, but nothing thereafter.

As soon as you sense you're outstaying your welcome, pack a light suitcase, slip the concierge a twenty or a fifty, and tell him you've got pressing business out of town which may detain you for the night. Or if he's that kind of concierge, give him a fat wink and say you have an obligation to a lady friend – oh, and will he kindly make sure your suite is safely locked because of all the valuable kit it's got in it? – having already made sure that whatever valuable kit you've got, if any, is already in your light suitcase. And maybe, for extra cover, you give the concierge your golf clubs to look after by way of reassurance, but only if needs must, because you love your golf.

But that dawn raid at the Dolder told Ronnie that the game was up. And today, forget it. They have your credit card details. They know where your children go to school.

*

Might Ronnie with his proven powers of deception have made a spymaster? True, when he deceived people he also deceived himself, although that wouldn't necessarily disqualify him. But if he possessed a secret – his own or anyone else's – he was positively uncomfortable until he had shared it, which would certainly have presented a problem.

Show business? After all, he'd made a good fist of looking over a major Berlin film studio under the pretext of representing myself and Paramount Pictures, so why stop there? And Hollywood, as we all know, has a well-attested habit of taking conmen to its bosom.

Or how about actor? Didn't he love the long mirror? Hadn't he spent his whole life pretending to be people he wasn't?

But Ronnie never wanted to be a star. He wanted to be Ronnie, a cosmos of one.

As to becoming a writer of his own fictions, forget it. He didn't envy my literary notoriety. He owned it.

*

It is 1963. I have just arrived in New York on my first ever visit to the United States. *The Spy Who Came in from the Cold* is riding at the top of the charts. My American publisher escorts me to the 21 Club for a grand dinner. As the maître d' shows us to our table, I see Ronnie seated in a corner.

For years we have been estranged. I had no idea he was in America, but he is, and twelve feet away, with a brandy-and-ginger at his elbow. How on earth did he get here? Easily. He called up my soft-hearted American publisher and plucked at his heart strings. He played the Irish card. One look at my publisher's name tells him he is of Irish origin.

We ask Ronnie to join us at our table. Humbly, he accepts, bringing his brandy-and-ginger with him; but only for a quick drink, he insists, then he'll leave us to ourselves. He is sweet and proud and pats my arm, and tells me with tears in his eyes that he hasn't been a bad father, has he, son, and we've done all right together, haven't we, then? Yes, yes, we've done fine together, Dad, just fine, I agree.

Then Jack, my publisher, who's a proud father as well as being Irish, says why doesn't Ronnie finish whatever he's drinking and let's have a bottle of champagne. So we do, and Ronnie raises his glass and drinks to our book. Note the *our*. Then Jack says, hell Ronnie, why don't you just sit here and eat with us too? So Ronnie lets himself be persuaded, and orders himself a nice mixed grill.

Out on the pavement we have our obligatory bear-hug, and he weeps, which he does a lot: big, sobbing shrugs. I weep too, and ask him whether he's all right for money, to which amazingly he replies that he is. Then he gives me some advice for life, in case I'm letting our book's success go to our head:

'You may be a successful writer, son,' he says through more sobs, 'but you're not a *celebrity*.'

And having left me with this incomprehensible warning, he sets off into the night without saying where he's going, which I guess means he has a lady on the go, because he almost always has.

*

Months afterwards, I'm able to piece together the back-story to this encounter. Ronnie was on the run, with no money and nowhere to live.

However, New York City's real estate agents were offering a month's free accommodation to first-time tenants in new developments. Under different names Ronnie was flat-hopping: a free month here, a free month there, and so far they hadn't caught up with him, but God help him when they did. It could only have been out of pride that he turned down my offer of money, because he was desperate and had already touched my elder brother for the better part of his savings.

On the day after our dinner at the 21 Club, he had called up the sales department of my American publishing house, introduced himself as my father – and of course as a close friend of my publisher – ordered a couple of hundred copies of *our book*, charged them to the author's account, and signed them in his own name for handing around as his business card.

I have by now received a score of such books, with the owners' requests that I add my signature to Ronnie's. The standard version reads 'Signed by the Author's Father', with an extra large F for Father. And mine in return reads, 'Signed by the Author's Father's Son', with an extra large S for Son.

But try being Ronnie for a moment, as I have done too often. Try standing alone on the streets of New York, stony-broke. You've tapped whoever you can tap, milked your contacts dry. In England you're on the Wanted list, and you're on the Wanted list here in New York. You daren't show your passport, you're using false names to hop between apartments you can't pay for, and all that stands between you and perdition is your animal wit and a double-breasted pinstripe from Berman of Savile Row that you home-press every evening. It's the kind of situation they dream up for you at spy school: 'Now let's see how you talk your way out of this one.' Allowing for the odd lapse now and then, Ronnie would have passed that test with flying colours.

*

The ship that Ronnie always dreamed of came home shortly after his death, in one of those drowsy Dickensian law courts where complex disputes about money are thrashed out over a very long time. For caution's sake, I will name the afflicted London suburb Cudlip, because it's entirely possible that the same legal battle is rumbling to this day, just as it had rumbled through the last twenty-odd years of Ronnie's life, then rumbled without him for another two.

The facts of the case are simplicity itself. Ronnie had befriended Cudlip's local council, notably its planning committee. How this had come about is easily imagined. They were fellow Baptists, or fellow Masons, or cricketers, or snooker players. Or they were married men in their prime who, until they met Ronnie, had never tasted the nocturnal pleasures of the West End. Perhaps they also looked forward to a slice of what Ronnie had assured them would be a big cake.

However it had come about, there was no question in law or anywhere else that Cudlip Council had signed over to one of Ronnie's eighty-three penniless companies the authorization to erect a hundred desirable houses in the middle of Cudlip's green belt. And no sooner had they done this than Ronnie, who had bought the land for peanuts on the understanding that it could never be built on, sold it complete with planning consent to a large construction company for a large sum of money. Champagne flowed, the Court was jubilant. Ronnie had pulled off the deal of a lifetime. My brother Tony and I would never want for anything again.

And as so often in his life, Ronnie was nearly right, had it not been for the citizens of Cudlip who, roused to action by their local newspaper, declared with one voice that any attempt to build houses or anything else on their precious green belt – their football field, their tennis courts, their children's playground, their picnic area – would take place over their dead bodies. And such was their passion that in no time they had obtained a court order leaving Ronnie clutching a signed contract with the construction company, but not a penny piece of their money.

Ronnie was as outraged as the citizens of Cudlip. Like them, he had never known such perfidy. It wasn't the money, he insisted, it was the principle. He rallied a team of lawyers, nothing but the best. They concluded he had a strong case, and agreed to take it on. No win, no fee. The Cudlip land thereafter became the gold standard of our faith in Ronnie. For the next twenty years and more, any temporary setback would be as nothing once the great day of reckoning came. Ronnie could be writing to me from Dublin, or Hong Kong, or Penang, or Timbuctoo, the mantra with its strange capital letters never varied: 'One day, Son, and it may well come After I am Judged, British Justice will Prevail.'

And sure enough, within months of his death, justice did indeed prevail. I was not in court to hear the verdict. My lawyer had advised me not to display a flicker of interest in Ronnie's estate lest I be stuck with its enormous debts. The courtroom was packed, according to my sources. The barristers' benches were particularly full. Three judges were sitting, but one spoke for all, and his language was so convoluted that for a while no layman could catch his drift.

Then gradually the news seeped through. The court had found for the plaintiff: for Ronnie. Outright. The jackpot. No ifs or buts. No on-the-one-hand and on-the-other-hand. Ronnie from the grave had won the slam-dunk victory that he had always insisted would be his: a People's victory over twerps and airy-fairies, for which read unbelievers and intellectuals, the posthumous vindication of all his striving.

Then a quiet falls. Amid the rejoicing a clerk has once more called the court to order. The handshaking and backslapping give way to a collective unease. A barrister who has not so far addressed the court craves the attention of their Lordships. I have my own arbitrary picture of him. He is puffy and pompous and pimply and his wig is too small for his head. He represents the Crown, he tells their Lordships. Specifically, he represents Her Majesty's Inland Revenue, which he describes as 'a preferential creditor' in the matter upon which their Lordships have just passed judgement. And to be precise, and not to waste their Lordships' precious time, he would like, with infinite respect, to petition that the entire sum awarded to the plaintiff's estate be sequestered in order to defray, if only in small part, the far larger sums, reaching back over a great number of years, owed by the deceased to Her Majesty's Inland Revenue.

*

Ronnie is dead, and I am revisiting Vienna in order to breathe the city air while I write him into the semi-autobiographical novel I am at last free to ponder. Not the Sacher again; I have a dread that the waiters will remember Ronnie crashing down on to the table and me half carrying him out. My plane into Schwechat is delayed, and the reception desk of the small hotel that I have chosen at random is in the charge of an elderly night porter. He looks on silently as I fill in the registration form. Then he speaks in soft, venerable Viennese German.

'Your father was a great man,' he says. 'You treated him disgracefully.'

34

To Reggie with thanks

You have to be closer to my age, I suppose, to remember Reginald Bosanquet, the impish, hard-living, hard-drinking television newsreader who captured the nation's heart and died ridiculously early, I never knew quite what of. Reggie was my contemporary at Oxford and had all the things I didn't: a private income, a sports car, beautiful women and a kind of premature adulthood to go with them.

We liked each other, but there is only so much time you can spend with a man who lives the life you dream of and can afford it when you can't. Besides, I was a shadowy fellow in those days, earnest and a bit haunted. Reggie was neither. Also, I wasn't just broke, but – halfway through my second year – seriously insolvent, since my father had recently made one of his spectacular bankruptcies, and his cheque for my term's fees had bounced. And though my College was behaving with exemplary forbearance, I really saw no way to remain in Oxford for the rest of the academic year.

But that was to reckon without Reggie, who drifted into my room one day, probably with a hangover, shoved an envelope at me and drifted out. It contained a cheque made out to me by his Trustees, large enough to pay off my debts and keep me at university for the next six months. The accompanying letter was also from the Trustees. They said that Reggie had told them of my misfortune, that the money came from his own resources, and that I should pay it back at my convenience and only when I was able. And that it was Reggie's wish that, on all matters relating to the loan, I should correspond directly with the Trustees, since he didn't hold with mixing money with friendship.

It was several years before I was able to repay the last instalment, and with it the interest that I reckoned the capital would have earned. His Trustees sent me a polite note of thanks, and returned the interest. Reggie, they explained, didn't feel interest was appropriate in the circumstances.*

* Written for Victim Support, 1998.

35

The most wanted man

The mysterious early-morning phone call came from Karel Reisz, the Czech-born British film director best known at that time for *Saturday Night and Sunday Morning*. It is 1967, and I am trying my hardest to live alone in an ugly penthouse in Maida Vale. Reisz and I have been working together, unsuccessfully as it turned out, on a screenplay of a novel of mine called *The Naive and Sentimental Lover*, not everybody's cup of tea to say the least. But Reisz isn't calling about our movie script, as I can tell from his voice, which is sonorous and conspiratorial.

'David, are you alone?'

Yes, Karel, very.

'Then if you could pop round here just as soon as possible, that would be a help.'

The Reisz family lived no great distance away in a red-brick Victorian house in Belsize Park. Probably I walked there. When your marriage is failing, you walk. Reisz opened the front door so fast he must have been watching out for me. Having dropped the lock, he led me to the big kitchen, which was where life in the Reisz household was lived: seated round a thick, circular pine table with sugar biscuits on a rotating lazy susan, with pots of tea and coffee strewn over it, and jugs of fruit juice, and a busy telephone on a long cord, and in those days lots of ashtrays; all this in part for the convenience of such improbable habitués as Vanessa Redgrave, Simone Signoret and Albert Finney, who would drift in, help themselves, chat a bit and drift out. I have always imagined that before Reisz's parents were murdered in Auschwitz, this was the way they had lived.

I sat down. There were five faces staring at me: the actress Betsy Blair, who was Reisz's wife, for once not talking on the telephone; the movie director Lindsay Anderson of *This Sporting Life* fame, which Reisz had produced for him. And seated between these two film directors, a smiling, nervous, charismatic younger man of classically Slav looks whom I had never seen before.

'David, this is Vladimir,' Reisz said gravely, at which the young man sprang to his feet and shook my hand vigorously – I could almost say desperately – across the table.

And seated close behind this effusive young man, a young woman who, judging by her studious concern for him, had more the appearance of a minder than a lover, or – in that setting – of a theatrical agent or casting director, for the young man, even at a glance, had presence.

'Vladimir is a Czech actor,' Reisz announced.

Great.

'And he wants to remain in Britain.'

Oh, really. I see – or something of the kind from me.

Anderson's turn: 'We thought that with your sort of background you'd know the people who handle this stuff.'

General silence round the table. Everyone waits for me to say something.

'So defect,' I suggest lamely. 'Vladimir wants to defect.'

'If that's what you want to call it,' Anderson says disparagingly, and the silence returns.

It is becoming apparent to me that Anderson has some sort of proprietorial interest in Vladimir, and that Reisz, the bilingual fellow Czech, is more intermediary than prime mover. This made for a certain awkwardness. I had met Anderson on three occasions at best, none of them comfortable. For some unexplained reason, we had got off on the wrong foot, and stayed there. Born to a military family in India, Anderson had been educated at a British public school (Cheltenham, which he later punished with his film *If . . .*) and at Oxford. In the war he had served in military intelligence in Delhi. And it was this last, I believe, that from the outset had disposed him against me. As an avowed socialist who was at daggers drawn with the Establishment that had spawned him, he had cast me as some kind of backstairs apparatchik in the class struggle, and there wasn't much I could usefully do about it.

'Vladimir is actually Vladimir *Pucholt*,' I hear Reisz explain. And when my reaction falls short of whatever they all expect of me – which is to say, I do not give out a gasp of admiration, or cry 'not *the* Vladimir Pucholt' – Reisz hurries in with an explanation, to be quickly enlarged upon by the rest of the table. Vladimir Pucholt, I learn to my humiliation, is a shining Czech star of stage and screen, best known for his leading role in Miloš Forman's A *Blonde in Love* (also translated, irritatingly, as *Loves of a Blonde*), which enjoyed international success. Forman also used him in his earlier films, and has declared Vladimir to be his favourite actor.

'Which means in short' – Anderson again, aggressively, as if I have questioned Pucholt's worth and he feels obliged to correct me – 'that *any* country that takes him can count itself *bloody* lucky. Which I trust you will make clear to your *people*.'

But I haven't got any *people*. The only *people* I have of the official or nearly official variety are my former colleagues in the spy world. And God forbid that I should call up one or other of them and tell him I have a potential Czech defector on my hands. I can readily imagine the kind of solicitous question that Pucholt would be invited to answer, like: are you a plant by Czech Intelligence and, if so, can you be turned? Or: name for us other Czech dissidents presently in Czechoslovakia who might be interested in working for us. And, assuming you haven't already bubbled your intentions to your twelve best friends, might you consider returning to Czechoslovakia and doing a little of this and that for us?

But Pucholt, I am beginning to sense, would have given them short shrift. He is no kind of fugitive, or not in his own eyes. He arrived in England legally, with the blessing of the Czech authorities. Before leaving, he discreetly put his affairs in order, fulfilling all outstanding film and theatre contracts and taking care to sign no new ones. He has visited Britain before, and the Czech authorities had no reason to suppose that this time he won't be coming back.

On his arrival in Britain, it seems, he at first went to ground. By some indistinct route, Lindsay Anderson then got to hear of his intentions and offered help. Pucholt and Anderson knew each other from Prague and London. Anderson then turned to his friend Reisz, and between the three of them a plan of sorts was drawn up. Pucholt had made clear from the outset that in no circumstance would he apply for political asylum. To do so, he argued, would bring down the wrath of the Czech authorities on those he had left behind – friends, family, teachers, fellow professionals. Perhaps he had in mind the example of the Soviet ballet dancer Rudolf Nureyev, whose defection six years earlier had been trumpeted as a victory for the West. As a result, Nureyev's friends and family in Russia had been cast into outer darkness.

With this stipulation foremost in their minds, Reisz, Anderson and Pucholt put their plan into effect. There would be no fanfares, no special-case treatment. Pucholt would be just one more disaffected young East European man walking off the street and seeking the indulgence of the British authorities. Together, Anderson and Pucholt set out for the Home Office and took their places in the queue for those seeking to extend their United Kingdom visas. Arriving at the desk of the Home Office clerk, Pucholt shoved his Czech passport through the little window.

'For how long?' the clerk asked, his rubber stamp poised.

To which Anderson, never one to mince his words, least of all when addressing a lackey of the class system he abhors, retorts 'For ever.'

*

I have a clear picture of the lengthy exchanges that now took place between Pucholt and the senior Home Office official assigned to his case.

In the one corner we have the laudable confusion of a ranking civil servant determined to do the right thing by the applicant, but also by the rulebook. All he asks is that Pucholt state unequivocally that were he to return to his home country, he would be persecuted. Once he's done that, fine, box ticked, visa extended indefinitely, and welcome to Britain, Mr Pucholt.

And in the other corner we have the laudable obstinacy of Pucholt, who flatly refuses to say what is asked of him, because by saying it he will have claimed political asylum, and thereby imperilled the people he has vowed not to imperil. So, no sir, I would *not* be persecuted, thank you. I am a popular Czech actor, and I would be welcomed back with open arms. I might be rebuked, I might suffer some token retribution. But I would not be persecuted, and I am not seeking political asylum, thank you.

And there is even a bit of black comedy to be had in this stand-off. Back home in Czechoslovakia, Pucholt had fallen into serious disfavour, and been forbidden to act in any film for two years. He had been invited – ordered is a better word – to play the part of a Czech borstal boy who, after being inspired by his dedicated borstal teachers in the highest principles of Marxism-Leninism, finds himself unable to handle life in the less enlightened, bourgeois-oriented society to which he has been restored.

Unimpressed by the script, Pucholt had asked to spend a few days as a borstal inmate. Having done so, he was more certain than ever that the play was rubbish and, to the dismay of his handlers, declined the part. Tempers flared, contracts were thrust at him, but he wouldn't budge. The result: a two-year ban that in better circumstances he could perfectly well have used as grounds for claiming he was the victim of political persecution in his home country.

A week passed before Pucholt was once more invited to the Home Office, this time to be informed by a conflicted official, in the best tradition of British compromise, that while he would not be forcibly repatriated to Czechoslovakia, he would have to leave Britain within ten days.

Which is where we are now, seated round the Reisz table in a state of muted alarm. Either the ten days are up, or they're about to be, so what do you suggest we do about it, David? And the short answer is, David has no idea what we do about it: and all the less so when somewhere in our circular discussions it emerges that Pucholt has not come to Britain in order to pursue his stellar acting career, but 'because, David' – as he earnestly explains to me across the table – 'I wish to become doctor'.

*

He concedes that becoming a doctor will take a bit of time. He calculates seven years. He has a few basic Czech qualifications, but doubts whether they will count for much in the United Kingdom.

I hear him say all this. I recognize the fervour in his voice and the zeal in his expressive Slav features. I try my best to look wise and smile approvingly at this noble vision of self-dedication.

But I know something about actors. And I know, as everyone round the table knows, how actors are able to latch on to a hypothetical version of themselves and become it; but only for as long as the show lasts. After that, it's off they go again, in search of the next new person to become.

'Well, that's great, Vladimir,' I exclaim, temporizing for all I'm worth. 'Still, I guess that while you're doing your medical training, you'll keep one foot in the acting world, won't you? Brush up your English, do a bit of theatre, take on the odd movie role that comes up?' – casting an eye at our two film directors for support, and not getting any.

Not so, David, he replies. He has been an actor since boyhood. He has been swept from one role to another – often roles for which he has no regard, for example the borstal boy – and now he intends to become a doctor, which is why he wishes to remain in Britain. I glance round the table. Nobody seems surprised. Everyone but me accepts that Vladimir Pucholt, Czech heart-throb of stage and screen, *wishes only to become doctor.* Do they ask themselves, as I do, whether this is an actor's fantasy rather than a life's ambition? I have no way to tell.

But it barely matters, because by now I have agreed to be the man they think I am. I will speak to my *people*, I hear myself saying, even though I haven't got any people. I will find the best way to bring this matter to a successful and speedy conclusion, as we backstairs apparatchiks have it. I will go home now, but I will be in touch. Exits left, head held high.

*

In the half-century that has since elapsed, I have occasionally asked myself why on earth I offered to do all this when Anderson and Reisz, as world-class film directors, had many more *people* within their reach, more friends in high places than I ever had, not to mention smart lawyers. Reisz, I knew for a fact, was hugger-mugger with Lord Goodman, *éminence grise* and legal adviser to Prime Minister Harold Wilson. Anderson, for all his socialist rigour, had impeccable upper-class credentials and, like Reisz, close connections with the ruling Labour Party.

I think the answer may be that, with my life in a God-awful mess, it was a relief to be sorting out someone else's. As a young soldier in Austria, I had interrogated scores of refugees from Eastern Europe on the off chance that one or two of them were spies. None to my knowledge was, but quite a few were Czech. Here at least was one I could do something about.

I am not sure any more where Vladimir slept over the next few nights, whether it was at Reisz's house, or the house of his companion, or Lindsay Anderson's house, or even mine. But I do remember that he spent long daylight hours in my ugly penthouse, pacing or standing at the big picture window and staring out.

Meanwhile, I am pulling every string I know to have the Home

Office decision overturned. I ring my genial British publisher. He suggests I phone the Home Affairs correspondent of the *Guardian* newspaper. I do. The Home Affairs correspondent has no direct line to the Home Secretary, who is Roy Jenkins, but he does happen to know Mrs Jenkins. Or rather his wife does. He will talk to his wife now, and call me back.

My hopes rise. Roy Jenkins is a brave and outspoken liberal. The *Guardian* correspondent calls me back. So here's what you do. You write the Home Secretary a strictly formal letter, no flattery, no schmaltz. 'Dear Home Secretary.' You type it, you set out the facts and sign it. If your man wants to be a doctor, say so in the letter and don't pretend he's going to be God's gift to the National Theatre. But here's the difference. You address the *envelope* not to Roy Jenkins, Esquire, but to Mrs Jenkins, his wife. She will make sure the letter is sitting on his breakfast table tomorrow morning, next to his boiled egg. And you hand-deliver it. Tonight. To this address.

I don't type. I have never typed. The penthouse contains an electric typewriter, but there's nobody around to use it. I call Jane. In those days, Jane and I are circling round each other. Today she is my wife. With Pucholt staring out at the London skyline, I write a 'Dear Home Secretary' letter and Jane types it. I address the envelope to Mrs Jenkins, seal it, and we set off for Notting Hill, or wherever Mr & Mrs Jenkins live.

Forty-eight hours later, Vladimir Pucholt is granted leave to remain in Britain indefinitely. No evening newspaper crows about a celebrated Czech movie star defecting to the Western cause. He may start his medical studies as soon, and as quietly, as he wishes. The news reaches me while I am lunching with my literary agent. I return to the penthouse to find Vladimir no longer staring out of the window, but standing out on the balcony in jeans and trainers. It's a warm, sunny afternoon. From a sheet of A4 paper on my desk, he has cut himself a paper glider. Leaning too far forward over the railings for my comfort, he waits for a favourable breeze, launches it and watches it potter away over the London rooftops. Up till now, he later

explained to me, he hadn't been able to fly. But now that he had permission to stay, it was all right.

*

This is not about to become a story about my boundless generosity.
It's about Vladimir's achievement in becoming one of Toronto's
best-loved and most dedicated paediatricians.

Somehow or other – and to this day I'm not sure how – I became
responsible for footing the bill for his medical training in Britain.
Even at the time, that seemed an entirely natural thing to do. I was
at the height of my earning power, Vladimir was at the nadir of his.
My offer of support deprived me of nothing. It caused me and my
family not one second of hardship, then or ever. Vladimir's financial
needs, by his own insistence, were frighteningly modest. His determination to repay every penny as soon as possible was ferocious. To
spare the two of us awkward discussion, I left it to my accountant to
settle the figures with him: this much to live on, this much to study,
this much for transport, rent, and so on. The negotiations went into
reverse. I pressed for more, Vladimir for less.

His first medical job was as a laboratory assistant in London. From
London he moved to a teaching hospital in Sheffield. In painstaking
letters of lyrical, greatly improved English, he extolled the miracle of
medicine, of surgery, of healing and of the human body as a work of
creation. His specializations are in paediatric medicine and neonatal
intensive care. With unabashed enthusiasm, he writes even today of the
thousands of children and babies who have passed through his care.

I have always found it humbling, and slightly embarrassing, to
have played the role of angel at so little sacrifice to myself and to
such extraordinary benefit to others. And more embarrassing still
that, almost to the day of his qualification, I never entirely believed
that he would make it.

*

It is now 2007, a full forty years since Vladimir launched his paper glider from the balcony of the penthouse that I have long since got rid of. I am living half in Cornwall, half in Hamburg, while I write a novel called A Most Wanted Man about a young asylum seeker, not from Czechoslovakia as was, but from today's Chechnya. He is only half a Slav; the other half of him is Chechen. His name is Issa, meaning Jesus, and he is a Muslim, not a Christian. His one ambition is to study to become a great doctor and cure the suffering people of his homeland, children a speciality.

Imprisoned in the attic of a Hamburg warehouse while the spies fight over his future, he fashions paper gliders from a roll of unused wallpaper and makes them fly across the room to freedom.

Sooner than I could have believed possible, Vladimir repaid every penny he ever borrowed from me. What he didn't know – and neither did I until I came to write A Most Wanted Man – was that he had made me the non-returnable gift of a fictional character.

36

Stephen Spender's credit card

I think it was in 1991 that I was invited to a private dinner in Hampstead to meet Stephen Spender, essayist, dramatist, novelist, disillusioned communist, knight of the realm, former Poet Laureate of America – need I go on?

We were six at table and Spender was holding the floor. At eighty-two, he cut a fine figure: white-haired, leonine, vigorous, full of wit. His theme was the evanescence of fame – his own, presumably, but I couldn't help thinking he was slipping me a veiled warning – and the need on the part of those touched by it to accept with grace their return to obscurity. By way of illustration he then told us the following story:

He had recently returned from a coast-to-coast car journey across the United States. Crossing the Nevada desert, he spotted a rare gas station and thought it prudent to fill up. A handwritten notice, presumably intended to discourage thieves, advised that the owner accepted credit cards only.

Spender presented his credit card. The garage owner scrutinized it in silence. Finally, he vented his concern:

'Only Stephen Spender *I* ever heard of is a poet,' he objected. 'And he's *dead*.'

37

Advice to an aspiring novelist

'Before I finish writing for the day I make sure I've left something under my belt for tomorrow. Sleep works wonders.'

Source: Graham Greene to self, Vienna, 1965

38

The last official secret

When I was a young and carefree spy it was only natural that I should believe that the nation's hottest secrets were housed in a chipped green Chubb safe that was tucked away at the end of a labyrinth of dingy corridors on the top floor of 54 Broadway, opposite St James's Park tube station, in the private office occupied by the Chief of the Secret Service.

Broadway, as we called it, was old and dusty and, as a matter of Service philosophy, inconvenient. Of the three creaky lifts, the Chief had one to himself which conveyed him, in its own sweet time, directly to the hallowed heights of the top floor. Only the chosen few had a key to it. We lesser mortals made our ascent to him by way of a narrow wooden staircase watched over by a fish-eye mirror and, on our arrival on the top-floor landing, by a stone-faced janitor seated on a kitchen chair.

I think it was we young entrants who loved the building most: for its perpetual twilight, its smell of the wars we hadn't fought and the intrigues we could only dream of; for the poky invitation-only bar, where old hands fell silent as you walked past; and for its dark, dusty library of espionage literature, presided over by an elderly librarian with flowing white hair who, as a young spy himself, had run with the Bolshevik revolutionaries in the streets of Petersburg, and tapped out his secret messages from a cellar next to the Winter Palace. Both the movie of *The Spy Who Came in from the Cold* and the BBC version of *Tinker Tailor Soldier Spy* capture something of this atmosphere. But neither came close to the mysteries of that old Chubb safe.

The Chief's private office was an attic room with layers of grimy netting over the windows and the unsettling quality of seeming to be underground. If he wanted to address you formally he remained seated behind his bare desk, shielded by portraits of his family – and, in my day, of Allen Dulles and the Shah of Persia. If he wished for a more relaxed atmosphere, there were the cracked leather armchairs. But wherever you sat, the green safe was always somewhere in your eye-line, staring at you inscrutably across the room.

What on earth could it contain? I had heard that there existed documents so secret that they were only ever touched by the Chief himself. If he chose to share them with another person, that person must first sign his life away, read them in the Chief's presence and hand them back.

*

And now the sad day is upon us when the final curtain will be rung down on Broadway Buildings, and the Service and all its chattels transferred to new accommodation in Lambeth. Is the Chief's safe exempt? Will cranes, crowbars and silent men convey it bodily to the next stage in its life's long journey?

After a debate at the highest levels, it is reluctantly ruled that the safe, however venerable, is no longer fit for purpose in our modern world. It will be opened. Whatever is inside will be examined by sworn officers, minutely documented and granted all the handling procedures appropriate to its sensitivity.

So who's got the bloody key?

Not the reigning Chief, apparently. He has made a point of never venturing inside the safe or needlessly familiarizing himself with its secrets. What you don't know you can't reveal. His surviving predecessors are urgently consulted. On the same principle, they too resisted trespassing on such holy ground. And they don't know where the bloody key is. Nobody, not Registry, not the Secretariat, not the department for in-house security, not even the stone-faced janitor on his kitchen chair, nobody has seen or touched a key, or knows where it is, or who last had it. All that *is* known is that the safe itself was installed at the command of the revered and pathologically secretive Sir Stewart Menzies, who served as Chief of the Service from 1939 until 1952.

So did Menzies take the key with him? Was he buried with it? Did he literally take his secret to the grave? He had every excuse. He was one of the founding fathers of Bletchley Park. He had conducted a thousand private interviews with Winston Churchill. He had negotiated with anti-Nazi resistance movements inside Germany, and with Admiral Canaris, the conflicted head of the German secret service, the Abwehr. Heaven alone knew what wasn't in that green safe.

In my novel A *Perfect Spy*, it appears as the chipped green filing cabinet that accompanies Ronnie's alter ego, Rick, on his life's journey. It is said to contain the sum of his debts to society, but it too is never opened.

Meanwhile, time is running out. Any day now, the new tenant will be asserting his legal rights. An executive decision is urgently called for. Very well, the Service has picked a few locks in its day, so it looks like time to pick another: send for the Service burglar.

The Service burglar knows his business. With disconcerting speed, the lock yields. The burglar hauls back the creaking iron door. Like the treasure seekers Carter and Mace before the open tomb of Tutankhamun, the spectators crane their necks for a first glimpse of the marvels within. There are none. The safe is empty, bare, innocent of even the most mundane secret.

But wait! These are sophisticated conspirators, not easily fooled. Is this a decoy safe, a dummy, a false grave, an outer bailey to protect an inner sanctum? A crowbar is sent for. The safe is gently prised from the wall. The most senior officer present peers behind it, gives out a muffled exclamation, gropes in the space between safe and wall, and extracts a very dusty, very thick, very old pair of grey trousers, with a label attached to them with a nappy pin. The typed inscription declares that these are the trousers worn by Rudolph

Hess, Adolf Hitler's deputy, when he flew to Scotland to negotiate a separate peace with the Duke of Hamilton in the mistaken belief that the Duke shared his fascist views. Beneath the inscription runs a handwritten scrawl in the traditional green ink of the Chief:

Please analyse because may give an idea of the state of the German textile industry.

Sources

The publisher gratefully acknowledges the following sources. Some of these articles have been reproduced as they appeared at the time. Many have been used only in part.

Chapter 10: Going out into the field
page 70: 'The Constant Muse' was first published in the USA in the *New Yorker* in 2000, and in the UK in the *Observer* and in the *Guardian* in 2001.

Chapter 24: His brother's keeper
page 175: 'His Brother's Keeper' originally appeared in different form as the Afterword to *A Spy Among Friends* by Ben Macintyre, published in the USA by Crown Publishing Group and in the UK by Bloomsbury in 2014.

Chapter 25: Quel Panama!
page 189: 'Quel Panama!' was first published in the USA in *The New York Times* and is used here with permission, and was first published in the UK in the *Daily Telegraph* in 1996.

Chapter 26: Under deep cover
page 200: 'Under Deep Cover' was first published in the USA in *The New York Times* and is used here with permission, and was first published in the UK in the *Guardian* in 1999.

Chapter 27: Hunting for warlords
page 204: 'Congo Journey' was first published in the USA in the *Nation* in 2006, and in the UK in the *Sunday Telegraph* in 2006.

Chapter 28: Richard Burton needs me

page 215: 'The Spy Who Liked Me' was first published in the *New Yorker* in 2013.

Chapter 29: Alec Guinness

page 228: 'Mission into Enemy Territory' was first published in the *Daily Telegraph* in 1994, and was reprinted as the Preface in *My Name Escapes Me: The Diary of a Retiring Actor* by Alec Guinness, published by Hamish Hamilton in 1996.

Chapter 33: Son of the author's father

page 255: 'In Ronnie's Court' was first published in the USA in the *New Yorker* in 2002, and in the UK in the *Observer* in 2003.